Cheers for
___ TeamThink ___

"*TeamThink* is a great idea that delivers what it promises. I have often thought that nothing in society blends as well into all our culture as sports. Here is an invaluable aid for your ultimate how-to list. Enjoy and use."

LARRY KING, CNN

"The sports business is difficult, to say the least. Motivating such high-salaried and mostly immature young players to perform to their potential is a most difficult task. *TeamThink*, blending sports and everyday business, is extremely well done, splendidly accomplishing its goal of educating business leaders on how to do the same in their companies."

ALAN L. AUFZIEN,
chairman,
New Jersey Nets

"Don Martin has used the most obvious metaphor of team sports to illustrate the fundamentals of business teams. His quotes from the great sports personalities are great reading. His linkage of these fundamentals to business teams is clear and illuminating. I think you'll enjoy this read. I did."

GERALD A. JOHNSON,
president and COO,
McDonnell Douglas Corporation

"Sports have always played an important part in my life. Don Martin has done a superb job of using sports to demonstrate and reinforce good management practices. Bravo!"

WILLIAM E. B. SIART,
president,
First Interstate Bancorp

"I am a sports nut and draw sports analogies all the time in my teaching. If you love sports too, Don Martin's *TeamThink* is for the reader who wants to develop, motivate and manage a winning team. I'm a believer."

KEN BLANCHARD,
co-author of
The One Minute Manager

"*TeamThink* is not only enjoyable reading for the sports fan and trivia buff, it is also full of insight and inspiration for business leaders. The principles on every page should be embraced and practiced by all of us who wish to improve our leadership skills."

RICHARD J. LOUGHLIN,
president and CEO,
Century 21 Real Estate Corporation

"Donald Martin may not have his MBA from that famous Northeastern school of business, but he has certainly captured the relevance of business to teamwork and leadership on the field of play. *TeamThink* is the game book for the big one and the one that happens every day. It is leadership by doing. It is the coming together of tradition on the playing field and corporate culture in the office and factory."

EDMUND A. HAJIM,
chairman and CEO,
Furman Selz Inc.

"Great basic skills learned, ideas gained, fundamentals introduced and a reorientation to principles long forgotten—all encompassed with sports trivia and insight—make Don Martin's *TeamThink* a must reading experience for all of us in business."

C. TERRY BROWN,
chairman and CEO,
Atlas Hotels

"Don Martin has provided us with a complete game plan for successfully managing a company. From mission statement to directing your employees to work as a team, to servicing the client—all the ingredients are here for success on the corporate playing field."

ROGER STAUBACH,
chairman and CEO,
Staubach Company

"Don Martin's *TeamThink* is a wonderfully practical guide to enhancing both the operations and value of a business using the experiences and wisdom from the field of sports."

JAMES D. JAMESON,
president, LIDCO, Inc.;
past international president, Young
Presidents' Organization

"Don Martin's new book, *TeamThink*, is a 'slam dunk' combination of business and sports. Since many of us in leadership roles are frustrated athletes or Monday-morning quarterbacks anyway, his book will connect with a wide audience. With today's increased emphasis on empowerment, team play, and the leader as coach, the book is both practical and enjoyable."

> David Davenport,
> president,
> Pepperdine University

"As in sports, certain companies seem to excel year after year, no matter what the circumstances. I've always felt that the link between winners in sports and business—leadership, motivation, intelligence, self-confidence and traditions—can't be merely accidental. Now Don Martin shows that where there are winners, there is *nothing* accidental. Anyone who works with people, and wants to be better at it, will benefit from *TeamThink*."

> Don Schuenke,
> chairman & CEO,
> Northwestern Mutual Life

"Americans love team sports—and winning. Don Martin has taken this desire and applied it to good management practices—a welcome, novel change from old theories. *TeamThink* should be taken seriously by American managers in both the private sector and, particularly, in the government, where working as a team *should* be the name of the game."

> Joseph R. Wright, Jr.,
> vice chairman,
> W. R. Grace & Co.

TEAMTHINK

TeamThink

Using the Sports Connection to Develop, Motivate, and Manage a Winning Business Team

---

Don Martin

Edited by Renee Martin

A PLUME BOOK

PLUME
Published by the Penguin Group
Penguin Books USA Inc., 375 Hudson Street, New York, New York 10014, U.S.A.
Penguin Books Ltd, 27 Wrights Lane, London W8 5TZ, England
Penguin Books Australia Ltd, Ringwood, Victoria, Australia
Penguin Books Canada Ltd, 10 Alcorn Avenue, Toronto, Ontario, Canada M4V 3B2
Penguin Books (N.Z.) Ltd, 182-190 Wairau Road, Auckland 10, New Zealand

Penguin Books Ltd, Registered Offices:
Harmondsworth, Middlesex, England

Published by Plume, an imprint of Dutton Signet, a division of
Penguin Books USA Inc. Previously published in a Dutton edition.

First Plume Printing, June, 1994
10 9 8 7 6 5 4 3 2

The Library of Congress has catalogued the Dutton edition as follows:
Martin, Don
    TeamThink : using the sports connection to develop, motivate, and manage a
    winning business team / Don Martin.
      p.   cm.
    ISBN 0-525-93609-2 (hc.)
    ISBN 0-452-27213-0 (pbk.)
    1. Success in business.   I. Title.
    HF5386.M363   1993   92-36020
    658.4'02—dc20   CIP

Printed in the United States of America

BOOKS ARE AVAILABLE AT QUANTITY DISCOUNTS WHEN USED TO PROMOTE PRODUCTS OR
SERVICES. FOR INFORMATION PLEASE WRITE TO PREMIUM MARKETING DIVISION, PENGUIN
BOOKS USA INC., 375 HUDSON STREET, NEW YORK, NEW YORK 10014.

*To Renee, whom I love very much, and to
Jennifer, Samantha, Michelle, and Susan,
who have enriched our lives.*

CONTENTS

___Acknowledgments___

Martin Writing Team

RENEE MARTIN   Not only for outstanding editing, but for the encouragement when I needed it and the willingness to sacrifice our discretionary time together to complete this book. Without her help this book would not have been written.

MARTIN LEVIN   His ideas and directions were invaluable. He remains a first-class businessman masquerading as an attorney.

BEVERLY CANIPE   Who spent many evenings and weekends finding old sport books and quotes long forgotten.

BRIAN SILVERMAN   For his additional assistance with the sports stories.

LESLIE RODRIGUEZ   Who continues to type forever.

ARNOLD DOLIN AND THE DUTTON TEAM   For their assistance and confidence in this project.

TEAMTHINK

_Team_Think_

Introduction

I always turn to the sports page first . . . it records people's accomplishments; the front page, nothing but man's failure.

Earl Warren,
former Chief Justice,
United States Supreme Court

I grew up in the Ohio Valley, where if you were as poor as we were, there were only three career options open to you: the coal mines, the steel mills, or, if you had the talent and some luck, a sports scholarship so that you could go to college. I was too frightened of working underground in the mines, too slight to work in the steel mills, and unfortunately, although I loved sports, I was not very good at them.

My father left us when I was three and my mother worked to support us. Young, poor, and uneducated, she did the best she could, which meant working days and evenings waitressing. I was pretty much left to fend for myself.

My most vivid childhood recollections are of often being hungry, having to make traumatic trips to the outhouse in near-freezing temperatures, and thinking we were in the lap of luxury when we moved to a house where we shared the one indoor bath-room with one other family. For several years my mother put cardboard inside my shoes to cover the holes because she couldn't afford new shoes or the $2 for glue-on rubber soles. During Ohio's frequent rainstorms and heavy snows, I learned to walk to school quickly because the cardboard didn't hold up well in those conditions.

Then my mother married an abusive alcoholic, and most of his abuse was directed at me. Fortunately, she didn't stay married to him very long, because during the time he lived with us, my usually high grades fell drastically. However, after my mother left my stepfather, my grades went from D's and F's back to A's and B's. Although scholastically I didn't make the upper third of my class, I became an officer in the Hi-Y and Head of the Order of DeMolay, a local junior Masonic organization, where I experienced my first role as a leader.

I had no clue about what to do after I graduated from high school, so I sought advice from two teachers whom I respected. One, the football coach, counseled me to go into the Marines. The other teacher pronounced, in no uncertain terms, that I was not college material. Fortunately, I ignored both and listened instead to a small inner voice that said, "Go to college." That was when I learned an important lesson: *Do not accept the limits that others place on you.*

Even though I had no role models, mentors, or money, I had a strong desire to succeed and a strong belief that I could. To this day I have no idea where that came from. I couldn't afford college in Ohio, so my mom packed us up and we moved to California; there I would have access to the state's affordable junior college system, and my grade average would not bar my acceptance.

I realized within the first few weeks at junior college that I had a problem; I didn't know anyone. I decided that one way to meet people was to run for freshman class president. The other candidates knew most of the freshman students because they were all from the local high schools. They seemed to have a lot of votes already sewn up, so I devised a strategy to visit the night school students, who were mostly returning Korean War vets. I went to the school cafeteria every evening, asked these night school students about their problems, and asked for their votes.

I won a close election, but I got 90 percent of the night school votes. As you can imagine, the losing candidates were asking,

"Who is this guy Martin?" And I learned another valuable lesson: *Go where the competition isn't.*

As freshman class president, I was abruptly introduced to challenging responsibilities and problems: budgeting, presiding over various committees, interacting with the student council, and representing the freshman class at various social and school functions. I had to develop new social and problem-solving skills.

After my election, I received invitations from several campus fraternities. I joined one because it seemed like a quick solution to my nonexistent social life. Although my social life did improve, I felt out of place in the fraternity and resigned. I decided to form a new fraternity, got the college's permission, drew up a charter, and solicited members. We did things differently. For one thing, we didn't have hazing. From this experience I gained still another bit of wisdom: *Don't conform to things that don't feel right—you can make things happen on your own terms.*

I had no idea what career path to pursue. In the eighth grade, I'd done well as master of ceremonies in a school show. This memory, and the fact that my high school peers thought I was witty, led me to think of becoming a radio announcer. To my mind, announcing required no "real skills," so I became a speech major in college.

When I heard about the college debate team, I joined it. Little did I realize that debate would be the most valuable learning tool of my entire college experience. College debate teams participate in local and national tournaments that feature a number of individual speaking competitions, impromptu and extemporaneous speaking, and oratory.

My partner on the debate team and I won a number of national tournaments, and eventually we were ranked as one of the top teams in the country. My days as a debater gave me one more insight: *Learning to work and strategize with other people, using teamwork, is a vital component for success.*

Debate taught me to think on my feet, to organize my thoughts, and to express myself convincingly. I gained self-confidence, which was the single most significant driving force that positively influenced my later years. Today, I encourage college-bound students to consider debate at school.

My strength as a debater elicited interest from some four-year schools, but because of finances, I chose a school that was part of the California State University system. At Cal State, L.A., I became president of a Greek fraternity, president of the debating fraternity, and president of the Interfraternity Council. In my senior year, I was named one of the five outstanding men at that school.

Still, money was always a problem. Working was difficult because of the demands of my classes and extracurricular activities, so I went looking for a job with flexible hours. There was a one-man insurance agency across the street from the apartment my mother and I shared. I put on my one and only suit, walked into the agency, and asked for a job selling insurance. The owner, figuring he didn't have much to lose, hired me, gave me a small salary, and put me on commission.

Although I studied and qualified for my insurance license, I really had no idea how to sell a product. In retrospect I realize I was successful in selling myself. Although short on experience, I had energy and enthusiasm. People responded, I made enough money to stay in school, and two years later the owner named me vice-president of his company. *In order to succeed, you don't have to be the most experienced or talented, just the most tenacious.*

I remained with the agency after graduation. Three years later at age twenty-five, I met a twenty-seven-year-old life agent who, like me, wanted to own an agency. We decided to become partners, form a corporation, and buy the agency. So, miraculously, in 1962 we bought the agency for $12,500 cash and the promise of future payments. My new partner borrowed most of the money and I contributed the only money I had in the bank, $100. Twenty-three years later, in 1985, we split into separate companies.

My organization presently consists of five separate entities known collectively as the Cal-Surance Companies. We employ 150 people, who generated over $100 million in sales in 1992.

My organization differs dramatically from the standard insurance brokerage, which only sells and services insurance policies. We address every aspect of the industry with our synergistic operation, which includes a retail brokerage company, a specialized wholesale insurance brokerage, an offshore insurance company, and a specialized claims adjustment service. The combination of all our entities makes us the largest privately held insurance broker-age firm in the state of California and thirty-sixth in size in the country, out of more than 200,000 firms. I still like to say to people that no matter what happens, I have only $100 at risk.

Looking back, I've asked myself, "How did I do it, especially since I never took one business course in college?" Despite my background, I did things right and made good decisions. But I had good role models and teachers, all from a very unexpected place: the sports world.

I have been a sports junkie since I was a kid. Whenever I watched a team sporting event, I was intent on more than just the action. I was avidly aware of the interaction between the coaches and their players. I devoured the sports section of the newspaper, not for the scores and statistics, but for the interviews and comments from the players, coaches, and team management. I raided the library and bookstores for books about coaches and teams. I began to see similarities among successful coaches and successful teams.

Subconsciously, by watching sports, I was learning about leading, motivating, managing, and strategizing. *I didn't have an M.B.A., but I did have the NBA, the NFL, and the NHL.* I was studying the various individuals and teams to decipher why what they did worked and, when it didn't work, what had gone wrong.

My experience is that many concepts from sports can apply in the business world; I believe they have worked well for me. In this book I share these concepts with you in the hope that they will be as useful for you as they have been for me.

TeamThink is a collection of concepts and principles that I have taken from sports and adapted and integrated to fit the business environment. The combination of these TeamThink concepts is geared to create a team atmosphere and a winning attitude in each element of your business.

This is a book for the busy, hands-on executive who is looking for ideas that work. In sports terms, it is a playbook with over 310 different plays, designed to trigger new thoughts and give you direct methods of improving the way you operate. I illustrate these ideas and principles with anecdotes from sports or business and then develop them using my own experiences.

I start out with the premise that you, the reader, are busy and engrossed in your business. I assume that you are interested and involved in one or more sports as a participant or spectator. I believe you want a book that helps you achieve your goals in your business. Being average is not enough—you want to be a winner. Perhaps you won't read this book in one sitting but in spurts on an airplane, or over a quick lunch, or whenever you have ten to thirty minutes of so-called free time.

As you read, visualize yourself as the head coach of a team that's out to win the championship—to be the best it can be. You are not alone. You have assistant coaches with their own specialties. The quarterback coach might be your sales manager, your linebacker coach might be your financial vice-president, and so on. The players are of course your employees. They determine whether you win big, have a so-so year, or languish in the cellar of your league.

Your job is to organize a team, to get the assistant coaches and the players to think as a team. It's up to you to provide the vision, the example, the skill to bring all the disparate parts of your business enterprise into a synchronized, effective unit.

I share with you my plays—and diagram them for you. When a play has bombed for me, I tell you frankly about that as well. But most important, you will read about successful ideas and concepts from over sixty-five different sports leaders, including Tommy Lasorda, Bill Parcells, Red Auerbach, Pat Riley, and Lou Holtz—and from business leaders such as Jack Welch, Peter Ueberroth, Peter Drucker, and numerous CEO's of medium-sized companies from all over the country.

By asking you to think of your organization as a team, by providing you with the plays used by successful coaches and business leaders, I hope to stimulate you to create your own playbook—ideas that will work for you in your industry, in your company. When I present an idea that is particularly important, I mark it "TeamThink." Stop when you see this marker (there are over sixty-seven TeamThink principles in the book) and take a minute to reflect. Read the quotes that illustrate the TeamThink principles to fix the ideas for you—or to stimulate your own ideas.

Approach the game of business as you would any sport—with strategy, skill, enthusiasm, and a passion to be the best.

> *In baseball and in business, there are three types of people. Those who make it happen, those who watch it happen, and those who wonder what happened.*
>
> Tommy Lasorda,
> manager,
> Los Angeles Dodgers

This book is for those who want to make it happen.

Postscript: I have always believed strongly that talent and skill in business are not gender-related. My company managers and officers are competent men *and* women. When writing this book, I attempted at first to impart that awareness by using "he" and "she" alternately. However, my editors thought this sometimes caused confusion, so for the sake of clarity only, I use the pronoun "he." Please be aware that it refers in all cases to either gender.

1

Learning the Name of the Game

We aren't where we want to be, we aren't where we ought to be, but thank goodness we aren't where we used to be.

Lou Holtz,
head football coach,
University of Notre Dame

When I started in business, I realized my company had to address four seemingly simple questions:

- What is our purpose?

- What do we stand for?

- Where do we want to go?

- Who are we?

Our purpose is defined in our mission statement. What we stand for is outlined in our corporate philosophy. Where we want to go is established by our yearly objectives and long-range goals. Who we are is reflected by our corporate culture.

The Mission Statement

"When I was told we needed a mission statement, I thought it was just a lot of M.B.A. jargon," says Ber Pieper, president of Brown & Root, the multibillion-dollar Houston-based construction firm. "But it's been a powerful tool to get our people working and moving in the same direction."

——————— TeamThink ———————
Create a mission statement for your organization that is clear and concise.

Pat Eilers, past senior flanker for the University of Notre Dame's football team, tells of the impact a clear mission statement delivered by coach Lou Holtz had on the team. "Coach Holtz gave us a big speech on how our new mission was to 'strive for perfection,' that we would accept nothing less, and that Notre Dame deserved nothing less than perfection. I think that set the tone for the entire road to the national championship, because we worked our butts off that winter during conditioning, during spring ball, and during the summer. I think that meeting was the start of it, the first chapter."

Whitey Herzog, former manager of the St. Louis Cardinals and now in charge of player personnel for the California Angels, states his mission this way: "to make the Angels one of the better organizations on the field, with their fans, and in their farm system." Before his arrival, the Angels did not have a mission; Herzog gave them one.

A mission statement sets forth in general terms the broad intent of the organization. It does not refer to anything specific such as plans, markets, or products. For example, Shell Oil's mission is "to meet the energy needs of mankind." Note that Shell does not refer to "gasoline," but to "energy needs."

Here are other examples of broadly stated yet clear and concise mission statements:

- Volkswagen: "To provide an economic means of private transportation."

- AT&T: "To provide quick and efficient communication capabilities."

- International Minerals and Chemical Corporation: "To increase agricultural productivity to feed the world's hungry."

Then there's Mrs. Gooch's, an upscale health-food market chain with seven stores in Southern California. Its huge success is in no small part due to its ability to live up to its mission statement, which is boldly printed on every shopping bag: "Mrs. Gooch's is committed to offering the highest quality natural foods, related products, service and information which optimize and enrich the health and well being of the individual and the environment, as well as our planet."

In 1986 Pizza Hut changed its mission statement to read, "To consistently demonstrate to America that Pizza Hut is the best choice for every pizza occasion." Steven Reinemund, Pizza Hut's former CEO, credited the new mission statement with developing the operation, then a pizza restaurant company serving only drive-in and carry-out customers, into a nationwide restaurant chain that now features pizza delivery as well. In five years, Pizza Hut more than doubled its sales and tripled its profits. Over one-third of current sales now come from segments of the business where Pizza Hut did not compete five years ago. The revised mission statement produced a change in direction that significantly affected the company.

Burson-Marsteller, the world's largest public relations firm, articulates its mission statement in a document called "Our Vision, Our Values" and held meetings on this topic in a three-month period at branches in their three units—the Americas, Europe and Asia—at a cost of more than $1 million. The document states, "As the world changes, we will change with it. The only constant is our dedication to excellence in thought and deed."

The mission statement of my organization, Cal-Surance, is "to become one of the dominant forces in the insurance brokerage business on the West Coast." How do we compare to our mission statement? All of our five operations are related to the insurance brokerage business. Although we have accounts in other parts of the country, we operate from one office in Orange, California. And as I've said already, we are the largest privately-held insurance brokerage firm in California and thirty-sixth in size in the country. Developing our mission statement gave Cal-Surance a purpose and a direction that enabled us to accurately and consistently—resisting distractions—focus our attention and energy.

CORPORATE PHILOSOPHY

Do what is right, do the best you can and treat others like you want to be treated. First we will be best, then we will be first.

Lou Holtz

In 1987, Notre Dame had a problem. With its winning tradition and national television exposure, the university had a built-in recruiting edge, but it needed someone at the top to give the proper direction. More than coaching skills were needed; the Irish needed someone to restore the gleam to the Golden Dome.

Lou Holtz was their choice. A man of impeccable integrity, Holtz succeeded. The restrictions put on him by Notre Dame were few: Be honest and live within our rules. This meant no redshirting or special athletic dorms and no special treatment from the admissions office. The university insisted that the players be students first and athletes second.

When Holtz took over the head coaching job, he set a standard for the team. By staying true to his beliefs and instilling them in his players, Holtz led Notre Dame to two National Championships and restored the university as a national football power.

—————— TEAMTHINK ——————
Formulate a corporate philosophy that expresses what you stand for. This is a statement of your values. Write it as you intend to live it.

The best way to make sure that your corporate philosophy is known and understood by your employees and customers is to put it in writing and communicate it. Your philosophy should follow these guidelines:

- **Belief.**

  Don't say anything that you don't believe and don't intend to enforce. I have seen many printed corporate philosophies that include the statement, "People are our most important asset." Yet often, as I look at one of these company brochures, I observe that no "people" are mentioned, only facts and figures, and I wonder, "Does this company really believe its statement?"

  Every year Cal-Surance's senior managers spend the first three hours of our off-site operational planning meeting reviewing in detail each statement in our corporate philosophy to make certain we really believe it and to question whether we really practice it. If we don't, we drop it, revise it, or recommit ourselves to it.

- **Simplicity.**

  Keep it simple and direct. The Lord's Prayer, the Gettysburg Address, and the Preamble to the Constitution are all under 300 words.

- **Actions.**

  Your actions in relation to these stated values and standards will tell your employees whether you are really committed to them. Actions do speak louder than words.

  When Whitey Herzog came to the St. Louis Cardinals to manage the team, he brought along his personal code of behavior. In 1979, after the Cardinals' star shortstop, Gerry Templeton, made an obscene gesture to the hometown fans, Herzog chastised the player in full view of his teammates. Regardless of how it would affect the team, Herzog went on to suspend Templeton and ultimately traded him. "Somebody in our society has to draw the line somewhere," he said, "and

I'm drawing it here." Herzog had a clear set of values and followed them with no exceptions.

One of our employees, who had been with us for sixteen years, committed a clearly unethical act in dealing with an insurance company. As painful as it was for me, I terminated him. Three years later, one of our managers told me that she had turned down a competitor's offer of a good job because our actions in that matter had demonstrated to her that we stood by our principles.

- **Communication.**

A corporate philosophy is useless if your employees don't know it exists. Our philosophy appears in every employee's handbook, is clearly and visibly posted in our lunchroom, gets highlighted and explained at every major meeting, and is thoroughly reviewed at our annual Outlook Meeting, which is attended by every employee. Finally, we present our philosophy as a major component of our corporate brochure.

This is our corporate philosophy:

- To provide our clients with the highest level of professionalism through quality service, reliability, and integrity.

- To treat our clients' interests as if they were our own.

- To be leaders in our field through new and innovative products, programs, and services.

- To grow and to earn a reasonable profit to ensure the continuity of the organization, and to provide opportunities for our employees.

- To attract and retain talented people.

- To recognize that people are important, and to encourage their dedication and commitment through teamwork, education, and recognition.

Anixier Brothers, a worldwide distributor of electrical wire and cable in Evanston, Illinois, has a direct and explicit ten-point corporate philosophy:

1. People come first.

2. Our word is our bond—we are reliable.

3. We are serious about service.

4. We cannot afford the luxury of a lousy day's business.

5. We want to be the best.

6. We are realists and we believe in candor.

7. We are accessible and easy to do business with.

8. We are aggressive—we are doers—we work hard.

9. We are often pleased but never satisfied.

10. We want our people to be properly rewarded.

———————— TEAMTHINK ————————

Your values should not be determined by the type of business you have; rather your values should govern your business.

Bob Haas, chairman and CEO of Levi Strauss, says, "Values provide a common language for aligning a company's leadership in its people. In an organization of 31,000 people, there is no way that any of us in management can be around all the time to tell people what to do. It has to be the strategy and values that guide them."

The General Electric Company has put together a value statement that is divided into business and individual characteristics. This format is so distinctive that I want to share their segment on individual characteristics with you:

Individual Characteristics
Reality

> What—Describe the environment as it is—not as we hope it to be.
>
> Why—Critical to developing a vision and a winning strategy, and to gaining universal acceptance for their implementation.

Leadership

> What—Sustained passion for and commitment to a proactive, shared vision and its implementation.
>
> Why—To rally teams toward achieving a common objective.

Candor/Openness

> What—Complete and frequent sharing of information with individuals (appraisals, etc.) and organization (everything).
>
> Why—Critical to employees knowing where they, their efforts, and their business stand.

Simplicity

> What—Strive for brevity, clarity, the "elegant, simple solution"—less is better.
>
> Why—Less complexity improves everything, from reduced bureaucracy to better product designs to lower costs.

Integrity

> What—Never bend or wink at the truth, and live within both the spirit and letter of the laws of every global business arena.
>
> Why—Critical to gaining the global arenas' acceptance of our right to grow and prosper. Every constituency: shareowners who invest; customers who purchase; community that supports; and employees who depend, expect, and deserve our unequivocal commitment to integrity in every facet of our behavior.

Individual Dignity

> What—Respect and leverage the talent and contribution of every individual in both good and bad times.
>
> Why—Teamwork depends on trust, mutual understanding, and the shared belief that the individual will be treated fairly in any environment.

Whether you call it a corporate philosophy or a value statement, it is geared to accomplish the same thing: to tell everyone what you stand for. This should become the guide for your future behavior.

YEARLY OBJECTIVES AND LONG-RANGE GOALS

TEAMTHINK

Your goals become the driving force in your organization; they trigger all the management functions, and determine your needs for people, equipment, and cash flow.

Picture this. It's June 1987. The Los Angeles Lakers have just won the NBA Championship. I'm one of 17,505 fans at the Forum, and I'm yelling my head off. Later, I hear the Lakers' coach at the time, Pat Riley, tell a TV sportscaster, "I guarantee you we'll repeat as champions next year." I'm stunned by his brazen promise, and assume he made it in the excitement of the moment. But it turns out that Riley said it deliberately. He knew he had to create a goal that would energize his team the following season.

Riley's goal to repeat as champions drove the Lakers' planning for the next year and created a series of subgoals. The first was to win the division so that the Lakers would have an advantageous playoff order. The second was to have the best win-loss record in the NBA so that they would have the home-court advantage throughout the playoffs. The Lakers accomplished these goals and won back-to-back championships.

When Tom Landry took over as head coach of the newly created Dallas Cowboys in 1960, he knew winning would not happen overnight. But after five subsequent losing seasons, he was frustrated. In 1965, he sent each returning Cowboy player a letter spelling out a set of goals for that season. He named a clear-cut objective for the team—to win the World Championship—and explained how he proposed they should go about achieving such a lofty goal: "The objective, the World's Championship, appears to be monumental . . . so it becomes more important to break down our major objective, the championship, into minor objectives—the resistances we must overcome. And each of the minor objectives must be a major objective until it is attained."

Landry also set forth his list of "minor objectives," which in reality were his subgoals. For 1965 the minor objective was to finish with a .500 record. And with a 7–7 record in 1965, his team achieved that objective. The following year the Cowboys won their next objective, the Eastern Division Championship, and they soon followed with their ultimate goal, the World Championship.

There is a subtle difference between a company's "mission" and a company's "goal." A mission is global and describes the company's overall purpose and direction. A goal is specific and normally has a time limit (such as one year or three years) or a particular numerical target (such as increasing sales by 20 percent).

The goals you select usually set off a chain reaction throughout your organization. If one of your goals is to increase your sales, this will probably trigger a need for more people. If your goal is to maximize profit, you may need to respond by cutting down on the number of people. If your goal is to expand, you will need more cash flow to buy more equipment or hire more people.

About fifteen years ago, I set a goal to double Cal-Surance's size in one year. This decision turned into one of my biggest mistakes. Because I had not taken into account the ability of the organization to keep up the pace, or the fact that we did not have adequate reserves to cover the cost of expansion, the chain reaction almost broke the firm.

On the other hand, about ten years ago, our organization was a major insurer of the transportation industry, which represented over 65 percent of our gross sales. We set a goal to reduce this ratio to 30 percent within the next four years, so that the firm would become more diversified and less dependent on this class of business. It's a good thing we did. Five years later, circumstances caused us to lose this product line, which at that point affected only 30 percent of our business, rather than 65 percent. Had we not set this strategic goal five years earlier, we might not be in business today.

Your goals determine where you want to go. You can only get

there by design, not by accident. Here are some guidelines on the goal-setting process:

- **Keep the goals clear, simple, and direct.**

A common reason that goals aren't accomplished is that they are not clearly defined. If employees don't understand their company's goals and its game plan, these goals won't be achieved. Plenty of organizations fail for that very reason. Football doesn't make this mistake. Its goals are always clearly defined. At the end of the field is a goal line. Why do we call it a goal line? Because eleven people on the offensive team huddle for a single purpose—to move the ball across it. Everyone has a specific task to do—the quarterback, the wide receiver, each lineman, every player knows exactly what his assignment is. Even the defensive team has its goals too— to prevent the offensive team from achieving its goal.

Jim Tunney,
NFL referee

You don't need to set a lot of goals. In 1969, his first year as head football coach at the University of Michigan, Bo Schembechler set only one goal for his team, "Beat Ohio State," then the dominant team in the country. Michigan beat Ohio State.

- **Make it measurable.**

A goal such as "improving the attitude in the department" is too subjective to be measured. All this kind of goal can do is create controversy about whether or not it was achieved.

In 1975, to achieve the primary goal of making their offense the best in the NFL, the Minnesota Vikings coaching staff focused on *pinpointing* measurable preliminary goals. For example, they knew from the record books that playoff teams over previous years had averaged four yards per rush. So, according to their quarterback, Fran Tarkenton, one of their preliminary goals was "an average gain of four yards per rush." They also found out what the previous playoff teams had done in terms of numbers of first downs, percentage of time scored once they were inside the ten-yard line, and so on. They made each of those items a goal on their offensive strategy list.

According to Tarkenton, "We made it to the Super Bowl that year, and I give a lot of the credit to the 'pinpointing technique' that enabled us to focus our motivation where it would do the most good."

- **The goals must become your team's goals, not just yours.**

  Red Auerbach, former coach and general manager and currently president of the Boston Celtics, says, "Good teams always have common goals. When you find that goals of certain members differ from the team's, then the team will usually do poorly."

  Your team has to buy into the goals. Unless everyone understands them, accepts them, and commits to achieving them, there is little chance of success. Only through acceptance and commitment by your key managers will you ever meet the goals.

  Deborah Coleman, now vice-president of operations, joined Apple Computer Inc. in 1981 as controller of its Macintosh division, from which several of her predecessors had been fired. Coleman says she "routinely pulled everyone in the plant together to set monthly goals and 'foster' a shared vision." As a result, assembly-line workers agreed to put in twelve-hour shifts at times to meet certain production schedules and the labor rate was reduced to less than thirty minutes for each Macintosh.

- **Communicate the goals to all employees.**

  Cal-Surance's annual Outlook Meeting is basically a state of the union address, presented by the company's senior managers, in which they outline the goals for that year. This meeting is held in early January for all employees, so that they can understand what each unit is attempting to accomplish during the upcoming year. We shut the organization down for half a day so that everyone can attend. This is one of our most important meetings of the year, because it enables everyone, from the mailroom to the boardroom, to see the complete picture.

- **Create accountability.**
We have quarterly accountability meetings at which the managers either report that they're on target or, if they are not, work on alternative plans. Each manager also prepares a monthly report comparing actual results to budget projections.

At the start of the 1988 season, in a meeting with his team—which the year before had lost to Penn State, Miami, and Texas A&M—Notre Dame coach Lou Holtz said, "Who in here wants to be great? Stand up." The entire team stood up. For the rest of the year, Holtz held his players accountable by reminding them of that meeting. He would say, "You guys told me you wanted to be great. I'm only doing what you guys wanted." Player Pat Eilers said, "Coach Holtz has a way of doing things like that to make us more self-motivated, instead of trying to motivate us." That year the team won the National Championship.

CORPORATE CULTURE

When you think of the Forty-Niners, you think of their tradition. When you think of all the good teams of the past, like the old Steelers, the old Raiders, they all had identity. Houston has an identity. We will have an identity in Atlanta. We want men who will stand up and be counted. Men who will make something happen.

Jerry Glanville,
head coach,
Atlanta Falcons

Invariably, when the media interview new draftees into the NFL or NBA, one or several report how thrilled they are to be going to a particular team because of that team's *tradition*. Although they may not say so, you know some draftees are disappointed because they were picked by a team whose tradition deflates, rather than inspires. All these players sense an intangible link between their own success and the tradition of their new team.

When Bill Walton, an outstanding center, became a free agent, he called the Boston Celtics to see if they would acquire him. He said, "The Celtics' reputation made it a team I always dreamed of playing for."

_____ TEAMTHINK _____

A positive corporate culture is essential if you want to attract and retain good people, enhance your image with clients, and increase the profitability of your company.

In sports it's called *tradition*, in business it's called *corporate culture*, but they both refer to the same thing. A sports team may have a tradition of being tough, hardworking, committed, disciplined, winning. A business organization may have a corporate culture that makes it professional, energetic, ethical, reliable, innovative, efficient. Your team's tradition or your company's corporate culture determines your reputation and establishes your identity.

The characteristics of your corporate culture are expressed and applied to your employees at all levels, from receptionists and mailroom clerks through managers and executives and on to the board of directors. These characteristics are the heart of a healthy company, enabling it to continuously grow, evolve, and renew itself.

Corporate cultures that empower employees and give them a real opportunity to participate fully in their companies create conditions that produce higher job satisfaction. When describing the characteristics of a healthy corporate culture in their book, *The 100 Best Companies to Work for in America*, Robert Levering, Milton

Moskowitz, and Michael Katz conclude that the one thing that characterizes all the best companies is that they are *fun* places to work.

In the book's "best companies," employees are allowed to make mistakes, do not feel compelled to prove their worth and industriousness by "acting busy," are treated fairly and aren't taken advantage of by the company, take pride in their work, and believe that they have responsibility for and control over their own work.

Company managers must discard the kind of narrow vision that dismisses such descriptions with the disclaimer, "We're in business to make money, not run a playground!" Enlightened managers realize that creating a company whose employees enjoy their jobs and get excited about coming to work is immensely practical, leading to reduced health-care costs, increased competitiveness, and greater profits.

W. L. Gore & Associates, a Delaware-based manufacturing firm, has consistently incurred total medical costs below national averages. During the five-year period before 1991, when the national average rose 94 percent, Gore's rose only 53 percent. One reason for this surprising record may lie in the fact that Gore's corporate culture is considerably different from that of most other companies.

At Gore, there are no titles except for president and secretary-treasurer, which are required by law. Everyone else is an "associate." Leaders emerge when their colleagues recognize their contributions and abilities. President W. L. Gore says, "We organize projects and functions by free commitment rather than by systems of authoritarian command. Open and direct communication, encouragement and trust, and the task-force approach to problem-solving are key components in the company's culture." Gore's corporate culture has not changed since the firm's founding in 1958.

In 1982, the same year the employees of Eastern Airlines went on strike against their management, the employees of Delta Airlines did a remarkable thing. To celebrate the company's fiftieth anniversary, they collected money among themselves and bought a new plane for the company. Clearly, Delta's positive corporate culture played a significant role in creating such goodwill among its employees.

In the spring of that year, the airline industry was beleaguered by a weak ecnomy and high fuel prices. Delta Air Lines had posted a quarterly net loss of $18.4 million, but still gave its employees an unexpectedly generous pay raise of some 8.5 percent in September.

"We couldn't believe it," remembers Ginny Whitfield, a flight attendant for over fifteen years. "We were just grateful to have our jobs, thanks to Delta's tradition of job security; we knew that forty thousand other airline employees had lost theirs."

Other employees were also impressed. "A bunch of us were sitting around one day saying how wonderful this company was," Ginny recalls. "So someone said, 'Let's buy them an airplane,' " A $30 million Boeing 767 airplane, no less.

With two other flight attendants, Ginny Whitfield organized a campaign to raise the purchase price from Delta's 36,000 non-union employees. Their idea was to ask the employees to sign a pledge card, voluntarily committing 2.5 percent of one year's pay to the airline purchase.

When told about the campaign, Delta president David Garrett insisted that it be totally voluntary. No records of individual giving could be kept by the volunteers, nor could they create "competitive" fund-raising drives.

Management agreed to convert an Atlanta storeroom into office space. It also provided access to Delta's communication system, including a B767 phone number, use of the payroll department for voluntary deductions, and advice on legal and technical details. (Employees could take a pay reduction and not be taxed on the deducted amount.)

Byron Carroll, a mechanic for eighteen years, remembers thinking, "That isn't a bad idea; Delta's been good to me and my family. When my dad died, the company helped my wife and kids fly to the funeral, sent flowers, and several managers wrote letters. It meant a lot to me that they cared." Carroll called the B767 number and volunteered, eager to give something back to Delta.

A retired maintenance inspector, Elmer J. Krebs, dropped into the project office to write a check, insisting they accept it so he could show the company his thanks. Management approved, opening the door for substantial support from Delta's retirees and other groups.

On the morning of December 15, 1982, seven thousand Delta employees gathered at Atlanta's International Airport to unveil the flagship of the 767 fleet. Ninety employees, representing cities in the Delta system, joined in lifting the curtain around the sleek silver and white jet emblazoned with "The Spirit of Delta."

Ginny Whitfield spoke for the employees: "This is to show our love and appreciation and to say thank you to a company that has always met the needs of the employees."

My own company's reputation is the product of its corporate culture, and I constantly see evidence that it is a major factor in generating financial dividends. Last year, two separate insurance companies asked us to work with them in developing two nationwide programs that would be new to their organization and ours. They told me they chose us because of our reputation for being highly ethical, innovative, and skilled in creating complex programs. Our corporate culture shaped our reputation.

TEAMTHINK

In sports, players often model their performance and behavior to conform to the tradition of their team. In business, people model their behavior to reflect the company's corporate culture.

An example of the impact of tradition on individuals is the performance of many baseball athletes when they don the pinstripes of the New York Yankees. Though the Yankees' reputation has become somewhat frayed recently, many players have made it their goal to put on those pinstripes—the same uniforms worn by Ruth, DiMaggio, Gehrig, Mantle, and Berra. When the Yankees were a dynasty, journeymen picked up by the team often had their best seasons. Something about wearing those pinstripes seemed to make the player work a little harder and push himself to levels never before achieved.

Johnsonville Foods has created an organization whose employees have modeled their behavior to reflect the corporate culture nurtured over the years by their CEO, Ralph Stayer. He has worked to create a culture that encourages his employees "to be self-starting, problem-solving, responsibility-grabbing, independent thinkers." As a result, at Johnsonville, teams make all decisions about schedules, performance standards, assignments, budgets, quality measures, and capital improvements.

Stayer claims that his organization's culture has developed in an environment where people *insist* on being responsible. He says emphatically, "The early 1980s taught me I couldn't *give* responsibility. People had to expect it, want it, even demand it."

TEAMTHINK

A negative corporate culture can have a devastating effect on the company's operations, causing higher turnover, higher health-care costs, and lower productivity.

In 1988, the UCLA Bruins basketball team had just lost to Washington State in the quarterfinals of the Pacific Ten Conference Tournament. Incredibly, on the bus ride back to their hotel, several members of the team were rejoicing and singing. Gerald Madkins, one of the players, explained their bizarre behavior: "Rather than prolong a 16–14 season by having a post-season berth, those players just wanted to end it, so they wouldn't have to play with Coach Walter Hazzard for one more week." Obviously this attitude had affected their play during the tournament—they lost. About a month later Hazzard was fired.

After the Yankees got off to a bad start one season, their much-disliked owner, George Steinbrenner, began flying to meet the team wherever it played on road trips. Alone among his teammates, Graig Nettles welcomed Steinbrenner's presence. "The more we lose, the more often Steinbrenner will fly in. And the more he flies, the better the chance there will be of his plane crashing."

Here's further evidence of the reaction to the Yankees' negative culture: a remark made by Don Baylor of the California Angels when Steinbrenner offered him a job as Yankees manager. Baylor rejected the offer, saying, "I came into this game sane, and I want to leave it sane."

There is a growing body of research into the drastic impact a negative corporate culture can have on a company's health-care costs. It has been found that psychological factors in the workplace influence the body-mind connection. The study of this connection is called psychoneuroimmunology. Corporate work cultures or environments that breed negative feelings and attitudes make employees more liable to become ill. In companies that create an environment in which workers are happy, the occurrence of illness is minimized.

Of the 12,000 workers surveyed by Bob Basso and Judi Klosek, authors of *This Job Should Be Fun*, only 20 percent of middle managers and 19 percent of lower-level employees answered yes to the question, "Do you truly enjoy your work?" Even more disturbing was the authors' report that 11 percent of middle management and 25 percent of nonmanagement employees went so far as to describe their workplaces as "a prison."

Surveys also confirm that a negative corporate culture results in high turnover. The employee benefits consulting firm of Johnson & Higgins conducted a survey to find out why service industries are losing so many top performers. The major reasons had to do with the companies' corporate culture: 75 percent of the employees were uneasy about making complaints; 57 percent felt they weren't appreciated by their supervisors; and 50 percent perceived that they were being treated unfairly.

While these revelations are disturbing, you must recognize that you can reorganize the work environment so as to reduce the risk of stress-related illness, reduce turnover of top performers, and increase productivity.

It is essential to accurately assess the quality of your own company's corporate culture. Robert Rosen, president of Healthy Companies, a nonprofit organization funded by the MacArthur Foundation to develop new global models of healthy, productive work, speculates that many CEO's who have companies with negative corporate cultures don't see the problem at all. "There are two causes for this perception gap," states Rosen. "One is that CEO's aren't getting out enough to hear the problems and the pain inside of their institutions. The other is that employees and managers are not being straight and forthright about the problems from the bottom up. We need employees who are willing to stand up and tell the truth."

The bottom line is, if you have a cultural problem, you have trouble with a capital T. A positive culture can't be mandated or eliminated by an executive order. It can only be built by a series of positive events over time.

Slogans and Mottoes—The Dynamic Duo

If you accept losing, you can't win.
> Vince Lombardi,
> former coach,
> Green Bay Packers

There is no substitute for work. It is the price of success.
> Earl Blaik,
> former football coach,
> West Point

Do it right the first time.
> Stew Leonard's "World's largest dairy store"

———— TeamThink ————
Slogans and mottoes can be extremely effective in delivering a concise message to your employees or customers. They are useful tools to help you motivate or inspire others or to emphasize a point.

The motto you choose for your company can be a rallying cry, such as "Back-to-Back," adopted by the Lakers in their quest for consecutive NBA titles; or it can be a promotional tool, such as "The NBA—It's FANtastic." A motto can succinctly make a statement about your organization, such as the Los Angeles Raiders' "Commitment to Excellence."

The 1990–91 Los Angeles Clippers' motto was "To Play in May." Although the Clippers, perennial league doormats, were a year removed from their preseason goal, they did eventually achieve it by making the playoffs in 1992.

Before Bo Schembechler became head football coach of the University of Michigan in 1969, spring practice had been a lark: light workouts and time off on weekends, with the only requirement being to stay in decent shape. Then Schembechler descended on the team like a giant, angry bear. Under his system, the team practiced twice a day every day, ran on Sundays, and after final exams, when the rest of the students went home, they had to come back to practice. He never let up. Drills were at full speed. Scrimmages were furious. He screamed, cursed, and constantly urged them on. He wanted to turn them into a team that could win a Big Ten Championship.

Schembechler decided he needed a slogan. He came up with "Those who stay will be champions." Of course, not everyone stayed. Many quit. One morning, Schembechler came in and saw that underneath "Those who stay will be champions," someone had written with a Magic Marker, "And those who quit will be doctors, lawyers, and captains of industry."

Stew Leonard has sprinkled slogans around his "world's largest dairy store," which generates almost $100 million in sales from its location in Norwalk, Connecticut:

"If you wouldn't take it home to your mother, don't put it out for your customers."

"Only happy customers come back."

"When in doubt, throw it out."

George Allen, coach of the Washington Redskins from 1971 to 1977 and of the Los Angeles Rams from 1966 to 1970, used a number of slogans to motivate and inspire his players:

"Every time you win, you're reborn; when you lose, you die a little."

"The winner is the only individual who is truly alive."

"One hundred percent is not enough; the world belongs to those who aim for 110 percent."

"Careers don't last forever and the season is short."

Vince Lombardi, the tough-minded coach of Green Bay, is remembered for the following slogans:

"Winning isn't everything, but making the all-out effort to win is the most important thing."

"Fatigue makes you a coward."

"Hurt is in your mind."

"I will demand a commitment to excellence and to victory, and that is what life is about."

His players liked to tell the story about the time Lombardi got a dose of his own medicine. Lombardi complained to his wife, "Marie, this damn knee is acting up on me again." Without a blink, his wife retorted with one of Lombardi's own well-publicized slogans: "You've got to be mentally tough." The players said the coach wouldn't talk to his wife for the rest of the week.

LEGENDS OF THE GAME

―――――――――――― **TEAMTHINK** ――――――――――――
Developing legends within your organization and keeping them alive contributes valuable benefits to the corporate culture because they can teach, inspire, or motivate your people.

The use of legends within a corporation can be a very effective means of conveying corporate philosophy and viewpoint. A strong company uses its oral legacy to embellish its history and focus its aspirations. These legends become folklore that can do a remarkable job of creating a positive and winning attitude. Because of this, storytelling is being touted in management seminars and workshops as a hot management tool.

An excellent illustration is the story of the Nordstrom Department Store employee who took back tires from a customer who claimed to have bought them a year before and alleged that they were defective. The employee accepted the tires even though that particular store had never sold tires and tires had been sold at Nordstrom only briefly, somewhere in Texas. This story has become a Nordstrom legend and helps the company promote its attitude toward customer service.

David Armstrong, vice-president of Armstrong International Inc., the industrial equipment manufacturer based in Stuart, Florida, uses stories galore. They are bound in books, hanging on bulletin boards, framed on office walls. Each one-page story was told by an employee to Armstrong, who wrote them up. Armstrong's book, *Managing by Storying Around*, was published in 1992. For example, there's one about the employee who had bypass surgery and alerted the company to hospital overcharges. Another story relates how road congestion problems dating back years led to a policy of letting office workers break for lunch five minutes ahead of factory workers. According to Armstrong, ''People remember stories and their morals a lot better than they remember written policies.''

Making employees laugh about a story is a better way to teach them something than reciting a list of rules. William Holekamp, president of Enterprise Rent-A-Car of Los Angeles, shared with me one of Enterprise's legends about a man who was nicknamed "Icepick Killion."

"Icepick gained his nickname," Holekamp told me, "based on the fact that he was so aggressive in pursuing renters who would not return our rental cars that one day he found himself in one of our cars attempting to drive it away from the front of the renter's house. The renter apparently was busily loading all of her personal goods into the car in an obvious plan to take our automobile to greener pastures. When Icepick looked up, he found our renter most unhappy about his attempt to take our car back . . . so much so that she had an icepick resting against the side of his neck. Needless to say, our employee decided that discretion was the better part of valor, and he elected to let the police handle this particular situation. However, the story of Icepick goes on and is part of our folklore, which has served to make what could be a negative activity of our work into something more of an adventure. There's also a hidden message of aggressiveness within the story which could never be trained. Safety and caution can be trained, but we have found that competitiveness and aggressiveness seldom can."

Every sports team has legends that have gotten exaggerated over the history of the franchise. Whether it is the Babe Ruth story, in which the Babe points out the spot and then hits the home run for a seriously ill child, or the one about Jack Youngblood, the Los Angeles Rams defensive tackle, who played a playoff game with a broken ankle, they all build up the folklore of the organization in a way that makes each new player want to become a part of that folklore.

Many baseball enthusiasts familiar with the Cy Young Award, given every year in the majors for pitching excellence, have heard the story of how the legendary pitcher got his name. While trying to impress an owner, Denton True Young tore some boards right off a grandstand with his high-powered fastball. Somebody said it looked like a cyclone had hit it, and cyclone became "Cy."

Legends shouldn't be tampered with. Everybody must know about the time a sparrow flew out from under Casey Stengel's cap. But not so well known is the time years later when the Dodgers tried to repeat the trick.

The first time, in 1918, was magical. When a sparrow crashed against the bullpen wall at old Ebbets Field in Brooklyn, the genius of inspiration alighted on Stengel, who was standing nearby. He cradled the stunned bird in his hands and returned to the dugout. An inning later, with the crowd watching him, Stengel bent over and doffed his cap, from which flew the now alert sparrow. The fans at Ebbets were no less amazed by what they saw than the early cavemen had been at the invention of fire.

Nearly a half century later an old and bent Casey Stengel, who should have known better, was prevailed upon to try his famous trick again at an old-timers' game in Dodger Stadium. The public relations people rounded up a sparrow, and to make the bird manageable, somebody had the bright idea of spinning it rapidly around by its tail. Casey obligingly did his part, but after he doffed his cap the bird fell to the ground like a rock. It wasn't dead, only dozing.

The moral: You cannot rubber-stamp genius. The muses will not be bullied; they come and go as they like, regardless of the opinions of public relations people.

THE BOTTOM LINE

This chapter has dealt with learning the name of the game—defining your company's purpose in your mission statement, addressing your organization's values in your corporate philosophy, focusing your direction by establishing your goals, and identifying who you are by assessing your corporate culture. These elements combine to determine your degree of success or failure. If these elements are not in place, all the other management techniques that you employ in your business will lack direction and purpose.

"Healthy companies [are] about shared ideals, shared goals, shared respect, and a shared sense of values and mission."

Max DePree,
former chairman and CEO,
Herman Miller, Inc.

2

Leading the Team

You don't become a leader because you say you are. It's much more what you do than what you say.

Sparky Anderson,
manager,
Detroit Tigers

To be an effective manager, you must become a leader.

onsider this message, published in *The Wall Street Journal* by United Technologies Corporation, Hartford, Connecticut: "People don't want to be managed, they want to be led. Whoever heard of a world manager? World leader, yes. Educational leader. Political leader. Religious leader. Scout leader. Community leader. Labor leader. Business leader. They lead. They don't manage. The carrot always wins over the stick. Ask your horse. You can lead your horse to water, but you can't manage him to drink. If you want to manage somebody, manage yourself. Do that well and you'll be ready to stop managing. And start leading."

Not everyone can be good at both leading and managing. Some people have the capacity to become excellent managers but not strong leaders. There are subtle yet apparent differences between a manager and a leader:

A manager administers; a leader innovates.

A manager maintains; a leader develops.

A manager plans; a leader sets a direction.

This is not to say that managers cannot be strong. The real goal is to combine strong management with strong leadership.

According to John P. Kotter, professor of organizational behavior at the Harvard Business School, "Most U.S. corporations today are overmanaged and underled. However, with careful selection, nurturing, and encouragement, dozens of people can play important leadership roles in a business organization."

MY PASSAGE TO LEADERSHIP

When I first started out in business, I was only a player. I had no idea how to manage, let alone lead. I found that the transition from player to manager can be hazardous, agonizing, and sometimes costly. The greatest danger to my organization came early, when I was trying to make the transition from star salesman to manager. Because I enjoyed selling so much, I always concentrated on the big sale of the moment and ignored pending management decisions. I failed to focus on or even recognize management problems. Although I put out a lot of fires, I finally realized that I was both the firefighter and the arsonist.

My transition from player to manager happened over a number of years, with a series of stops and starts. Eventually a transformation occurred and I found myself passing along the sales opportunities to others in the firm and concentrating on the management issues. As my industry became more volatile and competitive, I had to learn how to cope with change in order to survive and grow. Often that meant setting a new business direction, a tough and sometimes exhausting process. I recognized that my role in my organization was to create strategies and provide vision. I also discovered that while vision can gain high marks for originality, it is worthless unless it can be realistically translated to serve the interests of the company, employees, or customers. The final and perhaps most important lesson I learned in my transition into leadership was the absolute necessity to delegate operations and most problem-solving to others and to encourage and develop leadership in as many of my managers as possible.

In sports, and baseball in particular, the great players don't always make great managers—in fact, they rarely do. Babe Ruth, Ty Cobb, and Ted Williams all tried to manage, but with little success. They tended to expect too much from their players, to think that what came easily to them would come just as easily to the rest. They weren't good teachers. On the other hand, Sparky Anderson, Whitey Herzog, Earl Weaver, and Tommy Lasorda—mediocre players—all became excellent managers and leaders. These men have diverse styles, but they all possess some traits common to leaders.

LEADERSHIP TRAITS

————— TEAMTHINK —————
Leadership is not definable in simple terms because it has so many components. An effective leader has a combination of traits that motivate others to follow his direction.

I believe some of us must assume leadership, I believe young men thirst to be led to better themselves. Life is hard and success is survival. Leaders inspire us. Leaders show us the way.

Frank Leahy,
former head football coach,
University of Notre Dame

Here are some of the ways leaders inspire and give direction:

- **A leader has vision.**

  A leader must develop a mental image of where he wants the organization to go. Unless you know where you're going, you can't get there.

  The chief executive officer should spend 80 percent of his time thinking about tomorrow and only 20 percent working on today, whereas his chief operating officer should spend 80 percent of his time working on today and 20 percent thinking about tomorrow.

  Jack Welch, CEO of General Electric, says, "Good business leaders create a vision, articulate the vision, passionately own the vision, and relentlessly drive it to its completion."

- **A leader has scope.**

  This means having an expansive vista . . . seeing the big picture. I equate having scope with riding inside one of those elevators that has a glass wall on the building's exterior. The view expands dramatically as the elevator ascends from ground level to the top floor. You get a totally different perspective at the top than you had at the bottom. That's scope.

- **A leader is innovative.**

  Paul Brown, former coach of the Cleveland Browns and of the Cincinnati Bengals, was one of the greatest coaches in the history of football. His innovations have had a lasting influence on the game; he was a man ahead of his time. Brown was the first coach to hire assistants full-time, the first to make extensive use of notebooks and classroom techniques, the first to grade players with film clips. He was also the first to call plays from the sidelines by rotating his guards as messengers for his plays.

  Instead of simply carving out one little niche, as do a lot of cable television companies, Kay Koplovitz, founder, president, and CEO of USA Network, took on a mix of distinguished programming and shaped it to make USA the number-one cable network in terms of viewership and the first to use on-air advertisers. What has set USA apart is its diverse programming: major-league sports, an award-winning children's series, and movies.

Until fourteen years ago, all insurance agents nationwide purchased their own individual errors and omissions policy (similar to malpractice insurance). I came up with the concept of having the insurance company for whom the agent worked sponsor an errors and omissions program for *all* its agents. In effect, this new concept allowed one buyer (the insurance company) to act as the purchaser for five thousand agents instead of requiring those agents to be individually contacted. This innovative program was incredibly successful because it simplified enrollment, centralized collection, and significantly reduced administrative costs, which in turn reduced the premiums.

A successful leader has to be innovative. If you're not one step ahead of the crowd, you'll soon be a step behind everyone else.

> Tom Landry,
> former head coach,
> Dallas Cowboys

- **A leader is focused.**

General Electric's Jack Welch says, "A good leader remains focused. Identify your major objectives and don't be diverted by minor ones. Controlling your direction is better than being controlled by it."

- **A leader is *the* decision-maker.**

I always respected the players, but they have to understand that you are the boss. There are decisions that have to be made and you cannot be afraid to make them.

> Cotton Fitzsimmons,
> former coach,
> Phoenix Suns

Not every decision will be correct. The key is not to look backward, wasting time and energy trying to call Sunday's game on Monday. As Warren Buffett, CEO of Berkshire Hathaway Companies, says, "In the business world, the rear-view mirror is always clearer than the windshield."

Hank Peters, the former Oriole manager who traded for Reggie Jackson, only to see him become a free agent and leave the club, said, "If I knew then what I know now, I wouldn't have made the trade. But if I knew what I know now, I wouldn't have voted for Richard Nixon."

- **A leader must remain rational.**

A leader who has a quick temper or is erratic in his management style will make his employees nervous and upset. We've seen angry coaches throw chairs, grab facemasks, and charge fans. Who can forget the closing minutes of the 1978 Gator Bowl, when fans and players looked on in disbelief as Ohio State coach Woody Hayes ran onto the field and punched a Clemson player after a key interception. The next day Hayes was relieved of his duties as head football coach.

If the leader can't control himself, how can he ask others to control themselves?

The players don't want to see me rushing around and screaming. They want to believe I know what I'm doing.

Tom Landry

- **A leader must be able to handle pressure.**

How about pressure? It's tremendous. Internal pressure is the toughest. Nobody knows what it's like to be a head football coach unless he is one. An assistant only worries about his segment of the team, but the pressure on a head coach surrounds him. He has to decide everything. What is the starting lineup? What formations are we going to use? How do we practice? Whom do we recruit?

*If it doesn't work, I'll take the blame. You need that
courage to be a good coach.*
John McKay,
former head football coach,
University of Southern California,
Tampa Bay Buccaneers

- ## A leader must be trustworthy.

*If you set up an atmosphere of communication and trust,
it becomes a tradition. Older team members will establish your credibility with newer ones. Even if they don't
like everything about you, they'll still say, "He's trustworthy, committed to us as a team."*
Mike Krzyzewski,
head basketball coach,
Duke University

- ## A leader demonstrates a sense of humor.
John McKay has said, "A requisite for being a successful
coach is a sense of humor. It helps you survive. At times, such
as after a tough loss, my jokes are sort of a defense mecha-
nism."

McKay once said to his team after a bad loss to Notre
Dame, "Forget it, guys, do you realize there are seven hundred million Chinese who didn't even know that the game
was played?" McKay was wrong; the next week, he received
three letters from fans in China complaining about the loss.

The coaches of the Dallas Cowboys had designated park-
ing spaces. One day it rained just before team practice. Rookie
Steve Kiner didn't want to get wet and parked in coach Tom
Landry's spot. Landry came in soaking wet, looked over at
Kiner, and said, "I admire a man with courage."

- ## A leader teaches.
In 1992, Stanford University's women's basketball team became the NCAA champs after a hard-fought twenty-eight-

game regular season. Tara Van Derveer, their successful coach, says, "I look at coaching as very similar to teaching, except that we have twenty-eight public exams."

Branch McCracken, beloved longtime coach of Indiana University's basketball teams, who led them to win four Big Ten and two NCAA titles before retiring, once said, "Coaches, like teachers, occupy special places in life. They guide boys. We teach them to win. We also try to teach them to live. And we teach them to lose sometimes."

- **A leader encourages involvement.**

  You can encourage involvement through participative management, which allows employees at all levels to express ideas. This doesn't mean you take votes, because you can't run a business by committee, but it does mean you listen and ask for opinions.

  In the mythology of professional football, the quarterback is supposed to stand only one step down from the almighty coach in terms of field generalship and overall savvy. Everybody else on the team is supposed to be inanimate matter. The only reason linemen are needed at all, the theory goes, is to protect the genius who is the quarterback.

  Fran Tarkenton, who many believe is one of the greatest quarterbacks ever to play the game, refutes that theory. Although sportswriters lauded Tarkenton as a top-notch caller of plays, Tarkenton adamantly asserts that he practiced what came to be known as the "participative huddle" approach to play-calling. Tarkenton claims he only called about 25 percent of the plays himself. "The rest," he says, "were called by 'hunks' like guard Ed White and end Ahmad Rashad." As Tarkenton says, "This is just common sense. Nobody can solve every problem, every time, on his own. So if you're working with a group, doesn't it sound pretty reasonable to find out what the group thinks?"

- **A leader demonstrates the conviction of his principles.**

  When the legendary Bear Bryant coached the University of

Alabama's football team, he had a strict rule against drinking. He also had a star quarterback named Joe Namath.

There came a time when Namath admitted that he and some friends had been out drinking. Everyone, including the fans and the alumni, believed Namath was indispensable to the team. There were two games left in the season, against Miami and Mississippi. There was no question that Bryant thought their chances of winning either game without Namath was slim.

However, Bryant told Namath that he had broken the rules and was out for the year, and maybe forever. Bryant received over six thousand letters of protest, but he held firm. Alabama managed to win both games by narrow margins.

Namath returned the next year and led Alabama to the National Championship. Years later, he agreed that Bear Bryant was absolutely right to suspend him and to make the suspension stick.

You can bet the other Alabama players followed the rules not only for that season, but for future seasons as well.

In 1992, Indiana University basketball coach Bobby Knight kicked his son off the team after the younger Knight was arrested for public intoxication and disorderly conduct. This wasn't the first time Knight had ejected a player from his team, but it's got to be a lot tougher when it's your own son. Knight suspended five players and kicked three off the 1977–78 team after he walked in on a party where marijuana was being smoked.

Rest assured, nobody possesses all of the leadership traits just described. However, if you look closely at someone who is an effective leader, whether a manager or a CEO (or a winning coach), you will discern a number of those traits. But having a combination of successful leadership traits is only one step toward being an effective leader. The next step requires that you perform the functions of leadership.

LEADERSHIP'S FUNCTIONS

It's critical to address the functions that are the primary responsibility of leadership. A leader's success can be judged by his ability to recognize these functions and perform them. In my organization, I see leadership's functions as including *planning, establishing management philosophy, resolving conflicts,* and *establishing methods of accountability.*

Planning

I believe it is essential to formulate a *strategic plan* to enable your company to set its business direction over a period of years. Just because an organization functions on a calendar year for accounting purposes, doesn't mean that's the way the company operates in actuality. It is crucial to define and see the bigger picture because most issues are not resolved in one year: A new program doesn't get developed in one year; a branch can't be opened and become profitable in one year. Realistically, you cannot formulate a suitable annual plan if it does not support your strategic plan.

Harold Burson, chairman of the public relations firm Burson-Marsteller, emphasizes the importance of long-range strategic planning. Burson credits the firm's phenomenal growth to the overall vision developed in a long-range plan drawn up in 1960. Of his commitment to strategic planning Burson says, "It may be difficult for some people to believe, but in 1960, we wrote a long-range plan for this business that pretty well describes the business as it is today. We wanted to work for large multinational corporations; that was our prime client target. And we wanted to be internationally based. We wanted to go to Europe first, which we did, and then to Asia. In 1980, we went to Australia. We really had a vision for a long-term strategy, we plugged in the pieces as we went and changed it as we had to."

My organization operates on a rolling three-year strategic plan, which we reevaluate annually. Because the changes in the insurance industry can be rapid and dramatic, a longer-term plan would be futile. The planning committee consists of the board of directors and senior leadership.

After several days of discussion and deliberation, the committee developed this strategic plan:

1. To remain privately held.

2. To protect the company with diversification so that the loss of any one program, division, or specialty would not impair its future.

3. To develop programs that are product-driven.

4. To specialize as niche marketers whenever possible.

5. To operate under a profit center philosophy with each entity operating as a separate unit, but interrelating whenever possible with each other.

6. To place strong emphasis on profitability.*

7. To place major emphasis on attracting and retaining top personnel.

8. To develop a management team capable of managing each profit center as a separate self-sustaining company.

9. To develop a service philosophy and become a true service company throughout the organization.

You'll notice that no numbers turn up in any aspect of our strategic plan. Once numbers are attached, they become goals that belong in an operational plan.

Cal-Surance's *operational plan* is an extensive, highly detailed, one-year plan developed during a two-phase process consisting of two three-day off-site meetings attended by the senior leadership and managers of each profit center. The first round of

---

*There is a mistaken assumption that it is the goal of every company to be profitable . . . a company might choose to sacrifice profit for growth.

planning meetings deals only with key management and marketing issues. No numbers or budgets are discussed until the second round of meetings, two months later. The interval between these sessions allows everyone to prepare figures for the second round.

I have found that holding the meetings at a nearby resort facility is crucial because it provides a more relaxed atmosphere which stimulates creative thinking. Always in mind is the goal to develop a plan that supports the direction of the three-year strategic plan.

Establishing Methods of Accountability

At the completion of the operational planning meeting, each of my managers must *sign off* on his portion of the plan, so that it's clear that it's *his* plan. An operational plan is outdated as soon as it is made, in the sense that unexpected events do occur. Therefore, you must continue to *manage* the plan in order to achieve the projected results. By that, I mean you keep working on each issue in the plan and modify what doesn't work.

Cognizant of the need to monitor our progress, we hold monthly meetings with the head of each department and profit center to compare their results to the operational plan. I encourage my management team to focus more on certain key operating ratios that enable us to evaluate a number of factors, such as our revenue and expense ratios, employee cost ratios, etc.

Whatever system you use to evaluate your progress, you must establish a method of accountability that defines who is responsible, with target dates for their action plans.

For example, in my business, certain ratios seem to hold true over the years. If total salary to revenue exceeds 55 percent, we have a profitability problem; if revenue per employee is under $100,000 per year, we have a profitability problem; and if corporate overhead exceeds 15 percent, we have a management problem.

Establishing Management Philosophy

Let me first define what I mean by *management philosophy* so that you do not confuse it with management *style*. By philosophy,

I mean a *theory or principle* of management, whereas *style* refers to a *manner, fashion, or way* of management. Personality determines each individual's particular style of management, whereas the company has the ability to advocate the management philosophy to which its officers and managers should adhere.

The management philosophy I prefer is *participative management.* I try to create a business environment in which *everyone* has an opportunity to express his views on important subjects.

Watching Phil Jackson, head coach of the back-to-back NBA Champion Chicago Bulls, it's difficult to figure out his coaching technique. But those in the know attribute Jackson's success to the advice he seeks and relies heavily upon from his talented and veteran assistants.

According to assistant Tex Winter, "One of Jackson's strengths is that he likes a debate. He wants us to express our ideas on things, even to the point of an argument . . . he doesn't squelch us at all. Phil realizes the experience we have and that we can contribute, so he uses us." Winter adds that unlike most coaches, Jackson also encourages his players to express themselves.

Max DePree, retired chairman and CEO of Herman Miller, Inc., says, "I believe that the most effective contemporary management process is participative management. It begins with a belief in the potential of people, and guarantees that decisions will not be arbitrary, secret, or closed to questioning. Participative management is not democratic. Having a say differs from having a vote."

Management-By-Walking-Around

I see *management-by-walking-around* as a highly effective management tool that further implements participative management. I try to schedule my MBWA tour of the offices twice a day. I visit with a number of people, congratulate some for specific accomplishments, get a sense of what's happening, and act as a resource, particularly in sales strategy issues.

You want to avoid what I call *management-by-stumbling-around.* I suggest you keep the following suggestions in mind when you take your MBWA tour of your offices:

- ## Never use MBWA for criticism or checking up.
  This doesn't mean you should wear blinders. There's a lot to be seen. Just try to avoid the temptation to practice instant management on the spot.

- ## Be prepared for small talk.
  MBWA isn't meant to function like a formal management meeting. This is an informal opportunity to get a *feel* for how things *are going,* and gives people a chance to see you as *approachable.*

- ## If you don't like it, don't do it.
  People will sense it if you're not comfortable. MBWA does not work for everyone. If it's not your style, it could backfire on you.

- ## Don't make it a "ceremonial" or "state visit."
  If people prepare for the visit, or are on their best behavior, the spontaneity and relaxed manner of MBWA could be lost.

- ## Be willing to listen.
  I don't attempt to talk with everyone each time I do my MBWA, but I do make it a point to speak to everyone in my company at some time, from secretaries to supervisors to managers. People now anticipate my rounds and see them as an easy way to approach me to discuss a particular situation or problem. This lets people know that I am genuinely interested in them and that their operations are important to me.

Dan Finanne, president of the Golden State Warriors, claims he practices MBWA every day. "I have already been to the front of the offices and back, once today," he told me. "And before I leave, I always make one more trip around because I don't want my people to be able to say, 'Oh gosh, if I had caught you, I could have got this done.' So we get it done and that's that."

Encourage your company's officers and managers to try MBWA—they may find it a beneficial management tool. I've been faithfully practicing it for the past three years and it has served as an excellent bridge to help me get in closer touch with *all* the employees in my organization.

> *I stay close to the clubhouse and close to the players for two reasons. One, it helps break down their feeling that an uncontrollable source up there has total power to move their wife and kids three thousand miles tomorrow and they can't do anything about it. Two, it gives you a better chance to assess the players. You can see what they do on the field, but sometimes you can't assess mood and how they're reacting to winning or losing. If I'm down on their turf, they're comfortable and more inclined to say, "Can I talk to you?"*
>
> Buck Rodgers,
> manager,
> California Angels

Resolving Conflicts

> *A great leader doesn't treat problems as special. He treats them as normal.*
>
> Al Davis,
> general managing partner,
> Los Angeles Raiders

Another important function of a leader is to facilitate resolution of conflicts among his senior managers. The way conflicts are resolved can affect your relationship with your managers and can determine how they view you as a leader. In dealing with discord among managers in my organization, I try to follow certain rules.

First, I accept disagreement within the organization as inevitable. There can be strong differences of opinion wherein each opinion offers merits as well as drawbacks. Such divergent views often produce conflict between their advocates, but the conflict can be resolved in a healthy manner that produces positive results.

It is essential to prevent a conflict of opinion or interests from deteriorating into infighting, inappropriate remarks, or taking sides, which can have permanent destructive consequences. Claire Rothman, president of the California Forum and general manager of the Great Western Forum, home of the L.A. Lakers and Kings, declares, "I try to deal with conflicts immediately. There cannot be islands, territorial rights, or turf wars. We have to keep the feeling of teamwork that makes us so unique."

As soon as you are aware of a conflict, schedule a meeting with *all* the parties at the same time. Before that meeting, direct them to put their arguments, versions of the situation, or proposals in writing for your perusal. This forces them to rethink their positions and often diffuses the emotions that a verbal presentation can trigger.

At the meeting, try to remain neutral (for as long as possible). Depending on the situation, you can exercise one of three options: (1) send the parties off, directing them to try to resolve the dispute among themselves; (2) act as a facilitator, guiding the issue to a solution; (3) jettison the first two options and just step in and firmly make the decision or resolve things yourself. This is where you must assume the leadership role. Don't take votes; the decision must be yours, not the most popular or the consensus but what you deem the *right* decision.

Too many times a CEO or senior manager steps in too quickly to referee a conflict. The danger is that people will automatically look to you to resolve all differences. First, encourage the parties to work together to resolve their issues. Step in *only* if their process deadlocks or becomes too emotional or if time constraints necessitate your quick action.

My basic principle is that you don't make decisions because they are easy, you don't make them because they're cheap, you don't make them because they're popular; you make them because they're right.

> Theodore M. Hesburgh, C.S.C.,
> president,
> University of Notre Dame

WHO SAID IT NEEDS TO BE LONELY AT THE TOP?

Pepper Rodgers, recalling a bad year when he was coaching at UCLA, told a reporter, "My dog was about my only friend, and I told my wife that man needs at least two friends. She bought me another dog."

————————— TEAMTHINK —————————

Often it is difficult to share business problems or confidential matters with the people within your organization, so it's wise to seek support and advice from outside sources.

Even though the head coach at Notre Dame has many, many people around him, he's isolated in a sense. He can't air his own personal concerns with the public, with the team, not even with his staff. He's kind of contained in a little box, because everyone is leaning on him. Even when you're at the top, it's a bit lonely at times.

Ara Parseghian,
former head football coach,
University of Notre Dame

Lou Holtz, coach of Notre Dame today, has said, "It is not unusual for me to call other coaches; I do it all the time. It is not abnormal either, to have a variety of head coaches call me and discuss things."

Like Holtz, I try to recruit valuable advice from my peers outside my organization. Although my firm is privately held, I believe it is essential to have an outside board of directors. No member of the board works in the organization, which gives me the freedom to discuss any matter openly. All my board members are, or have been, CEO's of their own companies, and they make outstanding contributions not only during the quarterly board meetings, but also between meetings. Their main function is to provide a resource for me in the company. Not only is their counsel invaluable and their experience extensive, but because they've acquired an intimate knowledge of the company and my own goals, they can give me straight and informed responses to moves I'm contemplating. They are also strong enough to tell me when they disagree with me, or warn me when I'm about to make a major mistake.

James R. Martin, chairman of Massachusetts Mutual Life Insurance Company, believes one of his foremost assets is his company's outside board of directors. "Our board is very heavily involved in our strategic planning process," he says, "and when they go away with our top officers for the annual three-day strategic planning session, their influence is positive and strong."

As an alternative to a board of directors, you could form a group of advisers who can act as a sounding board for your thoughts and ideas. I formed a study group of six people from different parts of the country who operate in the insurance industry, and we have been meeting for over twenty years. We meet once a year for three days and alternate the site among our cities. We share ideas, problems, and successes as business colleagues. We discuss mutual management, product, and industry problems and concerns. We often speak by phone during the year, talking over a particular problem or issue.

Pete Newell, who coached University of California at Berkeley, which ranked number one in NCAA basketball in 1960, loves to tell this story. At that time, he was lecturing other head coaches and assistants in Minnesota when Fred Taylor came to his clinic. Taylor had just taken over the year before as coach at Ohio State, which had the worst defensive record in the history of the Big Ten. Taylor asked Newell if he could pick his brains on defense. Newell obliged and for three hours every afternoon went over defense with Taylor.

The next year, Taylor's assistant came to Newell with a list of questions a foot long that he said Taylor needed answers to. Newell answered all the questions, and later in the season more questions arrived.

"What do you think happened?" Newell says. "I end up playing Ohio State in the NCAA finals and he beats me with some of the defensive things we talked about." Newell asks himself, "Would I do it again? Hell yes, I'd do it again. And I would because so many coaches helped me along the way."

THE TROPHY CASE

―――――― **TEAMTHINK** ――――――
Rather than dwelling on mistakes, learn from the experience. Mistakes are not complete losses if they can be translated into valuable lessons.

Failure is good. It's fertilizer. Everything I've learned about coaching I've learned from making mistakes.
                              Rick Pitino,
                              head basketball coach,
                              University of Kentucky

One night, a Dodgers farm club coached by Tommy Lasorda was leading Tucson by one run in the eighth inning, but Tucson had the bases loaded with two outs. Lasorda decided to pep up his pitcher, a left-hander named Bobby O'Brien. Lasorda slowly walked out to the mound and said, "Bobby, if the heavens opened up right now and you could hear the voice of the Big Dodger in the sky and he said to you, 'Bobby, you're going to die and come up to heaven, and this is the last batter you're ever going to face,' how would you like to meet the Lord, getting this man out or letting him get a hit from you?" "I'd want to face him getting this guy out," O'Brien replied. "That's right, you would. Now, how do you know that after you throw the next pitch you're not going to die? This might really be the last hitter you're ever going to face and if it is, you'll want to face the Lord getting him out."

Lasorda, impressed by his own powers of persuasion, strutted back to the dugout confident that O'Brien was going to go after that batter with all the drive Lasorda knew he had. Unfortunately, before he even got back to the dugout, the batter lined a base hit to right field, knocking in two runs. "Bobby," Lasorda said at the end of the inning, "what happened?" "It's like this, Skip," O'Brien said. "You had me so worried about dying I couldn't concentrate on the batter." Lasorda probably never tried that strategy again.

Amateur and professional athletes display the trophies that symbolize their greatest achievements, but none of us wants reminders of our worst performances. However, I've seriously thought about setting up a trophy case in my office displaying some of my greatest disasters, to help me remember that all my decisions aren't winners. What are some of my all-time losers?

- The time I changed the compensation plan for our salespeople from commission to a salary with an annual incentive bonus. In their minds, each became an executive instead of a salesperson and new sales dropped dramatically. I changed back to the original compensation program three months later. **Painful lesson: If it ain't broke, don't fix it.**

- While in London, after a long dinner with too much wine, I impulsively hired the man I had been interviewing. He worked for me for one year in a sales capacity and never made one sale. **Painful lesson: Alcohol and good decision-making don't mix.**

- Twenty years ago I created a worldwide insurance program for marine insurance for the dredging industry. The problem was that at the time we were too small to match the resources of the competition. We finally "sunk" the program. **Painful lesson: Play within your limitations and ability.**

- I opened branch offices in Reno and Phoenix. We had no sound operational marketing plans and the offices were really established for the wrong reasons. We closed one office and sold the other with substantial losses from both. **Painful lesson: Establish a marketing plan and a sound operating budget before entering into any venture.**

Do Coaches Ever Make Mistakes?

Back in 1983, when Chris Ault was coach of the University of Nevada–Reno Wolf Pack, he literally ran out on his team. With eight minutes and thirty-four seconds remaining in the game between the Wolf Pack and the Fresno State Bulldogs, Ault's running back, Otto Kelly, scampered eighty-nine yards for a touchdown and a 22–21 lead.

During the run, Ault got so caught up in the excitement that he began racing down the sideline alongside Kelly. When Ault reached the Fresno State twenty-yard line, he realized he had gone beyond the marked-off area of the bench that restricted coaches and risked being penalized fifteen yards. So he just kept right on running. He dashed through the end zone, up a ramp, and out of Fresno State's Bulldog Stadium.

He was found hiding behind a truck by a fan, who asked, "Say, aren't you the coach for Reno?" Without a moment's hesitation, Ault replied, "I'm just looking for a hot dog stand."

When the chagrined coach made it back to the bench, he learned that in spite of his attempt to elude the referees, his team had been penalized fifteen yards on the subsequent kickoff because he had run afoul of the rules. This gave good field position to Fresno State, which went on to kick a last-second field goal for a 24–22 victory over the Wolf Pack and Ault—who simply ran out of luck.

When the L.A. Dodgers were still the Brooklyn Dodgers and playing in Ebbets Field, they had a fan by the name of Hilda Chester who was a regular at the games. She would sit in the bleachers displaying a sign, "HILDA IS HERE," bellowing encouragement to her Dodgers. She brought a brass cowbell which she would ring from time to time, making it one of the features of the park.

One night, she shouted at one of the Dodger outfielders, Pete Reiser, and dropped something onto the grass. "Give this note to Leo Durocher," she yelled. Reiser picked it up and put it in his pocket. As Reiser was going into the dugout, he saw the Dodger owner, Larry MacPhail, who waved to him. Reiser shouted back, "Hi, Larry." Reiser then sat down and gave the note from Hilda to Leo Durocher. Durocher immediately got on the phone to the bullpen and had a pitcher start to warm up. The pitcher on the mound was pitching pretty well, but in the next inning, Durocher removed him and a new pitcher came in for the Dodgers. This pitcher wasn't as good, but the Dodgers still managed to hang in and win the game.

After the game, Durocher shouted to Pete Reiser and angrily told him, "Don't ever give me a note from the owner again." Reiser replied, "I didn't give you a note from MacPhail." "Don't tell me that," Durocher said, "you handed me a note from him in the seventh inning." "That was from Hilda Chester, not McPhail!" Reiser said. Durocher looked at him and said, "You mean that wasn't from the owner?" What the note had said was "Get Casey hot, Wyatt's losing it." Believing it was from his boss, Durocher had changed pitchers. So Hilda Chester, sitting in the center-field bleachers, called the shots on the pitchers that day.

Just like these managers, I have made enough mistakes to fill my trophy case. But the purpose of these reminders is not to continue to beat myself up for making errors, it's to learn from these past mistakes to minimize the future ones.

The Bottom Line

I have been coaching the University of Kentucky basketball team for forty years. I've won four NCAA Championships. All groups need leaders. I'm the leader of this group. I know the way to win.

> Adolph Rupp,
> former basketball coach,
> University of Kentucky

Lou Holtz has said, "You've got to have great athletes to win, I don't care who the coach is. You can't win without good athletes, but you can lose with them. This is where coaching makes the difference."

These two great coaches sum it up. The bottom line is that no organization can win without good leadership.

Whether it's a sports team or a business, the quality of leadership determines the degree of success. In some, leadership is inherent; in others, it *can* be learned. When the seeds of experience, awareness, and imagination take root in an individual, he has the capacity to bloom into a leader. As Vince Lombardi said, ''The strength of the group is in the strength of the leader.''

3

Building the Team

How you select people is more important than how you manage them once they're on the job. If you start with the right people, you won't have problems later on. If you hire the wrong people, for whatever reason, you're in serious trouble and all the revolutionary management techniques in the world won't bail you out.

Red Auerbach,
president,
Boston Celtics

TEAMTHINK

None of your decisions is as important as the ones you make when selecting people, because they determine the performance capability of your organization.

Y ou need top people. It's so obvious it sounds silly to even state it. But hiring the best people isn't so simple. The truth is, it is not a science but an intricate art. You can't rely on references because former employers are reluctant to be honest. Because of government regulations, my company's application form is almost down to name, rank, and serial number. Professional résumé-writing services and courses that teach people to interview well further cloud the picture of the applicant. How then can you get a realistic assessment of anyone you're considering for your team?

The Sporting Edge

The Los Angeles Dodgers have twenty-four full-time and twenty-two part-time scouts looking for potential players. They use extensive computer analysis of performance statistics, interview the players, and watch them in action.

In this way, sports organizations have a tremendous advantage over businesses when they select new players. They have hard stats on an athlete's performance and the luxury of watching past performances on video. However, many coaches and trainers are skeptical about relying too much on past performance as measured by statistical averages. Former Milwaukee Braves manager Bobby Bragan voiced his reservations when he said, "Say you were standing with one foot in the oven and one foot in an ice bucket. According to the percentage people, you should be about perfectly comfortable."

What's scary is that even with the benefit of all those tools, a team can recruit a dud. Toronto Blue Jays scout Tim Wilken confesses, "A good scout, a very good scout, is only right twenty percent of the time on his main draft." Occasionally, a smart team can find a gem who was overlooked by previous teams. Twenty-six NBA teams passed over Dennis Rodman in the 1986 draft, but Detroit was smart enough to pick him. Rodman has become one of the most outstanding rebounders and shot blockers in the NBA. Incredibly, Joe Montana, perhaps one of the greatest quarterbacks in the NFL, was not picked until the third round of the player draft.

As business managers, we don't have dozens of scouts working for us; we can't videotape potential employees on the job, and we usually don't get measurable stats on their past performance. While there's no doubt that professional sports have an edge, there are things we can do to sharpen our team-building skills.

CREATE YOUR OWN WINNING EDGE

—————————— **TEAMTHINK** ——————————
Hiring needs to be a deliberate process, not a hurried and haphazard one: Many businesses rush into hiring, then live to regret it.

We're probably the most careful hirers of employees that you've ever met. We follow the Carpenter's Rule . . . measure twice and cut once; except we measure about four or five times and hire once.

> Dan Finanne,
> president,
> Golden State Warriors

The story about the day in 1981 when Pat Riley became coach of the Lakers is the best example I know of an expedient hire gone amok. Coach Paul Westhead had been fired. At a hastily called press conference, owner Jerry Buss announced that general manager Jerry West would become the new Laker coach. Before a stunned press, West contradicted Buss by stating emphatically that Pat Riley would be the new coach. Clearly flustered, Buss shot back that Riley and West would be co-coaches. Pandemonium reigned. A reporter asked Riley, "So, who's the coach?" Riley replied, "Beats me, I just want to go to lunch." The Laker-Riley story had a happy ending, but they got lucky.

At Cal-Surance, I expect everyone to follow certain hiring procedures. The following concepts have worked well for us:

- **Only hire someone for the specific position you are looking to fill and not for some future spot for which that person shows potential.**
  We once hired a receptionist because we thought she had great sales potential. What we got was a poor receptionist who didn't last long enough to become a salesperson.

- ## Always hire above-average people.

  Why take the time and spend the money to train someone who's only average? For the same investment of time, training, and money, you could end up with a superior employee.

  We coach better when we have better players; if I've learned one great truth over the years, it's that talent will always beat coaching. If I were advising a young fellow going into coaching today, I'd say, "Make sure you have better talent."

  > Ray Meyer,
  > former head football coach,
  > De Paul University

- ## Pay above-average salaries for the position; you usually will get better people.

  Smart people know they're worth more. If you don't know it, your competition will. We're all after the same top talent. Don't you want to give your managers an edge?

  If you're operating within a set salary range that won't get the job done, consider a sign-on bonus. If the person is as good as you think, future bonuses based on performance will meet everyone's needs. This avoids the risk of disrupting your overall salary levels.

- ## Before you start the hiring process, always complete an internal profile.

  Such a profile differs from a job description, which lists only the functions to be performed. In an internal profile, you consider the criteria that *determine future performance:* formal education, experience, ability to communicate, and factors that can be determined by testing, such as mental abilities, personality, and motivation.

  At Cal-Surance, we used to begin looking for someone before we knew exactly what we wanted. Halfway through the interviews, we would finally come to grips with what we were really searching for and have to start the time- and resource-consuming process over.

Set up a procedure for reviewing the profile *each and every time* the position comes open. Everyone hates to do this, but jobs change over time and the talent required changes too.

Frederick Turman, former provost of Stanford University, said, "If you want a track team to win the high jump, you find the one person who can jump seven feet, not seven people who can jump one foot."

- **Avoid the learning curve as much as possible.**

  If the person you're hiring has had limited experience in the position you need to fill, you'll pay the price. You don't want to pay for on-the-job training. Measure the cost of the errors this person is bound to make. Although he may not make the same mistake twice, you pay for the first one. The problem is, your new hire doesn't know what he doesn't know.

It's what you learn after you know it all that counts.
　　　　　　　　John Wooden,
　　　　　　　　former head basketball coach,
　　　　　　　　UCLA

- **Consider psychological testing for key positions.**

  According to president Dan Finanne, the Golden State Warriors use a psychologist to evaluate future employees. According to Finanne, "We don't tell the psychologist our opinion because we want him to be completely independent of us. He gives his view and then we compare it with ours."

  Cal-Surance employs an industrial psychologist. While the tests used cannot guarantee success, they can spot potential major problems. The characteristics that can be evaluated through testing include intellectual capability, work approach and style, motivation, emotional style and strength, and interpersonal and management style.

Dr. Pierre Mornell, a leading psychological business consultant, says, "Everyone comes in with problems. No one is problem-free. What you try to do is get the issues on the table before you pay for the moving costs. You want to be sure that the issues are manageable."

Mary-Ann Spencer, a vice-president with the executive search organization A. T. Kearney, suggests, "Assessment testing is most beneficial when the psychologist interviews your management team first and understands the types of business activities and decision processes that already work in your organization."

TeamThink

An important key in the hiring process is to have the right *fit*. You may hire a capable person with good talent, but if that person doesn't fit with the group, it won't work.

Los Angeles Lakers general manager Jerry West remarked of Boston Celtics president Red Auerbach, "He knows how to go into the draft and come out with exactly what he needs, but more important than that—someone who will fit into his system."

Cal-Surance hired a very bright individual, who had just earned his master's degree, as vice-president of one of our sales operations. The division he was to take charge of needed a strong leader who would work directly with the sales force. However, this individual turned out to be long on analysis and theory but short on rolling up his sleeves and digging in. After six months of studies, but no real action, it became apparent that we had what I call *a fish swimming in the woods*—a good person in the wrong spot, *a bad fit*.

I've discovered that not only must you find someone who is qualified for the job, but the candidate must also fit into your corporate culture. To achieve the *right fit*, you must go beyond the knowledge and skills that are requirements of the job and consider other factors as well.

Begin by evaluating your company's work environment. Is it formal and structured or informal and relaxed? A candidate coming from an informal work environment where dress was casual and work hours loosely organized might have difficulty adjusting to a more structured environment.

According to David Fagiano, president of the American Management Association, "Most managers don't fail because of incompetence; they fail because they didn't fit the 'style' of the job, the 'personality' of the peer group, or the company's 'management philosophy.'" The "style of the job" Fagiano refers to is *how* you want the job done, not *what* you want done.

You must identify the personality traits and culture within the particular unit where the vacant position is. As you assess these factors, you can better identify the needs, values, and interests a candidate must possess to successfully fit into that unit, as well as into the company as a whole. If, for example, you have a unit whose members function as a team with a fair amount of interdependence, you might not want a candidate who has operated on his own. For another example, you may find that a candidate who has worked in manufacturing has difficulty moving to a service environment, where the functions and attitude of the company are so different.

RECRUITING: THE GREAT TALENT HUNT

—————— TEAMTHINK ——————
The recruiting process is extremely important because it determines the talent pool from which you make your selections.

If you recruit good players and they play well, you're a genius. So for a year or two you'll be called a genius. Sometimes a "genius manager" will recruit bad players

*who play poorly, which will make people wonder how
come a genius got so dumb so fast.*

> Whitey Herzog,
> former manager,
> St. Louis Cardinals

According to a recent Dun & Bradstreet survey, the presidents
of small businesses listed "finding qualified, motivated employees
among their top five biggest headaches." Traditional recruiting
methods seem restrictive and ineffective because they only reach
people who are actively looking for jobs. To increase your ability
to reach elusive non-lookers and qualified candidates, you need to
go beyond the Help Wanted ads and broaden your recruitment
strategy.

Here are a number of recruitment strategies that have paid off
for my company:

- **Networking within your company.**
  Friends or relatives of top employees of the firm are potential
  good employees. If such a person is hired, we pay a finder's fee
  to the referring employee based on a scale tied to the new
  employee's salary.

- **Employing search firms.**
  When trying to fill senior management positions, our senior
  executives waste less time because the search firms only send
  us qualified people.

  I recommend that you treat a search firm like a prospective employee and interview its staff to make sure you have
  top talent looking for top talent.

  I'm always leery of a search firm that doesn't spend time
  to find out about our company, our structure, our needs. How
  can they interest someone in our firm if they don't know
  anything about us?

  Because the services of established search agencies are
  expensive, consider putting the agency at risk. If the em-

ployee isn't working out after ninety days, you should require that you get your money back and the agency start a new search.

Michael Arrington, president and CEO of Arrington Travel Center in Chicago, a company with over $90 million in annual sales, says, "We use six search firms to ferret out unhappy folks who might consider a change to our company. Our greatest assets are our human resources. The only impediment we have to growth and expansion is finding the right people to support expansion. That is my most difficult task. It's hard to find these people."

- **Using a recruitment database company.**
  These firms sell ready-made lists of specific types of candidates. They may require an annual subscription or charge a per-usage fee. Such database firms may focus on accountants, systems specialists, or college graduates.

- **Tapping into "Welcome Wagon" or newcomers' organizations.**
  Often when nearby companies bring in new employees from other parts of the country, the spouses of these new people are searching for jobs as well.

- **Contacting realty companies with corporate relocation departments.**
  These departments also address the job placement needs of families relocating to your area. Let them know about your employment opportunities.

You are not necessarily in for an unproductive search if you stick to traditional recruiting methods, but you have a better chance of reaching suitable people if you update your recruitment strategy.

The Turn-off Process

Potential employees are often lost because of careless hiring procedures. In 1923 the Detroit Tigers missed their chance to recruit the legendary Lou Gehrig just that way. Gehrig was playing baseball for Columbia University and making the eyes of major-league scouts pop by slugging the ball all over the field and often out of it, across the street, and onto the steps of the library.

Every scout thought his club should grab Gehrig before somebody else did. The Tiger managers were definitely interested, but dragged their feet deciding who should approach Gehrig. They finally settled on Wally Pipp, a onetime first baseman for Detroit who was then with the Yankees, to offer Gehrig a tryout with the Tigers. But they had taken too long. Much to Pipp's and Detroit's surprise and disappointment, Gehrig told Pipp he had just promised to join the Yankees. Pipp got Gehrig to promise he wouldn't tell Pipp's Yankee bosses that he'd tried to recruit Gehrig for Detroit.

Gehrig didn't tell anyone the story for many years. But he did join the Yankees. One day when Wally Pipp was sick, Gehrig took his place, and from that moment on he became the Yankees' regular first baseman. Pipp never did get his job back.

Pipp said later, "If only I'd talked to Gehrig a couple of days earlier, maybe I could have persuaded him to join the Tigers. And I might have stayed on at first base with the Yankees. I was just a little too late."

My firm has made mistakes that have turned off potential employees. Perhaps some of them will seem familiar:

- **Taking too long to make a decision.**
  Sometimes we've allowed a busy manager's schedule to slow down the process. The candidate gets turned off and accepts another position.

- **Failing to create an interest in the organization.**
  Poorly organized interview sessions that provide inadequate information about the company, or a negative or apathetic attitude on the part of the interviewers and careless treatment

of the candidate, can have a strong negative effect on the candidate's view of your organization.

- **Poor follow-through.**
Prompt follow-up after the interview conveys not only your interest but your professionalism.

- **Hazy job requirements.**
If you can't clearly specify what you're looking for and what the position requires, the candidate will think you don't have your act together.

Don't Drop the Ball

The wide receiver gets free, the quarterback sees him, and the offensive linemen give the quarterback the time to send a perfect spiral into the end zone. The ball is right on the receiver's numbers. He and the fans can almost see those six points on the scoreboard—and then the receiver drops the ball. Everyone groans, "How could it happen?" Usually it happened because he took his eye off the ball.

It's not unusual in the hiring process to get distracted, to lose focus. Many of us can probably recall with an appropriate groan when we dropped the ball and hired someone we shouldn't have.

When you are interviewing someone, follow certain steps and concentrate and you'll improve your results. To begin with, don't fall in love with the résumé. Professional résumé-writing services are widely used and can make anyone sound great on paper. On several occasions I've actually received résumés of people I had fired. Based on the résumés, I wondered how I could have let them go in the first place.

Since in all likelihood a résumé will be made available to you, here are some tips on evaluating résumés more accurately:

- **Start at the end.**
By reading the résumé from the back forward, you may collect the least desirable information about the candidate first—if

there is something unflattering, it is usually buried at the end. This may save you a lot of time.

- **Be suspicious of a functional résumé.**
  Because this type of résumé has no dates, only descriptions of past job functions and the candidate's qualifications, it could be an attempt to camouflage a job-jumper or hide the fact that the candidate has been out of work for a long time.

- **Don't be misled by a lengthy education list.**
  Candidates often try to use long (and often worthless) descriptions of seminars and special classes to conceal the fact that they lack an appropriate education.

- **Discount unimportant and unnecessary information.**
  A candidate who lacks appropriate experience or skills may attempt to cloud that fact by filling his résumé with trivia, such as sports interests, hobbies, family accomplishments, etc. Of course, if the candidate is overly involved in outside activities or commitments, you can question whether he has enough time for the job.

- **Be cognizant of the phrasing used.**
  If you are looking for direct hands-on experience, be alert to vague phrases such as "involved with . . .," "had knowledge of . . .," "was exposed to . . ."

- **Don't excuse a messy résumé or careless mistakes.**
  The candidate who isn't clever enough or does not care enough to make his résumé letter-perfect raises doubts about his desirability.

- **Don't read more into the résumé than is there.**
  Just because you hope, wish, or think you sense that something more is there, don't bet on it or count on it.

- **Look for the qualities that don't show up in a résumé.**
According to Dick Loughlin, CEO of Century 21 Corporate, "I feel that attitude and enthusiasm are more important attributes than skills. You can teach skills, but you can't alter attitude." After reading the résumé of a prospective salesman for our firm, I was very surprised that he had been scheduled to meet with me. His résumé did not reflect a pattern of previous success. However, when I voiced my reluctance to meet with him, my human resources director insisted that I proceed with the interview.

    After meeting with this individual, I knew why. He exhibited an intense desire to succeed and I sensed a dogged tenacity in his character. I didn't know what had happened to him in the past, but I felt certain he would be successful with us. My hunch paid off; he's been with us ten years now and is a real asset to the firm.

When I talked to a potential new player, I'd look him right in the eye and watch him respond to my questions. Numbers are important, but heart is as important to me. I want to know about attitude and intelligence and the ability to take it.

Bill Parcells,
head coach,
New England Patriots

Although in the 1980s interviews lost credibility and fell into disfavor as personnel managers focused more and more on psychological tests, that trend is now reversing itself. As studies reveal just how easily the ideal answers to these tests can be faked, professional opinion is shifting back in favor of the interview.

Interviews are unreliable *if* they are unstructured. Unconsciously, the majority of managers rely on personal chemistry, and although this is significant, it should not be the deciding factor.

Here are some pointers on interviews:

- **Schedule more than one interview for any serious candidate.**

  How can you make a valid decision on someone in a one-hour interview? Normally, by the third interview the bloom has come off the rose. A valid criticism of the way too many managers hire is that they don't spend enough time with job candidates and don't take enough time to find the right one.

- **Use team interviewing for key management positions whenever possible.**

  One-on-one, most people are skilled enough to present themselves favorably. Team interviewing creates tension and pressure and throws a candidate off from his comfortable or pat answers. In addition, it gives you an opportunity to observe his interaction with other people.

  Team interviewing has been implemented by several large companies which wanted to improve the validity and accuracy of their traditional interview procedures and increase the consistency and defensibility of the selection process. Companies are finding that team interviews often win a higher acceptance, or "buy-in," of selection and promotion decisions by both job candidates and their management team.

  It's wise to limit the size of the interview team to five people to prevent it from getting unwieldy and to avoid intimidating the candidate. The questions to be asked should be selected and approved by the interview team members themselves, and they should be job-related.

  Mary-Ann Spencer of A. T. Kearney suggests, "Clearly define everyone's role in the interview process *before* you start."

- **Remain the interviewer—don't change places with a prospective employee.**

  The person being interviewed should be talking about 80 percent of the time. While intelligent questions from the candidate are appropriate and a good sign, too many times I've observed my managers being interviewed themselves, rather than controlling and conducting the interview.

Probe for answers in depth. Don't move on until your question has been answered satisfactorily.

- **Take notes during and after each interview.**
  Taking notes improves your memory. You don't want to be overly influenced by the last interview and forget a better candidate whom you may have interviewed earlier. Too often after you've seen several candidates, their names and faces blur.

- **Avoid giving interviewees answers to key questions.**
  As an example: "People skills are important to this position. Do you have good people skills?" Is there anyone who wouldn't say, "Yes, I do"?

My approach in interviews is trying to get at the real person. We want someone who is introspective. We've found, for example, that if you get a person who has no insight about why he left other places, it's not a good situation for us.

Dan Finanne

- **Ask open-ended situational questions.**
  Try "How would you handle an employee who appeared tipsy after returning from lunch?" rather than "Do you approve of employees who return to the office after lunch slightly drunk?" Or say, "The distributor has screwed up the same order three weeks in a row. How do you handle it?"
  Studies conducted in 1984 by the University of Washington concluded that what people say they would do is pretty much what they *will* do when the real-life situation arises. This study also revealed that education and job experience are not necessarily indicative of future performance, which makes candidates' answers to situational questions a lot more useful than smug recitals of past achievements or pronouncements about where they want to be in five years.

- **Ask all candidates the same basic list of questions.**
  How can you compare the candidates unless you use some common measure? If you gave everybody a different test, what would an A or B mean? Also, if you ever have to defend your hiring decision, your ability to document that you asked all candidates the same questions will confirm that your hiring decision was unbiased.

- **Don't have departing employees conduct the interviews for their replacements.**
  This is almost always a mistake. You may no longer command a high degree of loyalty from the departing employees, and you don't really know what he is thinking or feeling. In addition, departing workers tend to want to hire candidates who are not as good as they are.

- **Consider having employees who have been promoted hire their own replacements.**
  Upon being promoted, the entry-level employees of Johnsonville Foods, Inc., hire their own replacements, instead of having the company fill the jobs through a central hiring office. This has proved a real benefit because the employees get to choose the new individuals with whom they will work and upon whom they will rely. They become coaches and mentors at early stages in their careers. And they learn the importance of good hiring early, when they're still at a level where mistakes won't badly hurt the company.

- **Avoid the prehiring syndrome.**
  Sometimes because he looks right and his résumé and references are perfect, a candidate is mentally hired before even being interviewed. But it's still very important that you force the candidate to prove he is right for the job. Make it clear that you plan to do a thorough reference check; you are likely to get more candid answers.
  Don't base hiring decisions on stereotypes. As one of my managers likes to say, "He looks like a duck and he walks like a duck, but am I really getting a duck?"

- **Make sure the applicant understands the good, the bad, and the ugly about your organization.**

  "Before you draft a kid, you got to know how bad he wants to play," says Bert Randolph, a scout for the Chicago White Sox. "So you don't tell him he's going to Hollywood. You tell him about the three A.M. bus rides, the greasy-spoon food, and locker rooms so filthy you suit up at the hotel. If he understands that and still wants to play, he's a prospect."

  For key management positions, we ask our interview team to be brutally honest about the problems within our organization and the problems associated with the position. We never try to sell a job by hiding its downside.

  Peter Drucker, the distinguished management guru from Claremont College, says, "The largest single source of failed promotion is the failure to think through and help others to think through what a new job requires."

  Every organization and every position has its share of problems; to pretend they don't exist is unfair to the candidate and the organization. You need to lay out what the negatives are and be certain the candidate is willing to accept the position with full knowledge of all the obstacles he will face. What you don't want is for a new employee to come to you six months later and say, "I didn't know what I was getting into."

- **Conduct the interview in a professional manner.**

  The way the interviews are conducted will make a profound impression on the candidate. Remember, just as you are evaluating him, he is also evaluating you in this process. An interview can turn off a potential recruit.

  Begin the interview by holding all calls. Inform the candidate about your interview process. Assure him that he will have time to question you at the end. Be certain you have taken the time to read his résumé or application *before* he meets with you. Have questions prepared based on his application, besides your usual interview questions. Set a time limit at the beginning of the interview; most interviews drag on too long.

Barry Switzer, former head coach of the University of Oklahoma football team, recalls his interview with Southern Methodist University. "They had about twenty-six people in the room, and we met at the First National Bank of Dallas. They had everybody there, including three of their players, some cheerleaders, and several alumni. It was a circus. I was genuinely surprised that the SMU band didn't parade through. I left there feeling there was real trouble lying ahead for SMU and I immediately withdrew my name from consideration."

- **Put the deal in writing.**

Once you have an agreement, put the financial terms in writing as soon as possible and have it signed *before* employment actually begins. I've had new employees come to me shortly after starting and say, "I didn't understand the financial arrangements"; there were times when we wound up giving more than we'd intended. We now have everyone sign an agreement before actual employment.

Very carefully go over the details of the job title, rate of pay, benefits, vacation time. Do not quote the pay rate as "monthly" or "yearly," since that wording could be construed as a contract.

THE HALFTIME INTERVIEW

"I'm just glad to be part of the team."
"I want to contribute in any way I can."
"We've got to look at this as just another game."
"They put their pants on one leg at a time, just like we do."

If it seems as if every athlete says the same thing when approached at halftime, that's probably because most of the interviewers ask the same predictable questions. In business too, because the candidate can anticipate most questions during the interview, the interviewer usually gets well-rehearsed responses.

To find talented people with good interpersonal skills, you

need to ask pointed and challenging questions during the job interview. The following interview questions to ask of candidates for management positions may give you a fresh perspective and reveal patterns that indicate how the candidate handles crucial people issues.

- **"Why are you giving up your job?"**
  Be wary of candidates who answer the question by bad-mouthing their current employer.

- **"How would you describe your management style?"**
  Will the candidate's management style be compatible with yours and the company's? This gets back to having the right fit.

A team should be an extension of the coach's personality. My teams were arrogant and obnoxious.
> Al McGuire,
> former head basketball coach,
> Marquette University

- **"Describe yourself, using three adjectives."**
  The candidate's choices can give you good insight into his self-image and creativity.

If only I had a little humility, I would be perfect.
> Ted Turner,
> owner,
> Atlanta Braves and Hawks

Joe McCarthy, the winning manager of the New York Yankees who coached Lou Gehrig and Joe DiMaggio, described his own qualifications as a manager this way: "A good memory, patience, ability, and ability to recognize ability."

- **"Since not everyone in a company is liked by everyone else, what would the people who don't like you say about you?"**

  The answer may reflect the candidate's people skills. For example, if he says that other people might complain that he always has to win an argument, you could then ask for instances of that excessive need to win. The response to that question may reveal flawed interpersonal skills—a red flag.

- **"Describe one of your greatest mistakes in business and what you learned from it."**

  If a person never acknowledges having made a major mistake, become very skeptical about that person's level of self-awareness, let alone his honesty. I'm even more interested to hear what he *learned* from that mistake.

  Red Auerbach readily recalls the major blunder he made in 1963. Auerbach was heavily involved with scouting back then; after intense scrutiny of Billy Green, a player from Colorado State, Auerbach made Green the Celtics' number-one draft choice. The kid looked great in training camp, but when he came into Auerbach's office just before the start of the season, he dropped a bombshell.

  It seems Green didn't fly and wanted to discuss his special "travel arrangements" with Auerbach. When Auerbach recovered, he realized too late that Green thought he could travel by train to meet the team in the various cities where they played. Auerbach couldn't talk Green into flying—the kid's fear was too great. Auerbach had no choice; he had to cut Green from the team.

  Although the Celtics wound up blowing a number-one draft pick, Auerbach claims he learned from it. "When a scout or ex-player told me about a kid who could 'fly,' I always made sure he did it both on and off the court."

*Last season we couldn't win at home and we were losing
on the road. My failure as a coach was that I couldn't
think of any place else to play.*

> Harry Neale,
> professional hockey coach

- **"What kind of people annoy you the most?"**
  The candidate's answer will alert you to the kind of individual he might have trouble working with. Sometimes the answer provides insight into the candidate's own traits.

- **"Have you ever fired someone?"**
  I'm wary of a manager who has never fired anyone—because
  maybe he can't make tough calls when necessary. Letting
  someone go is one of the most difficult things a manager has
  to do and I want to know how a candidate deals with that
  situation. Find out why he had to terminate someone and how
  he handled it.

*You have to improve your club, even if it means letting
your own brother go.*

> Tim McCarver,
> announcer for
> the New York Mets,
> former major-league catcher

- **"What criticisms would your previous manager voice
  about you?"**
  This forces the candidate to tell you a little bit about his
  previous employment; there's always the chance that you'll
  check to see whether his employer's answers are the same as
  his. Ask about his previous performance evaluations and their
  conclusions and recommendations.

Remember, interviewing is more than just a review of the pertinent facts or information about an applicant. It's a process of assessing the candidate's attitudes, values, and beliefs, and, most importantly, behaviors.

ALL THAT GLITTERS IS NOT GOLD

——————— TEAMTHINK ———————
The final stage in the hiring process is also one of the most important: reference checking.

Most employers perform reference checks perfunctorily, talking to only one or two of a candidate's former supervisors. Too often, this is done after a verbal offer has been made. Usually the hiring executive, who has already conducted a lengthy search, wants to hear only good things about the candidate because he does not want to be forced to start the hiring process again.

Many organizations will not give out a bad reference. Concern about lawsuits for slander has struck fear into many executive hearts. Therefore, it's safe to assume that the former employer will be less than candid when asked in a straightforward manner about the candidate. Another tack to take to try to glean accurate information from the reference is to quote comments from the candidate during his interview. For example: "The candidate told us he participated in a project to . . . ; what is your evaluation of the outcome? Could the candidate have done better? How so? Were you pleased with the result? Did it go over budget?" In other words, steer the conversation toward projects and gently probe into the candidate's contribution.

Although the former employer may not be reliable because of fear of litigation or because of a sincere desire for the former employee to do well, it may be possible to get a fair reading of a candidate's skill and character by speaking to his former peers and subordinates, who generally will not have been alerted about reference calls by the candidate. If a candidate is legitimate, he should have no problem supplying names to you. Former colleagues frequently paint a different picture of a candidate's abilities, so they can be a source of accurate, unvarnished information if the calls are approached properly. You may also be able to tap into your own industry network to find people who know the candidate or know someone who does.

SPRING TRAINING

TEAMTHINK

It is crucial for each new employee to be given a careful orientation into your company so that he will have the best chance to adjust, understand, and succeed in the organization.

In baseball, spring training is a critical time for the rookies, who need to be indoctrinated into the system, meet the coaches and other players, and develop the feeling of belonging. Both the NBA and major-league baseball have orientation camps for all the teams' rookies to offer them practical skills for coping with a variety of situations.

An effective orientation program is more than a personnel manual or a set of policies that anyone can read. I'm talking about really making sure that new employees are integrated into the team. The first thirty days of the employment relationship is a very critical time; it is then that the entire foundation for the future is established. Unfortunately, in most companies little is done to help new recruits learn their way around.

First impressions endure, which is why it pays to think about how new employees are introduced to your company. Sequent Computer Systems, Inc., doesn't leave anything to chance. Every new employee of the Beaverton, Oregon, company is assigned to a sponsor even before his first day of work. The sponsor is charged with taking the new recruit through Sequent's main streets and back roads—introducing the employee to others, rounding up office supplies, training the new hire on the electronic mail system, and imparting various aspects of company culture.

Sponsors, who volunteer for the assignments, commit about thirty minutes a day to their adoptees over the first couple of weeks. Sequent is convinced that the cost of that daily half hour of labor lost is far exceeded by the program's benefits. "One of the main values of this company is teamwork," says Barbara Gaffney, vice-president for human resources. "New employees work better if they know the other players, and a sponsor is one way to get to know people faster."

Top management at Corning Glass, realizing the absurdity of leaving new recruits alone to grope their way around their new surroundings, took a simple but highly effective step to eliminate the problem. Now most of the new managers are given the names of ten to fifteen veteran managers *throughout* the company. These veterans are required to schedule a lunch with the new recruit within his first few months at the company. The purposes are to build personal relationships throughout the company, to speed the newcomer's familiarity with the company, and to make sure that when problems arise, there is always someone to call for assistance. You may not have as large a company or as many managers as Corning Glass, but this is a good idea for a company of any size.

Not only in my own firm but in others, I've seen the following mistakes made in relation to new people:

- ### The sink or swim technique.
  Someone new is shown to his desk, introduced to his supervisor, and expected to know where everything is. One of his first problems is trying to find out where the rest room, copy machine, coffee machine, and exit are located. He can't come to work early because he doesn't know how to turn off the alarm system. He is a little like a lab mouse in a maze, expected to find his own way out to prove how smart he is.

  According to Carole Schwartz, a vice-president with A. T. Kearney, "New employees who feel unwanted often become dissatisfied with their employers and soon seek new opportunities elsewhere. The worst thing a company can do is hire an executive and then neglect to make the person feel welcome.''

- **Assigning ''widow-makers.''**
  These are jobs that regularly defeat even good people. Why give this type of function to a new employee and assume that a miracle will occur and he'll be able to do it when no one else could? Whenever a job defeats two people in a row, you should reassess the job to determine whether it can be handled by anyone.

GETTING OFF TO A GOOD START

To create a work environment in which new recruits have an opportunity to understand, adjust, and succeed in your organization, I suggest doing the following:

- Make sure the individual's office is ready on his first day of work and that you have already ordered his business cards.

- Introduce the new employee to as many people in the company as possible and arrange for yourself or an appropriate person to take him to lunch.

- Assign someone in the company to act as a mentor to whom the new employee can turn with questions.

- Include the new employee in as many memo distributions, meetings, and informal events as you can.

- Outline both the team goals and the corporate goals and define the new employee's role in meeting them. Taking the pains to see that a new employee understands the company and his role in it significantly increases the chances that he will become a part of the team.

THE COACH'S FUNCTION

TEAMTHINK

The CEO or president must become involved in the decision-making in hiring key people. As the company's leader, you are the one ultimately responsible for building the team.

Too often, because of time constraints, a CEO forfeits his role in the time-consuming hiring process. In my company, when the spot is for a salesperson, a middle manager, or a higher-level executive, I pass judgment on the final choice.

Richard White, author of *The Entrepreneur's Manual* (1977), said, "First-rate men hire first-rate men . . . Second-rate men hire third-rate men . . . These third-rate men will then employ the bulk of your company's employees and they tend to select fourth-rate people."

For those of you who think that because of the size of your organization, it is difficult or even impossible for you to take part in hiring decisions, think about the example of Admiral Hyman Rickover, who as head of the U.S. Submarine Command personally reviewed the nomination of every single officer under his command.

In the forty years during which he ran General Motors, Alfred P. Sloan, Jr., picked every GM executive down to the manufacturing managers, controllers, engineering managers, and master mechanics at the smallest accessory division. Sloan's long-term performance in placing people in the right jobs was virtually flawless.

Peter Drucker was on the money when he said, "Making the right people decisions is the ultimate means of controlling an organization well. Such decisions reveal how competent management is, what its values are, and whether it takes its job seriously. No matter how hard managers try to keep their decisions a secret—and some still try hard—people decisions cannot be hidden. They are eminently visible.

"Executives who do not make the effort to get their people decisions right do more than risk poor performance. They risk losing their organization's respect."

4

Keeping the Team

Keep good people by making the business as comfortable and challenging as possible, with good management, good working conditions, and the opportunity to grow.
Red Auerbach

TEAMTHINK
Money alone is not sufficient to attract or keep top talent.

In 1991 Wally Joyner, the star first baseman for the California Angels, rejected their four-year contract worth nearly $16 million for a one-year contract worth $4.2 million from the Kansas City Royals. The Angels were stunned. Joyner explained his decision by citing the deterioration of his relationship with the Angels, caused by doubts which he said had been cast on his commitment over the years by Jackie Autry, the club's executive vice-president and the wife of owner Gene Autry.

In the late 1960s, John Havlicek, a star player for the Boston Celtics, was offered a long-term, $2 million package by another team in the new American Basketball Association. Boston was paying Havlicek $105,000 a year—good money then, but dramatically less than the new offer. Boston increased Havlicek's salary, but it still wasn't close. Havlicek said, "I worked all my life and have always tried to do what was right. I never thought I'd earn more than $25,000. I just can't believe the money we're talking about, but to tell the truth, I love Boston. I value my reputation. I value what I think is right, so my answer is this: Even if they offered me another two and a half million, I would stay with the Celtics."

These two stories illustrate situations in which money was not a deciding factor. One star stayed because of his feelings about the organization and the other left because of his feelings about the organization. This situation occurs in business all the time; employees stay when they feel good about the organization, and leave when they feel bad about it. A recent survey by the Professional Employment Research Council found that eight out of ten workers at all levels would consider making a job change if the right opportunity presented itself. I find this statistic astounding; the conclusion would seem to be that company loyalty is dead.

In sports, loyalty often runs both ways, even in the age of free agency and $3 million yearly salaries. Several years ago, despite persistent overtures by his hometown team, the New York Knicks, explosive forward Chris Mullen made a decision in the off season to sign a nine-year contract with his team, the Golden State Warriors. Mullen says Warrior coach Don Nelson is the reason he decided to stay. Nelson played a key role in transforming Mullen from an alcohol-abusing, out-of-shape player to a perpetually-in-motion offensive force. The Warriors' organization credits Nelson with helping to save Mullen's career, and Mullen's loyalty to Nelson and the organization is the result.

How do you create an attitude that produces a group of employees who are loyal to your company? First, you must recognize that loyalty is a by-product of treatment. Next, you must believe that loyalty is strongest when built with emotional bonds, not material rewards. This chapter will deal with some ways to build loyalty and keep the team.

HOW TO LOSE THE TEAM

———————— TEAMTHINK ————————
People change jobs more often for personal reasons than professional reasons; emotions play the largest part in all human motivations.

Sports has a unique employment system. Once a player signs a team's contract, he belongs to that team. He can't leave because all teams in the league honor each others' contracts. The only exception is when he becomes a free agent; he can then negotiate with other teams. In business, even if you have an employment contract, your employee can always leave. We have a permanent free agent system. According to the U.S. Department of Labor, the average American worker has had eight employers by the age of forty.

Certainly no business deliberately creates situations that produce negative feelings in employees and ultimately lead to their departure. However, careless or unconscious attitudes or actions often contribute to turnover. The following are some of the kinds of things you should avoid.

- **Allowing salary inadequacies or inequities.**

  Employees want to be treated fairly. Nothing will turn someone off faster than feeling he's been taken advantage of through a salary inequity or inadequacy. The appropriate salary for a new employee is relatively easy to determine because in most cases the market sets the number—the employee knows what he wants or believes he's worth, and your competition establishes the salary it is willing to offer.

  The question to be addressed is "What are fair salaries for existing and long-term employees?" Cal-Surance uses three sources to keep us abreast of salary trends: a management association that provides quarterly salary surveys, information on current salary ranges from the search firm we engage, and the dissemination of salary ranges by industry membership organizations.

A potential for real trouble occurs when you have to pay a higher salary to a new employee than the one being received by a well-trained employee in a comparable position who has been with you for several years. Believe me, there is no way to hide this. The American Management Association contends that salary information is more widely known than management thinks, and once it gets out, you have a problem. The consequences of pay inequity within your company are employee dissatisfaction, withholding of effort, and lack of trust in the system.

When we face this problem, we try to use a signing bonus for the new employee rather than distorting our salary scales. If this isn't possible, there is only one way to deal with it and that's head-on. We have a meeting with our existing employees, explain the situation, and let them know when we will achieve salary parity.

- **Promoting non-achievers over achievers.**
  Here is a cardinal sin of management. Many times promotions are made based on longevity rather than achievement. Although longevity is admirable, it alone does not justify promotion. Besides not getting the best person for that position, you risk losing your achiever, who may go elsewhere to advance his career.

  No one in our firm has authority to promote someone in our organization without first securing approval from the supervisor to whom that person reports. This gives us an automatic system of checks and balances to make sure the promotion is justified.

- **Not promoting from within.**
  Remember, the grass is always greener on the other side of the fence. The person outside our company may only look better than your present employees because you are not yet aware of that person's limitations. By not promoting qualified people

from within your organization, you face the danger of turning off your own people.

Many professional sports teams say they like to award the head coach's job to a capable assistant coach within their own organization, but when it comes time to make the move, most hire an assistant coach from another club. Not so for Al Davis. The owner of the Los Angeles Raiders is a strong advocate of promoting from within. Three of the Raiders' past four head coaches worked in their organization before being promoted. And all three coaches, John Madden, Tom Flores, and Art Shell, have led the Raiders to winning seasons, Madden and Flores to the Super Bowl.

The one time Davis veered from his philosophy, when he hired Denver Bronco assistant coach Mike Shanahan, to replace Flores, the move backfired and Shanahan was dismissed.

• Not attending to an employee's personal needs.

Sometimes it's the little things that start to turn people off, such as incorrect payroll checks, improper handling of their employee benefits, or not fixing or replacing faulty office equipment.

When the San Francisco 49ers football team moved its offices from Redwood City to Santa Clara, California, it created a long commute for the organization's secretaries. Owner Ed De Bartolo paid attention. He bought a train pass for each secretary and had her picked up at the train station and driven the four blocks to the offices.

Sometimes a major personal problem needs attending to. The Cincinnati Reds blew it in the 1990 World Series, even though they won the Series in a four-game sweep over the Oakland A's.

Eric Davis, the Reds' left fielder, was seriously injured while diving for a ball in the fourth game in Oakland. He was rushed in severe pain to the hospital, where it was discovered he had a lacerated kidney. Although he was in critical condition for several days, the doctors told him he could go back to

Cincinnati, provided he hired a private plane. The cost for the plane would be $15,000.

His team had already returned home, so Davis tried to call Reds owner Marge Schott to ask whether the team would pay for the plane. She never called him back. Davis hired the plane himself.

His feelings were so hurt by the way he'd been treated that he took out a newspaper ad. The situation had been badly mishandled, and it made the whole Reds organization look bad. Davis was a valuable player and deserved better treatment. In 1991 he left the Reds to play for the Los Angeles Dodgers.

Richard Chandler, chairman and president of Sunrise Medical, Inc., headquartered in Torrance, California, says, "I always move to the top of my priority list any people issues or problems which arise in the organization. I view my job as a team coach, and if any of our thoroughbred athletes aren't happy or able to perform properly, I want to remove the impediment—any burrs under the saddle—so they can continue going in their respective directions at full speed. Then I can get back to my own priorities."

• Being insensitive to an employee's feelings.
When Don Shula was head coach of the Baltimore Colts, he became the first coach in the NFL to lose to the fledgling American Football League, in the Super Bowl of 1968. Afterward, because of this loss, Shula was concerned about his status with the Colts and his relationship with owner Carol Rosenbloom.

At a press conference, Steve Rosenbloom, the owner's son, introduced Don Klosterman, the new general manager. Shula had been made a vice-president of the organization. The question was asked, "How are Klosterman and Shula going to get along, and what are their responsibilities?"

Steve Rosenbloom replied, "Of course, we all know that the only reason Shula was made a vice-president is that we needed one more person around to sign the checks." Afterward Rosenbloom said his remark was *"just a joke."* It wasn't a joke to Shula.

Later that year, when Shula was offered a chance to coach the Miami Dolphins, he took the offer. He went on to become one of the highest-rated coaches in the NFL, taking the Dolphins to five Super Bowls and winning two.

I have a habit of joking with my senior managers about things that happen in the organization, but what may seem humorous to me isn't always funny to them. I know that this can put the managers in a tough spot. It obviously isn't a level playing field, and they may be uneasy about letting me know how they feel.

I became aware of this recently, when I made a joke at a manager's expense, thinking nothing of it. It wasn't until he called me at home on a Saturday to express his feelings that I realized how insensitive I had been. Fortunately he was able to raise the issue, forcing me to review my own behavior. How terrible it would have been to lose a good person or damage our relationship because of my own insensitivity.

- **Not keeping promises.**

Statements such as "In six months you'll get a raise," "The next opening in the department is yours," and "We're going to give you additional training" are all promises, perhaps well meant; but when not fulfilled, they have a dramatic effect.

I was very fortunate to secure a first-rate individual, highly regarded in my industry, to become president of my companies. He had been with one organization for over twenty years, but promises had been made to him that were not kept. As a result, this extremely loyal employee became so disenchanted that he felt he could no longer remain with that company.

- **Not according every employee dignity and respect.**

It is essential to treat each individual in your organization as a mature, intelligent, decision-making adult. This means, among many other things, no cutesy comments to young women and no condescending comments to older workers.

- **Being overly bureaucratic.**

  Forms, forms, forms + rules, rules, rules = frustration, frustration, frustration. Forms and procedures are necessary, but too many can be stifling. Be sure yours don't become speed bumps that slow down your organization and continually frustrate your employees.

  About twice a year, I give my executive team the task of finding ways to reduce bureaucracy in our organization. This continuing attention is necessary because bureaucracy has a tendency, like ivy, to come creeping back if you don't keep trimming it.

Any of the failings I've covered above can lead to turnoff or turnover. Lessening the threat of either boils down to being fair, honest, sensitive, and respectful to the people in your organization. When you slip up, they notice, so you'd best pay attention.

The Little Things That Count

TeamThink

Don't overlook the little things you can do for people that might contribute to an employee's positive feelings about your company.

Before the start of Game 1 of the 1981 World Series, Dodger manager Tommy Lasorda was busy managing—managing the turnstile at the press gate, that is. Lasorda spent ten minutes making sure the wives and girlfriends of his players were admitted into Yankee Stadium, despite their lack of tickets or credentials.

"You'd do the same thing for your wife, wouldn't you?" asked Lasorda. "Being a manager involves taking care of your players. I don't see any harm in this. I'm just making sure that everybody is happy."

When San Francisco 49ers fullback Harry Sydney and his wife, Nancy, had their third child, 49ers owner Ed De Bartolo sent flowers two hours after the birth. "Two hours!" said Sydney. When linebacker Jim Farnhorst's wife had twins, De Bartolo sent more than double the usual arrangement of flowers. Every Easter, every player and staff member gets two dozen long-stemmed red roses for his wife, mother, or girlfriend.

The managers of Underwriters Reinsurance Company in Los Angeles had a good idea when they installed a free popcorn machine for their employees. Everybody loves the smell of hot, fresh popcorn, and the employees appreciated the company's gesture.

So many factors contribute to an employee's feelings about a company that sometimes we overlook *the little things* that can make the biggest difference. You don't need to hit a home run on every one of these—a consistent single will do. Here are some things we do in my company:

- **First names only.**

  Baseball's Bill Veeck, flamboyant owner of the St. Louis Browns from 1951 to 1953, used to talk about the great differences between himself and his father. "My father was always 'Mr. Veeck' to everyone who knew him and I am always 'Bill.' Wherever I land, I make it clear to the girls at the switchboard and the guys who run the elevators that I am 'Bill.' I believe very strongly that we are all working together for the best interests of the ballclub. I cannot see why the fact that I own some stock and they don't should have any bearing on our personal relationship."

  As Claire Rothman, president of the California Forum, says, "We always call everyone by their first names; it's an important part of our culture."

  Similarly, at our company, regardless of position, we use only first names. Although I can't be sure what I'm called behind my back, when addressing me, everyone in the company calls me Don.

- **Lots of windows.**

  One of the reasons we selected our office building was because it had lots of windows, making the offices bright and cheerful. Being able to see the outdoors makes people feel better.

I recently visited the offices of an insurance company in New York where only senior executives had offices with windows. The balance of the staff functioned in poorly lit interior quarters. This is bound to create resentment.

- **Personalization.**
Each new employee in our company gets a coffee cup with the firm logo and his name on it. We also provide an attractive name plaque.

- **The seventh-inning stretch.**
During a recent visit to a client's office, I was horrified when a bell rang and I saw close to a hundred employees rise to their feet and file out for their *mandated* break. It's hard to believe that these archaic practices are still used in the 1990s. We don't have mandated break periods. I prefer that our employees take breaks whenever they need them.

- **Company lunchroom.**
In the lunchroom provided for our employees, we have full kitchen facilities, including a microwave oven, refrigerator, and soda and snack vending machines, as well as free coffee.

- **Personal days.**
Each of our employees receives two personal days off a year. Unofficially the employees call them "I Can't Cope Days." We can't always wait for a national holiday to tell us when we need a break. Why force employees to feel guilty by calling in sick when they just need personal time away from the office?

- **Flexible hours.**
To help us attract and retain people in a very competitive employment market, we give many of our employees flexible hours. They may start at 7:00 or 8:00 A.M., leaving at either 4:00 or 5:00 P.M.

The Harbor Sweets Company lets its 114 employees set any schedule that suits them, as long as it includes at least twenty hours of work per week. Part-time work is the norm, and the factory works four four-hour shifts a day instead of the more usual two eight-hour shifts. Most of the employees at Harbor Sweets are women from nearby affluent Marblehead, Massachusetts. They are paid only a little above the minimum wage, but they are attracted by the company's flexible hours.

- ## A stellar playing field.

At Dodgertown, the Dodgers' spring training center in Vero Beach, Florida, players are surrounded by the Dodger aura. The 450 acres include a stadium, five practice diamonds, two golf courses, hotels for the players, and a seventy-acre orange grove. The spherical streetlights have painted baseball stitches, and the streets are named after famous Dodgers. The message to the players and fans: We are a class organization. We're different, we're better, we have pride.

Cecil Fielder, the prolific home-run hitter for the Detroit Tigers, will be a free agent after the 1992 season. He has already proclaimed that he would like to remain with the Tigers, but only if the team commits to building a new facility. Though Tiger Stadium is beloved by fans, it is archaic, offering very few of the amenities players have come to expect. With their plush locker rooms, weight rooms, and air-conditioned dugouts, parks such as the new Comiskey, Oriole Park at Camden Yards, and the ultramodern Skydome in Toronto are the future. Before making a commitment to the organization, Fielder wants the Tigers to make a commitment to the players. He wants to see that they are willing to better their playing field.

What kind of message are you sending to your employees and clients when they're on your field? Is it well maintained? Is it clean? Is it professional? Does it create pride?

Dealing with Mistakes

TeamThink

When it is appropriate or essential to reprimand an individual, it should be handled directly, privately, and in such a manner that the person retains dignity and self-respect.

Every running back has had a game where he coughed up the ball. But, if he fumbles the ball in every game, or several times in one game, the coach can't overlook it. Come Monday, that player will likely find himself in a discussion with the coach.

Every employee in your organization is at some time going to do or say the wrong thing; otherwise he wouldn't be human. However, if an individual's mistake is flagrant or shows signs of becoming part of a pattern, you must deal with it. What you don't want to do is lose a good employee because you haven't handled it well. The desired result is to correct the situation while helping the employee maintain a positive attitude toward you and the company. What you don't want to do is blow the employee out of the water.

In these situations, you are more likely to achieve a successful outcome if you keep the following suggestions in mind.

- **Always have the discussion in private.**
  No matter how upset or angry you may be about the incident, you must pick an appropriate time and location for the discussion. No one wants to have other employees witness a reprimand or hear about his mistake. You want the employee to concentrate on the problem, not on how he looks to other people. Sometimes I use the individual's office or a small conference room for the discussion; it is neutral territory and less intimidating than my office. I try to help the individual relax so that he can be more receptive to what I have to say.

I prefer to deal with players in private. I had a philosophy about bawling a kid out. I'd always try to let him go home with a good feeling.

Ray Meyer

- **Be sure the discussion is face-to-face.**
  Too often a manager will resort to a memo rather than a face-to-face discussion. Because it does not give the receiver the opportunity to respond or dispute the facts directly and immediately, a memo can cause frustration and resentment.

  It's important that you be able to observe the nonverbal clues given by the individual so that you can assess his or her true attitude and receptiveness. Discuss the situation by telephone only if you cannot meet face-to-face in the foreseeable future.

I just try to treat the players like professional athletes. To me, this means treating them with respect, having enough courtesy to tell them face-to-face when they screw up.

Whitey Herzog

- **Avoid group admonishments.**
  First, it is unlikely that every individual in the group contributed to the mistake, and the guiltless will be offended.

  Second, it is difficult to get honest responses because many individuals are reluctant to speak out in a group.

  The University of Alabama was playing the University of Arkansas. Coach Bear Bryant was in a rage because the game was scoreless at halftime. In the locker room he went from player to player, telling them they were playing like dogs. When he came to a player named Henry Clark, he grabbed him by the shoulder pads, lifted him up, shook him, put him back down, and said, "Henry, you ain't playing worth a damn." Clark looked up and said, "Hell, Coach, I ain't even been in the game yet."

- **Only use effective criticism.**

  When delivering criticism, concentrate on maintaining a positive tone and a helpful, supportive attitude. Most people, when being criticized, are more sensitive to the tone than to the content of the criticism. As an example, a negative comment like "You messed up," provokes a defensive reaction. A more effective approach might be "Here's how this can be improved"; this should win a receptive response.

In keeping with the philosophy that whenever possible you should try to turn a negative into a positive, the way you confront someone who has screwed up is all-important: As described above, you should have a private, face-to-face discussion with individuals, not groups, and concentrate on using constructive criticism only. While this will not eradicate the mistake, it may help avoid a repetition while allowing the person being reprimanded to leave the meeting with a positive attitude.

> *People are human. If you're going to criticize them, compliment them first.*
>
> Bum Phillips,
> former coach,
> New Orleans Saints

RITUALS AND TRADITIONS: THE TIES THAT BIND

———————— TEAMTHINK ————————
Rituals and traditions that create goodwill are the ties that bind employees to the organization and create a sense of unity.

Pro sports have traditions that they take very seriously. When the Giants play at home, it's a tradition for the first-round draft choice to bring orange juice, coffee, and doughnuts for the whole team to Saturday practice. The doughnuts are serious business to the Giants. A few years ago, Eric Dorsey, the number-one draft rookie out of Notre Dame, brought the wrong kind of doughnuts the first couple of weeks and Bill Parcells nearly had a player revolt on his hands. Parcells had to send veteran Carl Banks with Dorsey to get the doughnuts, since Banks remembered from his rookie days where to go and what kind to buy. Said Parcells, "Some players came up to me and said, 'Bill, you've got to get Dorsey to shape up on this doughnut situation.' We're talking about doughnuts here!"

Since 1942, eight minutes before kickoff at each home game, the Clemson Tigers have boarded two buses that deposit the team at the top of a hill at the east end of the field. A cannon fires, and as the band plays "The Tiger Rag," the players gather to take turns rubbing a rock that supposedly grants mystical powers. The Tigers then run down the hill onto the field as the fans roar their approval. "The rock has strange powers," says former Clemson star Michael Dean Perry, now with the Cleveland Browns. "When you rub it, and run the hill, the adrenaline flows. It's the most emotional experience I've ever had."

In 1903, Clemson coach John Heisman—yes, that Heisman—wrote, "All colleges should have fixed athletic traditions and should be loyal to them."

The Golden State Warriors hold an annual picnic to which employees can bring their friends and families. Pictures can be taken with the players, but no autographs are given, so that the players can relax too. The purpose of the event is to tell the Warrior employees they are appreciated.

Every employee who has worked two or more years at Joseph and Laurie Cherry's Cherry Tire Service, Inc., a truck-tire road-service company, in Maybrook, New York, is entitled to take his spouse to Caesar's Pocono Resorts in Lakeville, Pennsylvania, for an all-expenses-paid weekend. Each year, the company upgrades the employee's suite—right up to the Champagne Towers, with a Jacuzzi shaped like a champagne glass and a heart-shaped swimming pool in the room. "The upgrading gives everybody something new to look forward to," says Joe Cherry. "When they come back, they are different people."

The benefit reflects Cherry's approach to management. "These guys work very hard at dangerous jobs. The reason they work hard is that they want a better life. We owe them a salary, just like they owe us the work, but the weekend is different. We're saying, 'This weekend is for you. Take it.' It's worth more psychologically than the six or seven hundred dollars it costs."

The Halloween day celebration at Cal-Surance has become an eagerly anticipated event. Starting months in advance, each department plans its theme in great secrecy, since departments compete for trophies and other prizes. We may be fifty miles from Hollywood, but the set designs our people create would do Movieland proud. One year the word processing department won first prize for transforming its headquarters into a Jules Verne undersea world, complete with underwater lighting effects, sounds of surf, fishnets, toy fish mobiles, and homemade mermaid costumes. Another year my office became a wartime unit. My secretaries were Private Benjamin and Rambo and they had me dressed as George S. Patton. We've seen everything from circus themes and *The Wizard of Oz* to *Star Trek*. Not only does everyone in each department go from unit to unit with awe and admiration, but so do all the visitors we get from the other companies in our twenty-two-story office building.

Our 150 employees select an Employees' Activities Committee that serves for one year. Last year they started a monthly potluck lunch—Mexican, Western, Italian. Only those who want to participate do so. The potluck is a chance for people to socialize and build camaraderie, and it makes work more fun.

Whether serious or silly, rituals and traditions become part of the company's culture and contribute profoundly to creating a sense of unity and belonging. They also enable everyone to step away from the pressures of business and have fun as a group. These experiences translate into good feelings toward your organization and help keep people with you.

MANY HAPPY RETURNS

―――――――――――― **TEAMTHINK** ――――――――――――
By remembering and acknowledging an employee's birthday, wedding, or parenthood, you convey a message that you are thoughtful and care about him.

When, in the 1940s, "Jolly Cholly" Grimm managed the Milwaukee Brewers, then of the American Association, he was approached by his boss, Bill Veeck (that was before Veeck became owner of the St. Louis club), who knew Grimm's birthday was coming up. Veeck asked what his manager would like. "A good left-handed pitcher," Grimm said jokingly.

Milwaukee had a long-established practice of honoring its manager's or coach's birthday with a lavish on-the-diamond fete before the game. Grimm was toasted at the pitcher's mound and a huge cake was wheeled onto the field, whereupon he was presented with a $1,000 savings bond. When Grimm picked up the giant knife to cut the cake, he discovered that his wish had been granted. Hidden inside the cake was one Julie Acosta, a left-handed pitcher whom Veeck had secretly purchased from Norfolk for his manager's birthday.

For his thirty-sixth birthday, the Brooklyn Dodgers' captain Pee Wee Reese was hailed with an entire evening in his honor. He was overwhelmed with gifts, including an automobile (in which his mother, to Pee Wee's surprise, was sitting), but the *pièce de résistance* came when the house lights dimmed and 33,000 fans lit matches and sang "Happy Birthday."

I'm a sucker for anyone who remembers me on my birthday. And I don't think I'm the only sucker around. Most people, whether they say so or not, like to be remembered at least once a year. So, at Cal-Surance, we make a big deal out of birthdays.

First, of course, we send birthday cards to everyone. If you have too many employees to write them by hand, have your personnel department prepare them from the computer records—you've already got the dates on file. Each month we have an enormous cake with the names of that month's birthday celebrants on it. I share the September cake with fifteen of our employees. For members of my executive team and other employees with whom I interact directly, I give a personal gift such as a fruit basket, a fine wine, or a selection of Swiss chocolates.

Many managers believe it's important to acknowledge an employee who has been with them for some time with a special gift. Lotus Development Corp. awards a paid sabbatical of four weeks, to be taken within twelve months of an employee's sixth anniversary. For fifteen-year employees Maytag's anniversary gifts include a twenty-inch Mallorca pearl necklace with the division crest on the clasp, a set of crystal tumblers etched with the division crest, and a Winchester carriage clock with the crest. Also at the fifteen-year mark, 3M invites the honoree and five guests to its autumn wingding at the St. Paul, Minnesota, headquarters, and IBM kicks in with a letter of congratulations from CEO John Akers, a $1,000 check, a string of pearls or a Rolex Oyster watch, and a lunch.

At Cal-Surance we also celebrate the anniversaries of our employees' hirings. We give them a "business" gift to remind them every day that we're glad they're with us. The first-anniversary gift is a distinctive pen with the person's initials. On the third anniversary, it's a handsome desk clock with the employee's name on it. For the fifth and subsequent anniversaries, the employees can choose among several gifts. For the tenth anniversary, for example, the value of each gift exceeds $3,000. To me, that's not too much for people who have given ten years of their business lives to our company. I also have dinner with them at a good restaurant so that I can personally tell them how much I appreciate them.

THE HERO'S FAREWELL

———————— **TEAMTHINK** ————————
Your commitment to rewarding the loyalty and hard work of long-term employees is reflected in the manner by which you honor their retirement.

At what was to be the last ballgame at the historic Polo Grounds before their move into Shea Stadium, the New York Mets, in a wonderfully cozy, sentimental ceremony paying tribute to seventy-three-year-old Casey Stengel, awarded him home plate. As Stengel made the long walk with the dish to the clubhouse 600 feet away, behind the center-field fence, "Auld Lang Syne" wafted down from the speakers. The 10,304 spectators stood, some weeping openly. "And we all stood outside the clubhouse," recalls Hot Rod Kanehl, "and *we* cried."

When Kareem Abdul-Jabbar retired from basketball in 1990, the Los Angeles Lakers' organization prepared to honor their incredible center for his consummate professionalism and outstanding performance and effort over the years. At a halftime ceremony at the Forum, Kareem was seated on the court with his family and other distinguished sports figures who were there to pay tribute to him. To the thunderous approval of the fans, Kareem was showered with both plaudits and gifts, including a Rolls-Royce from his teammates.

Every time I attend a basketball or hockey game at the Forum, I see the spotlighted retired jerseys hanging high above the stands with the names of former Los Angeles Laker and King superstars. The numbers on those jerseys cannot be used by any other player on the team, and the jerseys serve as enduring testimonials.

Twenty-two years ago, I competed for an account with a guy named Mike Bogen who had a one-man agency. Although I got the account, I was so impressed by Mike's professionalism and knowledge of the industry that I called him and talked him into joining my firm. My instincts about him proved right. For twenty-one years, he was loyal, committed, hard working, and a real asset to the company. He became a vice-president of the firm and managed our commercial division. He was funny and fair and his people and clients loved him. When Mike told me he was going to retire, I wanted to show how much I appreciated his efforts over the years.

We planned a surprise retirement gala for about a hundred guests, including family and clients of Mike's as well as everyone in the division, and held it in one of the ballrooms on the *Queen Mary*, berthed in Long Beach, California. After a super dinner, a riotous roast, some memorable plaques, and humorous gifts, we gave Mike two airline tickets to Europe. How could I do less for someone who had given me his all for twenty-one years?

If you've been fortunate enough to have a reliable and hard-working employee, you too must recognize and honor him on retirement. The way you do it will send a message to your present employees that effort and loyalty do not go unnoticed in your company.

BURNOUT

TEAMTHINK

An employee doesn't have to physically leave the business to be gone. If he is mentally turned off, either through boredom or exhaustion, he has already left the firm.

When Dick Vermeil coached the Philadelphia Eagles, his day started at 8:00 A.M. and lasted at least until 1:00 the next morning. He slept on the pull-out sofa bed in his office three nights a week. He opened Christmas presents a week late at home so that the hubbub wouldn't disturb his preparation for his first playoff game. Although he set curfews for himself, he broke them. He canceled vacations. He had coffee for breakfast, ate a Carnation Breakfast Bar for lunch, and sometimes had a hoagie for dinner while sitting on the toilet.

By his fifth NFL season, Vermeil was a Super Bowl coach. But the Eagles lost to the Raiders in the 1981 Super Bowl. Vermeil was criticized for burning out his team with long practices and meetings. He reacted by adding another hour to his already grueling daily schedule. It wasn't until the 1982 players' strike that Vermeil was forced to take time off. He never came back with the same intensity, and he finally quit coaching. His escalating overkill, he admitted, eventually burned him out.

One of my top producers came into my office one day and said his doctor had advised him to either take time off or quit entirely because his nerves just couldn't handle the stress anymore. He had been with me for over ten years and had always performed well. I had been totally unaware of his condition. I immediately worked out a six months' leave—paid his salary until his disability kicked in and told him the job would be waiting if he came back. Fortunately, he did. He's now working on a reduced schedule and can cope with the lessened stress of the job. I now realize that all the signs of burnout were there. I simply chose to ignore them.

"Basically, burnout is a process in which a *person's motivation is somehow diminished or damaged,*" says Beverly Potter, Ph.D., a Berkeley, California, management consultant and workplace psychologist.

If you look around, you are likely to find people who suffer from burnout without knowing it. Recognizing the signs of burnout is important so that you can gauge the depth of the problem and perhaps reverse it. Here they are:

1. An individual who once loved his job begins to complain about tiredness, lack of energy, and perhaps sleep disturbances.

2. An individual who was once functioning effectively now displays lower creativity, avoids making decisions, begins to believe there are too many things to do and not enough time to do them. He feels he is never caught up.

3. An easygoing person who has always appeared calm becomes chronically angry, often at his coworkers or the company. He indulges in sarcastic humor aimed at the management, the company's goals, or coworkers.

4. An individual displays signs of exhaustion or symptoms such as tension headaches, body aches, or nausea.

5. An individual "hits the wall," becoming unable to continue in his job. This is the final stage of burnout. Some people may develop a dependency on alcohol or drugs for relief; others may have a physical or mental breakdown.

When John Madden was asked what the first signs of burnout for him were, he replied, "You won't have the energy because you won't have the interest. Suddenly, you don't care about the draft. You're not interested in minicamp. You don't care who the best college linebacker is. You don't care if they've signed any of your veteran players to contracts. When you don't care, it's time to go . . . you're history . . . you're done."

If you or any of your employees or coworkers are showing any early signs of burnout, do something now, before they reach a crisis. People suffering from burnout can create a demoralizing environment in their effort to send out clues that they need help.

Here's what an organization can do to reduce burnout:

- Build reward systems that make employees consistently feel like winners.

- Set targets that people can meet. Better yet, give them a chance to set their own targets so that they gain a sense of initiative, confidence, and control.

- For employees already showing signs of burnout:
  Get them professional counseling.
  Force them to take time off.
  Change their job functions and create new challenges.
  Move them to a place where they can win—get them out of the mess.

As Peter Drucker says, "People aren't always burnt out; they are simply bored and need to be repotted, need the challenge of a new job, of a new environment, and of new associates."

Awareness, attention, and intervention to prevent burnout make good business sense. It is clear that deflecting burnout saves employers money by reducing absenteeism and increasing productivity. Most importantly, it helps companies keep good employees.

CHALLENGE AND GROWTH

Athletes thrive on challenge. Even the most successful are always looking for ways to improve their game. After Magic Johnson won an MVP award, he spent the following off season working on his free throws, which he believed needed improvement. It may seem incredible that the Most Valuable Player in the NBA sought to find a challenge for himself, but he did. The following season, Johnson won the title of best free-throw shooter in the NBA.

Sports teams prefer the games in which they go up against a tough competitor. The athletes really get up for those games. Whether it's completing the crossword puzzle in *The New York Times* or climbing a mountain, it's human nature to love a challenge.

Professional baseball succeeds in providing solid opportunities for its players' growth. Fans of the sport are aware that, with a few exceptions, most baseball players do not start their professional careers playing in the majors. Big cities are the home of the major-league teams, but smaller cities and towns all across America are home to the league's farm teams. The main purpose of these clubs is to help their young athletes develop into skillful and experienced players. These ballplayers know they have a golden chance, with the help of the team's coaches and manager, to become fine enough to get to the majors.

Businesses can't operate their own farm clubs, but they must provide the techniques that challenge their employees to grow. If business avoids this challenge, the risk is employees who are bored, burned out, or bummed out. The following practices will help alleviate potential problems:

- **Performance evaluation as a tool for growth.**
  A performance evaluation should be used as an opportunity to promote growth rather than simply to be critical. If the evaluation incorporates specific suggestions that will result in improved performance, it becomes a valuable tool for both the manager and the individual. The best evaluations are those that develop a game plan for progress and a remedy for shortcomings.

  It is crucial that the evaluation be well prepared and honest. Any manager who doesn't level with an employee is doing a great disservice; employees have no opportunity to either enhance or rectify their performance if they don't know where they aren't performing.

  At Cal-Surance, we never combine a performance review with a salary decision. The employee's concentration should not center on whether or not he got the raise he wanted.

- **Career path planning.**
  Many employees would like to further their careers. They would like to know what the next step is and what they have to do to qualify.

  In constructing career path plans, the first step is to designate the jobs that offer upward mobility. Not every position affords a career path opportunity, and not every employee wants to move up. The second step is to identify the educational, training, or personal qualifications for advancement.

It takes a lot of time, thought, and work to develop career path planning. A career path plan requires a serious commitment from the company and the individual if it is to succeed. If the plan is not in writing, signed off on by both parties, there can be real misunderstandings about the commitments both parties are making.

I am in favor of career path planning, but it's wise to remember that not every position opens up when planned, business cycles cannot always be controlled to create job openings, and sometimes the employee has a faster schedule in mind than the company can meet.

- **Committing to education and training.**
  Cal-Surance has developed an educational policy, included in every employee's manual, which spells out what we are willing to do for our people. We require that the education be job-related. Helping someone in sales go after a degree in accounting doesn't make sense. I also want to know that there's a reasonable chance that this is a long-term employee; I'm not interested in educating a short-term employee for my competitor. Each manager signs off on the employee's courses.

Nurtured for Success

Deep down, your players must know you care about them. This is the most important thing. I could never get away with what I do if the players felt I didn't care. They know, in the long run, I'm in their corner.

Bo Schembechler,
former head football coach,
University of Michigan

Remembrances and rituals will show your employees that you care, that you are in their corner. Their importance in keeping the team together cannot be overestimated.

What is it most of us want from work? We would like to find the most effective, most productive, most rewarding way of working together . . . we would like a work process and relationships that meet our personal needs for belonging, for contributing, for meaningful work, for the opportunity to make a commitment, for the opportunity to grow and be at least reasonably in control of our own destinies. Finally, we'd like someone to say, "Thank you."

Max DePree

5

Motivating the Team

When a club wins, it's difficult the next year to get the players to dedicate themselves the way they did the year before. The players aren't as hungry the next year.

Frank Robinson,
former manager,
Baltimore Orioles

I n the 1992 NBA playoffs, the Chicago Bulls tried to repeat as the NBA Champions, but they were almost out-hustled in the semifinals by the determined Cleveland Cavaliers. Michael Jordan explained the Bulls' lapse: "The hunger has not been the same as it was last year, which is part of the difficulty of trying to repeat. It's tough to have that same hunger."

─────────── TEAMTHINK ───────────
Improved performance comes from motivation, from arousing and maintaining the will to work effectively—not because the individual is coerced, but because he is committed.

According to John P. Kotter of the Harvard Business School, "Motivation and inspiration energize people, not by pushing them in the right direction as control mechanisms do, but by satisfying basic human needs for achievement, a sense of belonging, recognition, self-esteem, a feeling of control over one's life, and the ability to live up to one's ideals.''

Although I'm not minimizing the importance money plays in motivation, beyond the financial rewards that big-time winners earn there is a hunger for recognition—a desire to be acknowledged and remembered for a meaningful accomplishment. These feelings affect people deeply and can produce a powerful response. Here are a few examples:

- **Greg Louganis.**

  In Seoul, Korea, at the 1988 Summer Olympics, Louganis, one of the world's great divers, pulls himself out of the water after a diving mishap and, with a nasty gash on his head, continues to compete . . . and wins a gold medal.

- **Willis Reed.**

  It's the seventh game of the 1969–70 NBA finals, the New York Knicks against the Los Angeles Lakers. Reed, the Knick captain and inspirational leader, is hobbled by tendonitis in both knees. It's doubtful that he'll be able to play in the crucial game. But despite his obvious pain, Reed limps onto the court to start and scores the game's first basket. Inspired by his presence, the Knicks go on to beat the Lakers and win the NBA Championship. Reed gets his championship ring.

- **Kirk Gibson.**

  The Los Angeles Dodgers are playing Game 1 of the 1988 World Series against the powerful Oakland Athletics. Down by one run in the ninth inning, Dodger manager Tommy Lasorda sends up a sore-ankled Kirk Gibson to pinch-hit against the game's best relief pitcher, Dennis Eckersley.

  Gibson isn't even supposed to be able to limp. He strained his left hamstring in Game 5 of the National League Championship Series and hasn't swung at a pitch since compounding his woes by injuring his right knee in the seventh game of that series. He hasn't even been introduced before the game. In fact, twenty minutes earlier, he didn't even have his uniform on. But Gibson pleads with Lasorda to let him play.

After hitting three straight foul balls, Gibson hits the next pitch into the seats to win the game for the Dodgers. His home-run hobble is probably the slowest passage around the bases of all time. Only by hitting a home run could Gibson even have made it to first base. His teammates go on to win the series.

Bill Sharman, former coach of the Los Angeles Lakers, said, "Motivation is so important in pro sports. After so many games and so many road trips, players start feeling tired. The airports and hotel lobbies get you down after a while and it's up to the coach to keep you motivated. It's the coach's hardest job—motivating his players for each game, keeping them as high as they can be for every minute of every game."

In a much different arena from sports, business managers have the same problems of motivation as Bill Sharman. How do we get our employees to put forth a sterling effort, day after day, year after year, in order to achieve top results? Your employees may not be sports superstars. But once in a while, they do need to bask in the sunlight of recognition.

The National Science Foundation reports that of all the factors that help create highly motivated and highly satisfied workers, the principal one appears to be for effective performance to be recognized and rewarded in whatever terms are meaningful to the individual: financial, psychological, or both.

RECOGNIZE AND REWARD

TeamThink

Personal recognition from a boss or his peers is probably one of the most effective ways to motivate an employee.

*There's nothing greater in the world than when some-
body on the team does something good, and everybody
gathers around to pat him on the back.*

> Billy Martin,
> former manager,
> New York Yankees

When one of the Dodgers hits a home run, makes a fine play,
or pitches a good game, Tommy Lasorda doesn't just shake his
hand or pat him on the rump—he hugs him. "I don't believe all
that hugging with his players works," said Billy Martin. But Martin's third baseman Graig Nettles disagreed: "Hey, if we can ever
break up Lasorda and his players, we're going to beat them."

Athletes thrive on the recognition they receive when they've
performed well. Whether it comes from the coach, the teammates,
or the fans, it's the gas that drives their engines. Sports wisely
provide a number of avenues to challenge athletes to do well or be
the best.

It's every athlete's dream to make it into the Hall of Fame—to
be recognized as one of the greatest in his sport. The Hall of Fame
is the pinnacle for most athletes, the culmination of sustained
success. But there are many other levels of achievement that they
push hard for every working day. Election to an all-star game, a
league MVP, all-defensive team in the NBA, baseball's batting
crown, most sacks in a season for an NFL defensive lineman; these
are just a few examples of the many honors an athlete continually
strives to win.

The sensational guard Magic Johnson won the NBA's MVP in
1987 but the following year lost it to another great, Michael Jordan.
The loss of the MVP award in 1988 did not significantly affect
Johnson's income; he worked harder than ever in the off season to
regain the honor in 1989. For Johnson, winning the MVP was a
matter of personal pride.

When Bear Bryant was coaching at Alabama, he had an important game against Arkansas. With less than a minute to play,
Bryant's team was ahead 7–6 and had the ball on the Arkansas
thirty-five. Roddy Osborne, his quarterback, threw a poor pass and

the Arkansas defensive back, a student named Moody, also a champion sprinter, intercepted it and was immediately in the open field, running at full speed. Osborne, who was no sprinter, ran him down from behind, near Alabama's twenty-yard line. Alabama held and finally won the game, 7–6.

The next morning Georgia Tech coach Bobby Dodd called Bryant. He had read about the game and said he couldn't believe it. He asked, "How in the world could a slow guy like Osborne catch a speed demon like that Moody?" Bryant replied, "The difference was that Moody was running for a touchdown; Osborne was running for his life."

You'll discover that most of your employees, like athletes, have their own degrees of personal motivation. Recognizing and acknowledging an employee's contribution to the company makes him feel good, gives him status, and encourages others to go after recognition.

A few years ago, a member of our financial department named Bill was moving to another state. I decided to interview him before he left to get some feedback on the company. Bill said, "Remember that memo you sent me last year praising me after I suggested a new accounting procedure? That made me work harder for this company than anything else you people did. I'm taking that with me."

Bill took me by surprise. I vaguely remembered that our controller had called me and complimented Bill's contribution. On the spur of the moment, I fired off a memo to Bill, then promptly forgot about it until that exit interview. I quickly ordered some thank-you notes and asked all my managers to tell me anytime someone did something special. When I get the word, I write a note right away or drop by that employee's desk and tell him how much I appreciate his work.

The Xerox Corporation recognizes people through its "You Deserve an X Today" program. Any employee can give anyone else in the company a certificate redeemable for $25 for excellent support, service, work, or cooperation. American Airlines supervisors hand out coupons to employees for superior effort which can be traded in for gifts or free vacations.

Here are some other ways to show recognition for deserving employees:

- **Titles.**

  A title is the least costly thing you can give but one of the most rewarding to its recipient, and can bring unexpected returns. A title makes a statement to everybody. To the people inside the organization, a title designates a person's place in the hierarchy of recognition and authority.

  But conferring titles requires achieving a delicate balance. Although you'd like to give out as many as you can, each one has to be meaningful. Your employees will know when they or anyone else are handed a hollow title. Any inequities can have a lasting effect on the way people view their own and their colleagues' titles.

- **Quality circles.**

  This is a fancy way of saying: Make your achievers part of a select group. Sports does it superbly with the Pro Bowl in football and the All-Star Games in baseball, basketball, and hockey.

  Tommy Lasorda created a quality circle one year in spring training when he was supervising the non-roster players: He established the 111% Club. He and several other coaches selected the group of players who had hustled the most that day, and the players themselves voted for the winner. The first winner received a guided tour of the major-league locker room, where he had his photograph taken sitting in the locker of his favorite major-league player while eating a major-league ham and cheese sandwich. On another day, the winner was allowed to use Lasorda's personal electric heater inside the cold dugout during practice. One of the most desirable prizes was the privilege of helping the Chief of Clubhouse Sanitation feed the ducks in the adjoining pond. The grand-prize winner was invited to lunch with Walter O'Malley, the Dodgers' owner.

  The Continental Insurance Companies in New York

have created a special category they call "Circle Agents." To qualify, an agent must produce a certain volume of profitable business. Circle Agents are identified throughout the organization so that they earn extra commissions, receive preferred underwriting reviews, and have all expenses paid on trips with the senior management of the company.

I know of other businesses that have created a "President's Club" which gives special achievers extra recognition and status.

- **Honor walls.**

At the Baseball Hall of Fame in Cooperstown, New York, the inductees are represented by bronze plaques bearing their likenesses. Bronzing the mugs of some of your high achievers might be carrying it a bit too far, but pictures of such employees on a designated Honor Wall make a good way to recognize exemplary work.

When you enter the reception area of the home office of Century 21 in Irvine, California, you immediately see seventeen pictures prominently displayed. This is their Sales Associate Hall of Fame, created two years ago. Through an elaborate selection process based on leadership, quality, service, and exceptional performance, these individuals were selected from over 70,000 other associates. Each new member of their Hall of Fame is introduced first to Century 21's prestigious Centurion Group (their quality circle) and then to their national convention of over 10,000 people.

- **Newsletter recognition.**

Most professional athletes do not suffer from lack of recognition. Their performances are reported daily by hundreds of papers. While you and I and the people who work for us can't expect to be written about in the local press, many companies do have in-house publications.

In our newsletter, *Personal Lines*, we run a column called "Unsung Heroes," in which we salute the people who ordinarily wouldn't get the recognition they deserve for consistently doing a good job. The more names and the more pictures, the better I like the issue.

The Burroughs Company posts a regular notice titled the *Brag Sheet* at the employee entrance of its Canadian factory which details outstanding efforts.

Stew Leonard's, the highly successful dairy store in Connecticut, publishes a biweekly newsletter and a monthly magazine called *Stew's News,* which tout employees and announce births, birthdays, and promotions. The newsletter abounds with photos of employees and titles like "Superstar of the Month."

- **Perky perks.**

For the MVP's in our office, I like to award what I call "Perky Perks"—items such as special business cards, personalized stationery, unique desk accessories, anything that sets a deserving employee apart, both inside and outside the company. At a cost of only a hundred dollars for specially embossed business cards, for example, you can give a person a thousand opportunities to say to others, and to himself, "I'm special."

- **Wall plaques and certificates of achievement.**

One of a professional athlete's prized possessions is his collection of trophies and plaques. These treasures aren't locked away in the attic; they're prominently displayed.

If you're looking for another way to recognize good work, wall plaques and certificates of achievement might just do the trick. And it's important that the employee be awarded such recognition in front of as many coworkers as possible. If you don't think these are important to your employees, walk into a recipient's office and look around. You won't find them stuffed in a desk drawer—they're *always* on the wall, prominently displayed.

- **The personal touch.**

One of the best chances I had to see the personal touch in action came at the Broadmoor Hotel in Colorado Springs, run by the Tutt family. Frankie Tutt, the wife of then owner Bill Tutt, took a group of us on a tour of the huge resort, which has 57 departments and over 1,400 employees. No matter whom we passed on the tour, Frankie called all the employees by their first name, introduced them, and then proceeded to tell us about their family backgrounds, which of their relatives also worked for the hotel, and what they did. What she really was saying to each of those employees was, "I recognize who you are. I know what you do. You are a real person in our organization and not just a name on a paycheck." No wonder the hotel runs so smoothly and with so little turnover.

Alabama's Bear Bryant was never seen on the football field without his houndstooth hat. Whatever the weather, sun, rain, or snow, that hat remained atop Bryant's head. However, after a memorable goal-line stand against Penn State, Bryant showed his personal recognition of their tenacious performance and paid tribute to his players by quietly taking off his trademark houndstooth hat and lowering his eyes as they passed. Few of them have forgotten it yet.

Sometimes the best forms of recognition are the personal ones. A thank-you note or a pat on the back can work wonders. And don't underestimate the warming power of simple courtesy toward your employees. A pleasant "good morning" to every employee you see and an enthusiastic "good night" to everyone you pass on your way out certainly can't hurt.

DON'T TAKE YOUR WINNERS FOR GRANTED

Fran Tarkenton, an undisputed quarterback great, recalls the only time he called a play that required him, as quarterback, to block. (A blocking quarterback is about as rare as a three-legged giraffe.) His Minnesota Viking teammates were getting nowhere against St. Louis, and Tarkenton knew he had to pull out a surprise play to save the game. There is nothing more likely to surprise a defense than a play in which the quarterback blocks. The play worked; when Tarkenton's block took out a tackler, it allowed his teammate, John Gilliam, to score a touchdown and win the game.

Watching the game films the next day, Tarkenton's coach, Bud Grant, came around to talking about that particular play. Tarkington felt he had "sacrificed his body for the team." Although he was ready to bask in the glory, it never came. Everyone involved in the play was praised except Tarkenton. After the film, Tarkenton said, "You saw my block, didn't you, Coach? How come you didn't say anything about it?"

This coach's answer exemplified the "you don't need it" fallacy. Grant replied, "Yeah, I saw the block. It was great. But you're always working hard out there, Fran, you're always giving one hundred percent. I figured I didn't have to tell you."

"Well," Tarkenton replied, "if you want me to block again, you do."

The lesson is clear. If you want somebody who's performing well to keep performing well, say so, or you risk losing the good performance.

WANTED—REWARDS THAT WORK

───────── TEAMTHINK ─────────
An appropriate reward provides you with the opportunity to show appreciation to an employee who has gone beyond what his job requires.

During a dry spell, when Tommy Lasorda wasn't getting enough hits from the Dodgers, he promised a new suit to any player who would drive in two runs in a game. The following week, two Dodgers got new outfits.

Contrary to what you might be thinking, this was not a reward; instead, Lasorda used a bribe. There's a not-so-subtle difference between the two. A bribe holds out a carrot and says, "If you do this, you will get that." Now, I'm not saying all bribes are bad (or illegal). If the bribe sets up a win-win situation, there's nothing wrong with it.

A reward, on the other hand, is something that you get for doing something right that you didn't expect to get. Psychologically, a reward is much more powerful than a bribe. Here are some examples of effective rewards:

- **Personal gifts.**

  Our supervisors try to keep up with the interests of our employees so that we can reward them for their hard work by giving them something special. To an avid golfer, we might give a set of floating golf balls; to a football fan, maybe an initialed blanket to take to the games. A case of good wine might go to someone who likes to entertain. When you tailor a gift to an individual, your employee knows you're paying attention and you care. Try to steer clear of the uninventive, standard gifts such as pen sets and desk diaries. They're better than nothing, but they don't pack the same wallop a more personalized gift does.

- **Time off with pay.**

  It doesn't matter if it's one day or one week, time off with pay is always appreciated. Sometimes, if one of our employees is on a business trip overseas or doing business in a resort area, we'll throw in a few extra vacation days with all expenses paid.

  When Bill Walsh was head coach of the San Francisco 49ers football team, he would reward his players after they'd won a big game by giving them a day off from practice—to them a big treat.

- **Dinner for two.**

  Dining at a really nice restaurant is a favorite reward in my company; it's something that everyone loves. They get both the steak and the sizzle. You and I may take eating out in style for granted, but I'll bet many of your employees don't.

- **Tickets to a special event.**

  It can be the theater or the circus or anything an employee

might not normally get to. To honor our firm's Unsung Heroes, we recently bought tickets to a special concert, and we frequently get seats for a sports playoff. Since we are located in Southern California, a much-desired bonus is a pair of tickets to a Lakers, Kings, Dodgers, or Angels game.

- **Special trips.**
We have on occasion sent an employee and his spouse on a weekend vacation or a weeklong cruise. This is a major status reward that shouts to family and friends, "I'm a winner." But obviously this is an expensive reward that is only given for a champagne-popping achievement.

- **Group trips.**
One year, we put together a sales contest called "The Goalkeeper's Award." Every salesperson who met his sales goal qualified for a weekend at a local golf resort. Each person competed not with colleagues but with his own previously set goals. The desire to win the trip was strong—no one wanted to be left behind and be noticeable by his absence.

THE BONUS

––––––––––––– **TEAMTHINK** –––––––––––––
To reward a special performance, you may be better off giving a cash bonus rather than a salary increase. You want to avoid paying during the next ten years for a performance that might not be repeated.

I believe in performance clauses and incentives. If I had to do it over, when I went to Alabama, I'd have had them buy me a twenty-year annuity, say for half a million dollars, and if I stayed there for twenty years, it would be mine.

Bear Bryant,
former head football coach,
University of Alabama

The New York Mets' Dwight Gooden's base salary averages $5.15 million per year for three years. But as if that's not enough, Gooden's contract is loaded with bonus incentives. He can make more money if he wins the Cy Young Award or the league MVP. If he pitches more than 200 innings in any year of his contract, he can earn another $250,000, or a total of $750,000 if he pitches 500 or more innings in the three years.

Although my company has cash incentives for our managers and salespeople, we also give bonuses throughout the year called Special Achievement Rewards. Our managers have the authority to award a cash bonus of up to $1,000 for an employee's extra effort or achievement. There are two criteria. First, the request for the reward bonus must be submitted in writing to the other managers in the company, who must approve it. This procedure protects against favoritism. Second, the reward bonus must be presented to the recipient in front of every employee in his department at a departmental meeting.

Instead of giving bonuses once a year, you might consider spreading them out over the course of the year. Twelve months is a long time between rewards. If you divided and disbursed the same bonus quarterly, the company would get four times the appreciation.

STRIKING OUT

——————— TEAMTHINK ———————
Your recognitions or rewards will lose their significance for your employees if they are given to undeserving individuals.

Mark McGwire, the slugging first baseman of the Oakland Athletics, was voted by the fans to the starting American League All-Star team in 1991. McGwire won this honor even though he was hitting a paltry .190 at the time. No question about it, McGwire is a good first baseman and a legitimate long-ball threat, but he did not deserve to start, much less be involved in a true gathering of All-Stars. Other first basemen like Wally Joyner of the California Angels and Don Mattingly of the New York Yankees were much more deserving but didn't even get invited to the game. What some saw as an injustice was responsible for bad feelings among many players and fans.

Do the right people in your company get the right recognition or rewards? Or do people in the right place at the right time luck out? That's something you have to be wary of. Look back at all the people who have been honored in your organization. Were their awards legitimate? Did they really deserve them? Chances are, you may not know—but I'll bet your employees do.

Here are some ways to avoid undermining your reward program:

- **Don't give bonuses impulsively.**
  The temptation could be to reward a current favorite and ignore a high achiever who is out of favor at the moment. That can cause resentment and confusion.

- **Be careful of group rewards.**
  Everyone should be working toward a common goal, but when you recognize an entire department with a group bonus, or everyone in the organization with a profit-sharing bonus, you are rewarding both the achievers and the non-achievers. I call this the Being Alive Award. The annual Christmas bonus for everybody, which I view as a big taken-for-granted mistake, could qualify for this category. Rely on your department heads to keep you informed as to the people in their departments who are shining and really deserve a reward.

- **Make sure the gift is perceived as valuable.**
  If your employee has no appreciation for a clock or a pen and

pencil set, then giving this type of gift is hardly a significant event to him.

It still hurts when Bear Bryant recalls the time he won football's Southeastern Conference Championship for Kentucky, the only time a Kentucky football team had ever won. When Kentucky basketball coach Adolph Rupp won it in basketball, he had been given a blue Cadillac with whitewall tires. Bryant received only a cigarette lighter.

- **Give the gift in a meaningful way.**

  The way an award is presented is often as important as the award itself. In a group award meeting, not only does the recipient receive satisfying recognition, but everyone else gets fired up to win recognition.

DOING THE RUMBA

One of the first things I learned about giving awards and rewards is that the criteria must be concrete and measurable—no abstract ideas. You could never quantify the Most Improved Attitude in the Department. Obviously, your judgments would be subjective, and you'd risk leaving yourself open to some heavy criticism. Remember the NBA controversy in 1989 over whether Magic Johnson or Michael Jordan should receive the league's MVP award? The skating, platform diving, and gymnastic events at the Olympics, too, almost always generate some heat because the rating system is partially subjective.

The best reward systems rely on specific criteria. Steve Mulvaney, CEO of Management Tools, Inc., in Orange County, California, devised a criteria he calls "doing the RUMBA":

- **Results.**

  Reward an accomplishment, not an activity. For example, losing ten pounds is a goal. To accomplish this, the activity might be to cut down calories, eliminate sweets, and exercise more. The accomplishment is actually losing the ten pounds. Anytime you can add the phrase "so that" to your activity, you articulate your objective.

- **Understandable.**

  Everyone in the company must understand each objective and the available rewards. It helps if both are stated in writing so that everyone knows exactly what needs to be done to win— and the non-recipients know exactly why the other person got it.

- **Measurable.**

  You don't want to honor "the most improved player"—how could you measure that? You want to acclaim the person who hit the most runs, stole the most bases, or set a new record.

- **Beyond routine efforts.**

  There's no point in rewarding people for doing what they are already paid to do. You want to recognize the achievers, those golden employees who are exceeding your expectations and their job descriptions.

- **Achievable.**

  Remember, you want your people to succeed, to feel like winners, so the goals have to be achievable. I used to make the mistake of setting departmental goals too high, with the idea of stretching people to reach them. What happened was that my expectations were not just high, they were unreasonable. Consequently, I made people of accomplishment feel they had failed. Now I'm careful to set reasonable goals. We reward people who hit the ball out of the park; they don't have to hit it into the next county.

If your reward system passes the RUMBA test, you're on your way to a good dance program.

TAKING PRIDE

Pride is one of the great motivators in sports and business; pride of the individual in his own accomplishments, and pride in the organization of which he feels himself a part.

Every year, as the season draws to an end and the National Football League playoff contenders are pretty much decided, there are a few teams left that are definitely out of the playoffs, yet have one more game left to play in the regular season. Sometimes this last game turns out to be their best game of the season. Why is this? What motivates these players when there's no chance a win will change the playoff picture for them? One word says it all: pride. Listen to the coaches, listen to the sportscasters—they all say, "This team has pride, this team is out there today playing its heart out." Usually in these situations, the opposing players realize they're in a real war; they may still need the win because they have a chance in the playoffs, but they also know that the other team's pride is as great a motivator.

When Tommy Lasorda was asked in 1976 if he would manage any other team, he said, "I don't want to manage some other team. Cut my veins and I bleed Dodger Blue." He had such pride in the organization that he stayed with them for twenty-seven years before they made him a manager.

He went on to say, "I'm proud of the organization that I represent and I love what I'm doing. I think that we should be proud when we get up in the morning. If I was an executive of a corporation, I would work at my people the same way I work at these ballplayers—no different. I'd have them proud that they work for AT&T or IBM. I tell them to be proud and to hold their heads up high. You're working for the greatest organization in the world. I would make them feel like they were a very important part of the organization. I would let them know that if they put forth all the effort that they have, and they all get together, they could be number one."

How do you instill pride in people? Recognition and reward, which have been discussed in this chapter, can instill a sense of self-pride in the individual. But how do you get to the next step, instilling pride about the organization? A number of ingredients, mixed together, serve as a recipe for pride.

- **Good treatment of your employees.**
  This goes beyond employee's personal experience with the company. It encompasses how he sees the company treating everybody else in the organization. If an employee is treated well but others in the organization are not, he is not going to feel good about the company. If the organization that employs him treats its people in a fair, considerate, and caring manner, he is consciously or subconsciously proud of the organization.

- **Honorable dealings with your clients.**
  If you are honest, fair, conscientious, and professional in your treatment of your clients, you create pride in your employees.

- **Reputation for honesty and high ethics.**
  Again, people feel good about working for a company that is respected. There can be no question that they feel real pride if someone says to them, "Say, I've heard that's a great company."

- **A strong relationship with the community.**
  Cal-Surance encourages its people to serve on committees or boards of community associations such as Goodwill Industries and the Chamber of Commerce. We conduct an annual blood drive within the company, and every Christmas our employees donate toys and gifts for needy families in the community. As an organization, we try to do things to make a difference, and I know from feedback I've gotten that our employees are proud of this.

  Dick Loughlin, the CEO of Century 21 Corporate, discussed his organization's decision to adopt Easter Seals as their corporate charity. "We selected Easter Seals not only because it helps people with disabilities of all ages, races, and creeds, but also because wherever the money is raised, it goes back into that local community." With over 72,000 salespeople nationwide, Century 21 wanted to involve their people in a unified commitment to this worthwhile charity. Organizing marathons, volleyball-a-thons, cook-offs, and fund-raising events of all kinds over the last thirteen years, Century 21 has contributed $35 million to Easter Seals.

In Minden, Nevada, a tiny community outside of Reno, Patty Clark, a Century 21 franchisee, decided to have a house built to sell so the proceeds could go the local Easter Seals organization. She used persuasion and perseverance to convince suppliers, contractors, and subcontractors to donate their material and labor. After the completion of the house, the entire office turned their efforts toward selling it. Their success resulted in $150,000 for Easter Seals.

"Our involvement with Easter Seals is just awesome and a real unifying venture," says Loughlin. "It makes our people feel good inside and gives them great pride that they have helped the people with disabilities in their community."

- **Concern for the environment.**
  We've all become strongly aware of problems with the environment. If your company disregards these concerns or contributes to the problems of pollution or waste, many of your employees may feel embarrassed, ashamed, or angry though they may not voice it. On the other hand, in this age of environmental enlightenment, companies that exhibit a genuine concern and take actions (even if small) to counteract the problems will instill pride in their employees for *doing the right thing.* Since Cal-Surance is in the insurance industry, we do not create manufacturing pollutants, but we still can make some small contributions, such as switching from the traditional yellow legal pads (which we used to consume by the thousands each year) to recyclable white legal pads.

- **Being a "successful" company.**

  It's not necessarily financial success that I am addressing, but success in achieving the goals you set out to achieve. The responsibility of the company is to regularly communicate these goals and periodically report to everyone the progress being made toward them. People have pride in their company if they perceive it as successful.

THE COMPANY MANTRA

TEAMTHINK

A fired-up sports team wins games even if it's not the best team. A fired-up company can achieve the same results.

The time, effort, and expense you put into instilling pride and using recognition and reward in your company can reap big dividends. If you use these tools wisely and well, they can motivate your employees in a number of positive ways. When you create an environment in which people experience pride and feel appreciated and valued, they will be more energized and more productive and will want to stay with you.

Here is the message or "company mantra" you want to deliver to your employees:

> I recognize the extra effort you put forth on behalf of the company.
>
> I want to reward your efforts as a way of saying, "Thanks, I appreciate it."
>
> I know you are here.
>
> I'm glad you are here.

I appreciate you.

I respect you.

I'm proud of you.

You are important to me and this company!

6

Sending the Players to the Showers

The most difficult thing for me to get used to as a manager was releasing players. The people who sign professional contracts have been stars in their own high school, college, or amateur leagues. They were used to succeeding. It became my job to tell them that their lifelong dream was not going to come true.

Tommy Lasorda

───────── TEAMTHINK ─────────
Because firing an employee is one of a manager's most dreaded and distasteful responsibilities, the task is often preceded by resistance, procrastination, or avoidance.

In 1966, when Dan Reeves, the owner of the Los Angeles Rams, hired George Allen as head coach, he gave Allen a five-year contract. For the preceding seven years, the Rams had finished only fifth in their division. In Allen's first year as head coach, the Rams won more games than they lost. In his second year, they won the divisional playoffs. In 1968, although they had a number of injuries, they were just nosed out of the playoffs. On the day after Christmas Reeves called Allen. Allen said, "Merry Christmas." Reeves said, "I'm sorry, you'll have to go."

The enraged Rams fans threatened to boycott games. Thirty-eight of the forty Rams players sided with Allen, and six actually appeared with him at a televised press conference during which he pleaded to be reinstated. Ten days after the firing, Reeves met with Allen, and then in a meeting with the press Reeves reluctantly announced that the coach's contract had been restored for its remaining two years and they would try to resolve their differences.

Allen stayed on for two more years. Five days after Christmas in 1970, Reeves again fired him. Allen recalled that Reeves did it on a park bench in downtown Los Angeles. "He did not say good luck, he didn't even say thank you for all that I've done." Allen went on to Washington and built the Redskins into a top contender, and in 1971 he was voted Coach of the Year.

It would appear that Reeves had wanted to fire George Allen (for whatever reason) since 1968. However, he backed down because he was being labeled a bad guy by the press and the fans. The three years Reeves forced himself to wait to fire Allen, until Allen's contract expired, are a prime example of the avoidance many of us go through.

TEN EXCUSES NOT TO FIRE

The decision to fire someone is often unconsciously sabotaged by irrational excuses. The following may ring a bell for you:

- **"Just give him time . . . I'm sure he'll work out."**
  How many times have you heard this excuse from a manager when it has already become clear that the individual cannot perform?

- **"We haven't given him enough attention."**
  At this point, you've tried nine different managers for him and you still haven't seen any improvement.

- **"He's not right for this spot, but he's going to be great in the next one."**
  Perhaps the heavens will open up and he'll be struck by lightning, transforming all of his shortcomings into virtues.

- **"His father owns the firm."**
  This can be pretty sticky. The question is, has the father been fair to his son? Realistically, can the son be fired or expected to meet the performance standards of other employees? If not, the managers are placed in an unfair position and so is the son, because he's not required to stand on his own.

- **"He's my son-in-law."**
  You could be the master of your own disaster. A good rule of thumb in employing any relative would be to become brutal in the hiring process, so that you don't face the awkward situation of suggesting early retirement when your son-in-law is only twenty-six years old.

- **"It makes me feel bad to fire people."**
  Now we know the heart of the matter and why most people who should be terminated are not.

- **"I'm too busy to fire him; I'll do it later."**
  Delaying action on an employee who is not working out can not only damage the business, but adversely affect the employees who work with him.

- **"I can't fire him because I don't have a replacement."**
  This is usually just a cover for "It makes me feel bad to fire people."

- **"He's better than nothing."**
  Again, "It makes me feel bad to fire people."

- **"He's better than me."**
  That's the start of a different problem.

The truth is, you could throw away nine of the ten excuses and focus on the issue that it makes you feel bad to fire someone. Everything else becomes a smokescreen, no matter how valid the reason for firing. But ultimately, you must make the right decision for the organization.

> *Perhaps the toughest call for a coach is weighing what is best for an individual against what is best for the team. Keeping a player on the roster just because I liked him personally, or even because of his great contributions to the team in the past, when I felt someone else could do more for the team would be a disservice to the team's goals.*
>
> Tom Landry

Why *Do* We Fire People?

Analyze the reasons for the decision to fire someone. The decision may have its origins in any number of problems: You can't get him to perform his job to your standards; he screwed up big-time and cost the company money or its reputation; he lied, stole, or cheated; the company is being downsized or reorganized; etc. While the proliferation of wrongful termination suits illustrates the need for rational reasons for firing someone, it does not preclude the continued use of subjective factors. For example, incompatibility may be a more common reason for firing someone than incompetence.

ORGANIZING THE FIRING SQUAD

TEAMTHINK

Management can create situations that result in people being fired for the wrong reasons: poor management, promotional firings, over-hiring, and downsizing.

Poor Management

In sports, when a manager or coach of a losing team gets fired, you often hear the following cliché: "You can't fire the players, so you fire the coach." Tony LaRussa, manager of the Oakland Athletics, said, "When I first became a manager, I asked Pittsburgh's manager, Chuck Tanner, for advice. He told me, 'Always rent.' "

In 1982, *Sports Illustrated* made the statement, "There are close to 11,000,000 unemployed and half of them are New York Yankee Managers," a reference to the constant firing of Billy Martin and others by owner George Steinbrenner. Billy Martin's comment on these frequent firings was, "All I know is, I pass people on the street these days and they don't know whether to say hello or to say goodbye."

In business, it normally works the other way around. It's more common to fire the employee than the manager, when in reality poor performance is more often due to mismanagement. Robert Hogan, a psychologist at the University of Tulsa, completed a two-year study on workplace stress and managerial competence. The results indicated that up to 75 percent of U.S. managers may be incompetent because of poor training, lack of meaningful feedback, inability to learn from mistakes, or personality disorders. Inadvertently, you may be *sending players to the showers* when the individual who is really *all wet* is your manager.

If you keep a record of turnover in each unit of your organization, it may alert you to a pattern of higher turnover in one unit. This raises a warning flag.

An example from my company: In a unit with only seven employees, there were six exit interviews over a period of eighteen months. I finally realized (too late) that the problem was not the former employees, but the manager. One major benefit of reviewing exit interviews and keeping statistics on terminations by each unit is that you can study how many employees a manager loses.

Promotional Firings

I've already said that when possible, I like to promote from within the organization. However, on two occasions in the past, I wanted to reward someone who was doing a particularly good job at a certain level by bestowing on him a *battlefield commission*, so to speak, and moving him into a higher slot which opened up in the firm. Although my motives were good, I failed to perform a proper evaluation to determine whether the person was really qualified for the new position.

The results of these inappropriate promotions were disastrous. We were dissatisfied with the performances in the new positions, without recognizing our role in creating the situations. Moreover, the two people's failure to perform well caused them to become dissatisfied. We had to let both of them go. In essence, what we did was take two good performers and promote them beyond their level of competency or training, preordaining them to fail (commonly referred to as the Peter Principle).

Overhiring

At one time I had a president who insisted that we needed fifteen additional employees. Coincidentally, we had recently brought in an outside organization to review our work flow. These consultants not only disagreed about the number of people my president wanted, they were able to show me that we should eliminate three of our existing employees. We followed their advice and found that the unit became more efficient with fewer people.

By hiring those three employees in the first place into positions that weren't necessary and consequently forcing them to expand their functions to fill their workday, we did them a terrible disservice. Having to terminate them because of our own inept management was inexcusable.

Downsizing

Most businesses are cyclical and at one time or another may face a financial crisis. Other businesses experience financial problems caused by overexpansion rather than downturns. For whichever reason, it becomes necessary to substantially cut expenses, and because salaries always take a big bite, that usually means cutting down on the number of employees.

Whether you announce it as "dynamic consolidation" or "downsizing," the terminology is not important to your employees. All they know is that people are going to *lose their jobs.* To reduce employee anxiety (if not outright panic), it is important to handle this situation wisely. Make the necessary cuts quickly, all at once, and communicate openly, clearly, and directly to the remaining employees that the cuts are now over. Allowing anxiety to persist among your remaining employees may affect their work and could move them to send out their résumés just to be safe, or to start job-hunting. Once they begin to receive job offers, you could lose good people for the wrong reasons.

—————— TEAMTHINK ——————
The most important factor in an organization's post-downsizing success is open, honest, and factual communication.

When our organization had to reduce our staff, we organized a "task force" of several managers to handle the situation. Their primary purpose was to ensure that we were well organized, consistent in our treatment of the employees, and communicating at all levels before the termination day and afterward. Employees want to know that they are secure in their positions and that they can go on with their lives without fear of losing their jobs. On the other hand, you should not *promise* that future reductions will not occur. Such promises can be construed as the equivalent of offering employment guarantees or contracts, which may be binding on the company in the future.

RENEGOTIATING THE CONTRACT

───────────── **TEAMTHINK** ─────────────
By setting the stage early for reasonable salary negotiations, you lessen the risk of losing a good employee because of injured pride or bad feelings.

One afternoon just before the start of the 1964 football season, an attorney unexpectedly presented himself to Vince Lombardi, coach of the Green Bay Packers, in his office. In an arrogant manner the attorney said, "I'm here to renegotiate the salary of Mr. James Ringo." Ringo was an outstanding center who had been the strength of Lombardi's offensive line and was considered a fixture at Green Bay.

Lombardi merely asked the lawyer to excuse him for a moment, disappeared into another office, and returned twenty minutes later. Lombardi looked the attorney straight in the eye and said, "I believe you've come to the wrong city. Mr. James Ringo is now the property of the Philadelphia Eagles." Needless to say, very few players presented their contracts to Lombardi to be renegotiated that year.

In some cases employees simply price themselves out of the market during salary negotiations. When we can't meet the demand, the unhappy employee, with injured pride and feeling undervalued, leaves our company in hopes of finding another position with better pay.

If an employee stays on after being turned down for a salary increase, you may be faced with another dilemma. He is clearly not happy because he didn't get what he wanted. Chances are good that while he's still on your payroll, he will start looking for another job. He could feel justified in letting his work slip, or leaving you with inadequate notice. The problem then is, does he leave on your timetable or his? You really don't want to lose him, but you don't want him walking out on you at a bad time either. It's a tough call.

We try to reduce the chances that these situations will occur by setting the stage early for reasonable salary negotiations.

- To keep the right perspective on the appropriate salary for each individual, we find it best to review the salary of *every* individual in the firm at the same time near the end of our calendar year. We look at everyone's salary in context so that we can avoid inequities. This concurrent review and overview makes more sense to me than reviewing individual employees' salaries all during the year on their employment anniversary dates.

- To keep future salary expectations realistic at senior management levels, we have salary caps that are plainly spelled out as part of the employment contract. Some staff positions also warrant salary caps. Without a salary cap, when an annual salary increase is usually given and therefore expected each year, the danger exists that you will price the position or the employee out of the organization.

- Senior managers have measurable performance bonuses that are adjusted annually. (See RUMBA criteria for performance bonuses in Chapter 5.)

- Salary ranges are established for staff positions and are tied to performance and longevity. This information is disbursed regularly to employees.

The Four W's

————————— TeamThink —————————
Prepare for a termination meeting by addressing the four W's: who, where, when, and what time.

- **Who will conduct the dismissal?**
  This meeting should *always* be face-to-face rather than through a letter or by telephone. The employee's immediate superior should perform the task. The employee deserves the consideration of hearing from his boss the reasons why he's being fired.

  Joe Belmont recalls his firing from the position of coach of the Denver basketball team. He was riding in the car with his family, listening to the car radio. "They announced on the radio that I had been fired. That's how I heard, and that's a hard way to hear it. You're driving along and suddenly you hear on the radio that your world has been shot out from under you. My wife started to cry and I got upset and I just couldn't believe it. If that was it, that was a hell of a way to find out about it. Hadn't I done my best for them? Hadn't I done good for them? Wasn't I a human being? Couldn't they have told me to my face?"

  The next morning Belmont went to meet with the managers of the organization. He got there at 8:00 A.M. and was told the managers were in a meeting. He was made to wait for two hours. After that humiliation, he was told that the firing was the result of a unanimous vote of the board of directors and was in the best interest of the team. No excuse or apology was made for making the announcement to the media before notifying him face-to-face.

- **When should you schedule the dismissal meeting?**
  Although many firms terminate people on a Friday, the early

part of the week is a better time from the employee's perspective. This lets the discharged employee use the rest of the week to make phone calls, set up interviews, and make contacts. This extra time gives him a stronger sense of control over his job future and eases his feelings of helplessness or abandonment.

- **What time of the day is best?**

  To prevent the office grapevine from slowing down that day's work, schedule the termination meeting for the end of the day. This also allows the employee to clean out his desk without the embarrassing presence of his coworkers. Someone from the human resources department should be present while the employee empties his desk and returns the office keys, ID cards, or security badge, and that person should accompany the employee as he leaves the premises.

- **Where should you have the meeting?**

  Rather than having the meeting in your office or the employee's office, schedule it for a neutral setting such as a conference room. This will allow you to tactfully leave the room after the meeting and return to your office and gives the discharged employee some time and privacy to collect himself. It also affords an opportunity for someone from your human resources department to step in to address any questions the employee may have.

  Red Holzman, coach of the New York Knicks from 1967 to 1982, once released a player while he was on the road. It was early in Holzman's coaching career, before the big-money days, and he had a small room in a small hotel. The player he was letting go was a six foot ten, 250-pound bundle of raw aggression. Holzman had always prided himself on his ability to let a guy down easy. He invited the ballplayer to his room, but his smooth talk didn't quite work out. The player stood up and advanced menacingly on the coach as Holzman retreated slowly to the door. With his back against the doorknob, Holzman reached back, managed to open the door, and nervously wished the ex-player good luck and goodbye. Fortunately, the player finally left.

Holzman later offered this advice to other coaches: "Never release a guy in a small room. Always do it in an open area, a dance floor, a gym, or a football field."

The Four C's

You've got a hundred more young kids than you have a place for on your club, Every one of 'em has had a goin'-away party. They been given the shaving kit and the fifty dollars. They kissed everybody and said, "See you in the majors in two years." You see these poor kids who shouldn't even be there in the first place. You write on the report card "4-4-4 and out." That's the lowest rating in everything. Than you call 'em in and say, "It's the consensus among us that we're going to let you go back home."

Some of 'em cry. Some get mad. But none of 'em will leave until you answer 'em one question: "Skipper, what do you think?" And you gotta look every one of those kids in the eye and kick their dreams in the ass and say no.

If you say it mean enough, maybe they do themselves a favor and don't waste years learning what you can see in a day. They don't have what it takes to make the majors. Just like I never had it.

> Earl Weaver,
> former manager,
> Baltimore Orioles

_____ **TeamThink** _____
During the termination meeting, use the four C's: care, consideration, compassion, and clarity.

When an individual is fired, for whatever the cause, for him the bottom line is always the same: He has lost his job. So many employers are now concerned with the legal implications of termination (and understandably so) that they fail to address the more personal issues that this event triggers.

Because getting fired is often a devastating experience with huge potential effects on the employee's self-esteem and standard of living, you must handle it with a great deal of care, consideration, compassion, and clarity, while at the same time taking the necessary precautions to protect your organization. It is incumbent on the organization to train its managers to handle both the legal and personal aspects of the process.

The following suggestions may provide a framework to address the needs of the employee while providing you with the protection you require.

- **Never fire anyone in the heat of an emotional moment.**
  In our firm, no one has the authority to fire anyone who reports directly to him without first obtaining approval from the person to whom he himself reports. Even as CEO, I cannot fire anyone who reports directly to me without the approval of my board of directors. This system of checks and balances avoids impulsive terminations.

  As previously mentioned, George Steinbrenner was infamous for his quick firings. Yankee manager Billy Martin, fired several times by Steinbrenner, joked, "The only real way to know you've been fired is when you arrive at the ballpark and find your name has been scratched from the parking list."

- **Always treat the employee with dignity and professionalism.**
  Whatever the reason for dismissal, never humiliate or degrade the employee. Attempt to put the employee at ease. Do not phrase the reason for dismissal in personal terms, but state them in a straightforward manner within the context of the job.

  When Golden Richards of the Dallas Cowboys was traded in 1978, he remarked on how well coach Tom Landry had handled it. "He called me into his office and took the time to carefully explain why he traded me. He said I was a fine player, and didn't believe it would help me, as a former starter, to be a backup. He said I'd be starting in Chicago. He was very straightforward in explaining the situation and seemed to have my best interest in mind. I had respect for him while I was in Dallas, and respect for him after I left.''

- **Be clear and direct in your delivery. Keep the message brief, concise, and businesslike.**
  Be sure the employee understands that the decision is firm and final. Be careful not to give the impression that the situation might change.

- **Clearly state the effective date of the termination of employment.**
  Before the meeting, determine the effective termination date. In the case of a layoff rather than a firing, you may want the employee to remain on the job longer.

- **Don't fire someone on a date significant to him.**
  Be sensitive to the date on which you schedule a termination meeting. Avoid releasing an employee on a birthday, wedding anniversary, or service anniversary with the company. Check the personnel record for this information. It's bad enough to lose your job, but worse to lose it on your birthday or some other significant anniversary.

- **Be prepared to answer the employee's questions about job reference, severance pay, benefits, pension or profit-sharing payouts, and accrued vacation time.**
  If a human resources person will not be immediately available to give this information, or if you don't know the answers to these questions, get them *before* you give the employee the bad news.

- **Be open and honest when you discuss the reference you will be giving for the departing employee.**

  The question uppermost in the employee's mind is, "Will you give me a good reference?" By telling the employee up front exactly what response you will give to future inquiries, you can significantly reduce his anxieties and avoid potential future problems.

- **Don't give a poor reference for any former employee that you can't substantiate.**

  You're asking for trouble—spelled libel, slander, or defamation of character. As a matter of policy, Cal-Surance will not give out references on former employees; however, I will give a verbal reference if it is requested by someone I know personally.

- **Don't give a glowing letter of reference until you have a signed termination agreement.**

  Otherwise, your letter could help set up a lawsuit against you for wrongful termination. Our termination agreement holds us harmless from any future lawsuits and includes a clause for protecting our trade secrets.

- **Inform the employee how inquiries about him from staff and coworkers will be answered.**

  Don't give the dismissed employee one reason for his discharge while giving a different reason to the remaining employees. Such behavior can invite legal action and injure management's credibility with the remaining employees. While you need not go into details, you can give a general yet truthful answer such as "He wasn't getting the job done."

- **Don't make promises to a terminated employee that you can't keep.**

  Statements such as "We'll help you find a job" and "If you

don't find a job by a certain time, we'll talk about additional severance" might legally obligate you to a future payment.

- **Consider a specific policy pertaining to severance pay.**
In our company, any discharged employee receives a minimum two weeks' severance pay. If the individual has been with the organization at least two years, we follow the rule of an additional week of severance pay for every year exceeding two years. This is in addition to accrued vacation and sick leave pay. For senior management positions, our employment contract provides a three-month severance benefit upon termination of the individual for whatever reason.

  Neither Dan Topping nor Del Webb still owned the New York Yankees when Whitey Ford, one of their best pitchers of all time, suffered an injury and was unceremoniously sacked after eighteen years with the team. According to Ford, "When the general manager told me they were going to pay me until the end of the month, I was shocked. After eighteen years, I was getting two weeks' severance pay. I couldn't believe it."

- **Before committing to severance, make sure that you secure a signed termination agreement from the employee.**
Why give someone money and then have him use it to hire an attorney to sue you? If possible, have the separation agreement include the specific last day of employment, unused vacation pay, bonuses, commission, and other compensation due (state whether these are included in the severance amount).

  On more than one occasion, I've had a signed termination agreement, only to have the former employee indicate that it didn't include vacation time. I've also found that senior executives had a habit of not recording when they'd taken vacation time because the company itself hadn't kept good records. Invariably we'd end up paying substantial amounts for duplicate vacation benefits over a multiyear period. This is a strong argument for keeping accurate records of employees' vacations in their personnel files.

- **If the severance is substantial, spread the payments out over several months.**

  By treating the severance like regular payroll you not only retain the loyalty of the former employee, but you provide the opportunity to keep his benefits in force. This also gives you the ability to discuss work-related problems and ask questions that come up after he's left.

Although you cannot take the pain out of job loss, by showing consideration and compassion to the individual and giving careful attention to the process, you can see that the employee emerges with self-esteem and dignity intact while also ensuring that the company is legally protected. If the employee is treated respectfully, the organization is less likely to suffer recriminations and legal action down the road.

PREPARING A GOOD DEFENSE

Unfortunately, there are realistic reasons that you must also take precautionary steps to protect yourself in termination situations. If you follow these suggestions, you will lessen your vulnerability:

- Be sure that your human resources department has completed all required documentation and received necessary written confirmation from the employee's managers according to company policy.

- Consult with a knowledgeable labor attorney to educate your managers on potential legal issues. The fee for a legal consultation is minimal compared to the penalty that could be exacted by a court.

- Contact the customers, clients, and other individuals who will be affected by the dismissal of the individual to inform them and reassure them that the company will continue to serve them.

- Be sure all company-related property is accounted for before the employee leaves the premises, including office keys, identification cards, computer disks, and company manuals.

- Change computer access codes and security codes to the building or offices.

- If you are dismissing a sizable number of people at one time (thirty or more), prepare a news release. If your organization has a public relations person or consultant, decide whether that person should release the information or just have it prepared in the event there are media inquiries.

- Be prepared for the remote possibility that a discharged employee may react irrationally or even violently during the dismissal or in the weeks following.

Hap Day's reaction to his firing does not seem irrational given the circumstances. Day worked for the Toronto Maple Leaf hockey team from the day in 1926 when the franchise was born, first as player, later as coach. During his coaching reign, he led the club to five Stanley Cups in eight years. You'd think Day would be rewarded for his accomplishments. However, manager Conn Smythe did not reward Day, but fired him so that he could give the job to his son, Stafford Smythe.

Post-Termination Procedures

If your organization does not provide outplacement, you might consider supplying the discharged employee with the names of agencies or executive search firms, along with services that might be helpful. You could also consider having someone from the company designated to call the discharged employee occasionally to see how he is doing until he secures another job. Especially in situations where circumstances forced the release of the individual, this concern conveys to him that company management cares about his welfare. We have assisted former employees by sending their résumés with a cover letter from us to other organizations.

GOOD OLD CHARLIE:
THE TOUGHEST MANAGEMENT PROBLEM

—————————— **TEAMTHINK** ——————————
When a loyal long-term employee is no longer productive, it's important to deal justly and fairly with him. Often your ingenuity can allow him to leave with his dignity and self-respect.

Charlie Hough had done a consistently good job as a winning pitcher for the Dodgers over the years, but finally those years were catching up with Hough, and Tommy Lasorda realized he had a tough problem on his hands. Hough's pitching had gone so sour that the fans were booing him as he warmed up. Lasorda recalls how bad he felt. "Seeing players traded or released is part of baseball, but when someone you've lived with, laughed with, and cried with leaves the team, it hurts." Lasorda was so close to Hough's family that Hough's daughter called him "Uncle Tommy."

Lasorda took it upon himself to find another team for Hough. He persuaded the Texas Rangers that all Hough needed was a change of scenery; and Lasorda said he would stake his reputation on the fact that he could still pitch. The Rangers agreed to acquire Hough for the waiver price and in 1984 he led their pitching staff with sixteen wins and was second in the American League with 266 innings pitched.

Lasorda had handled a tough management decision admirably. Difficult as it was, he appropriately cut Hough from the team, but he did it with compassion and helped find Hough a spot where he could go on playing baseball.

The most creative solution to the "good old Charlie" problem concerned a CEO I know. His brother-in-law had hired him into the firm twenty years before and was now the "Good Old Charlie" in the company. The CEO was torn up about how to handle the situation, but he finally came up with a workable solution. The CEO called the local Heart Association and by pledging sizable annual donations convinced them to name his brother-in-law as their local director. In addition, he made certain that his brother-in-law received the same salary by having his company make up the difference between its salary and what the Association could pay. He sold his brother-in-law on the idea that the business had an obligation to contribute to the community and he could do it. Everybody won. The Heart Association got a top executive, the brother-in-law felt he was making a meaningful contribution, and his departure opened up his slot for someone else.

Richard Gordinier, president of the Henry Group of Companies, a conglomerate located in California, needed to replace a division president who had been with the company for twenty years. Gordinier told that individual that he could have six months to look for another position, agreed to keep the matter confidential, and added that if a job was found before the six months were up, the individual would be paid a bonus in addition to his severance package. The man had a real incentive to move fast. He found another position, he was treated with dignity, and his fellow employees never realized that he had actually been terminated. He left the company with his head held high.

Not all businesses can afford to follow these two examples, but there are many other creative options available to solve the problem. For example, early retirement plans are a win-win situation for everybody. In essence, the company offers a sweetened pension package to its "good old Charlie." The employee who accepts this package signs a release that immunizes the company from age discrimination liability, provided he knows what he's signing, signs voluntarily, and signs the release in return for the extra severance pay (valuable consideration).

The employee who may not want to continue to work is given a chance to opt out with dignity, and with a better pension package than he would otherwise have had. The company gets people who really aren't interested in working anymore to leave with little risk of a lawsuit.

MANDATORY RETIREMENT PLANS

*A lifetime contract for a coach means, if you're ahead in
the third quarter moving the ball, they can't fire you.*
                                                    Lou Holtz

In 1960, from a public relations standpoint alone, the New
York Yankees did great damage to themselves by the coldblooded
manner in which they jettisoned their legendary manager, Casey
Stengel, because he had passed his seventieth birthday. At a
hushed and historic press conference, a grim and unsmiling Stengel
announced that he had been told that "his services were no longer
desired." Stengel refused to use the word fired. Dan Topping,
co-owner of the Yankees with Del Webb, had nervously read a
prepared statement full of empty words that never did say bluntly
whether Stengel had quit of his own accord, was fired, or what.

In his twelve years with the Yankees, Casey Stengel brought
them the most productive period in their glamorous history—ten
pennants and seven world championships. He brought warmth to
a cold organization, giving it a colorful appeal it couldn't have
bought for a million dollars.

The Yankee owners decided to adhere rigidly to the letter of
a new law of their organization that could have waited for im-
plementation until Stengel decided to quit on his own. Although he
was priceless and strongly indicated his own preference to continue, all Stengel got was a word of thanks, the sum of $160,000
from a profit-sharing plan, and the back of Topping's hand. It was
a shabby way to treat the man who had given the club firmer
footing than it had ever had and brought it glory as well. Stengel
later joked, "I'll never make the mistake of being seventy again."

I recently visited with the senior partner of our own outside
legal firm because he wanted me to meet the head of his new
corporate division, who had just joined him. This man was
seventy-two years old and had been told to leave his previous law
firm because of its mandatory retirement age. What his firm didn't
count on was that when he left it, all his accounts followed him,
along with two of the firm's top attorneys, to form the unit at the

new firm. Not only did the previous firm lose the services of a still competent and capable attorney, it lost a dramatic amount of business as well.

Even in the high-pressure arenas of the sports world, age should not be a deterrent. Sid Gillman, the former coach of the San Diego Chargers and Los Angeles Rams who is noted for his innovations on offense, worked full-time well into his seventies, devising plays for Dick Vermeil when he coached the Philadelphia Eagles and serving as general manager of the Oklahoma Outlaws of the USFL. When Mike Gottfried was coaching the University of Pittsburgh, Gillman served as an unpaid consultant. Gottfried, now an analyst on ESPN, recently said of Gillman, "I don't care if he's going to be eighty or ninety. If I'd gotten a head coaching job in the new World League, my first call would have been to Sid."

If you have a mandatory retirement plan, my recommendation is that you review it. If you don't have such a plan, now is a great time to check out those who do; they may have some great talent available for you soon!

Handling the Tough Calls

Better get rid of him a year too soon than a year too late.
         Branch Rickey,
         former president and general manager,
         Brooklyn Dodgers

The human tendency to avoid confrontation can push your company into the trap of complacency and subpar performance. Upgrading the organization often requires us to make tough decisions. We may have to fire some people, bypass others, and tell poor performers where they stand. How we do this affects the growth, strength, or vulnerability of our company. It also defines the character of our company.

No one enjoys delivering the bad news, but as CEO or manager, you need to understand how critical it is to your long-term success, and you must set the example for the rest of the organization.

> *Hiring and firing people is the most unpleasant part of being an employer, but it is a major part of the responsibility a proprietor has to himself, his organization, the persons who are dependent on that organization for their living, and those who support it.*
>
> Jack Kent Cooke,
> owner,
> Washington Redskins

7

Prime Time

There are certain things in this world we all have in common, such as time. Everybody has sixty seconds to a minute, sixty minutes to an hour, twenty-four hours to a day; the difference is what we do with that time and how we use it.

Lou Holtz

TEAMTHINK

Anyone who works eighteen hours a day and then spends the remaining six hours dreaming about his work is either ruining his health, scared to death, having marital problems, a lousy parent, or all of the above.

In the same year, Mike Ditka, former head coach of the Chicago Bears, had a heart attack; Sparky Anderson, manager of the Detroit Tigers, became ill from nervous exhaustion; Jerry Reynolds, coach of the Sacramento Kings, passed out during a game; Frank Layden, coach of the Utah Jazz, quit basketball entirely because he had to get off the ''roller coaster,'' and Bill Walsh, who has since returned to college coaching, retired as coach of the San Francisco 49ers. Walsh said, ''There were years when I was so enmeshed in my work that I lost energy—lost the will to handle the job." All of these coaches were caught up in the myth that their jobs required almost a total commitment of their time.

Until about twelve years ago, I was convinced that the only way to be successful was to work a seventy-hour week. I accepted the constant stress of time pressures as a necessary evil. Even though my wife and children didn't see much of me, and I was too tired for it to matter when they did, I rationalized that I was really doing it for them. I finally got my wake-up call when my marriage broke apart and my blood pressure hit the ceiling.

Since then, I have made every effort to reduce the daily and weekly hours I spend at work by consciously streamlining my operational techniques. I realized that in years past, I had *wasted* time in a number of ways. By focusing on *working smarter*, I have succeeded in cutting my work week down to fifty hours that are eminently more productive and efficient.

Jack Welch is CEO of General Electric, an organization with over $38 billion in sales and fourteen different companies, yet he's able to handle all his responsibilities within a balanced work week. In fact, he says, "If someone tells me he's working ninety hours a week, I tell him he's doing something terribly wrong. I go skiing on the weekend, I go out with my buddies on Friday and party. You've got to do the same, or you've got a bad deal. Put down a list of twenty things you're doing that make you work ninety hours, and ten of them have to be nonsense, or else somebody else has got to do them for you."

While Peter Ueberroth was completing the sale of his company, one of the largest travel agencies in the country, he became the head of the 1984 Los Angeles Olympic Committee and was named *Time* magazine's Man of the Year. At the same time, he served as international president of the prestigious Young Presidents' Organization. Throughout this period, Ueberroth maintained strong ties to his family and friends by restricting his work week to fifty hours.

The American Management Association has consistently contended that unless you are going through a major business crisis, your average work week should not exceed fifty hours. In this chapter, I suggest a number of ways to save time and make the hours you work more productive.

Are You Living in a World of Deadlines?

When deadlines determine which tasks we perform, rather than the task dictating the time frame, we establish a pattern of constant stress that becomes a way of life.

Here's a scene that has become familiar in the NFL. With two minutes remaining, the team with the football back at its own fifteen-yard line needs to drive at least sixty-five yards to set up a field goal to win the game. The players go into their two-minute drill. Their adrenaline starts pumping, they become completely focused, and they march down the field and gain enough yardage to permit their kicker to deliver the ball between the goal posts and win the game. You look around amazed and say, "If they could do that in just two minutes, why didn't they do it all during the game?" The answer, of course, is that no sporting team can operate for the whole game at the peak that a crisis generates.

The same goes for you as an individual and for your organization. Therefore, the imposition of constant crisis deadlines takes its toll on both.

If you make every game a life and death proposition, you're going to have problems. For one thing, you'll be dead a lot.

Dean Smith,
head basketball coach,
University of North Carolina

Look at your daily schedules and ask yourself these questions:

• How many deadlines do I normally face each day?

• Are these deadlines self-imposed?

- Could any of these tasks have been postponed?

- How many of these tasks must be handled only by me?

- What would happen if I didn't do this?

Also ask yourself, "How do I feel at the end of the day? Am I exhilarated, tired, satisfied, frustrated, or worn out? When I need more time, do I cut back on my sleep?" The real question is, are you in control of your work, or is your work in control of you?

Avoiding Bored Room Meetings

TeamThink

By conducting only meetings that are necessary, well prepared, and well organized, you set the pattern for business efficiency throughout your organization.

Antony Jay, chairman of London's Video Arts Ltd., says, "Certainly a great many meetings waste a great deal of everyone's time and seem to be held for historical rather than practical reasons; many long-established committees are little more than memorials to dead problems."

Effective meetings serve a number of worthwhile functions. First, they give your staff a chance to be brought up to date, as a group, on what's happening. Second, meetings can become a main focal point for decision-making where consensus is necessary. Finally, meetings can create a commitment to decisions which become binding on the group.

But too often meetings are unproductive and waste valuable time for everyone. A survey of 200 executives conducted by Accountemps indicated that executives waste an average of 288 hours a year attending unnecessary meetings. Here are some suggestions on meetings that can help you use time more effectively and productively.

- **Start every meeting on time.**

  If all your staffers aren't present, they will be for the next one. Notre Dame's Lou Holtz says, "I normally will walk into a meeting at precisely the proper time. The first thing we do on a continuous basis is set our watches. We go by LLH time. This stands for 'Louis Leo Holtz' time."

  When Vince Lombardi coached Green Bay, he instituted "Lombardi time," which meant fifteen minutes early. Often when the team bus was scheduled to leave at 10:00, he would direct the driver to pull out at 9:45. If you missed the bus, you had to find your own way of catching up with the team.

  General Electric's Medical Health Group in Milwaukee always has one less chair in the room than people invited to the meeting. The purpose is to get people to the meetings on time.

  The CEO of Southland Corp., which operates the 7-Eleven stores, starts every meeting at seven or eleven minutes *after* the hour. The CEO figures the odd starting time ups the chances of punctual attendance.

- **Clearly define the purpose of the meeting.**

  If you can't state the purpose, don't have the meeting. Recognize that there are two types of meetings—the kind where ideas are generated and the kind where decisions are made. It's difficult to mix the two successfully.

- **Always have an agenda.**

  The agenda should be completed and distributed enough in advance that all participants can prepare for the meeting.

  High-priority items should appear first on the agenda. The early part of a meeting tends to be livelier and more energetic. The top of the meeting is also the place to approach the tough problems—you'll have the time to deal with them.

  The more detailed the agenda, the better everyone can prepare. Terms such as "discuss new venture" are too vague.

- **Control the timing of the meeting.**

  Besides setting the starting time, it's important to fix the ending time. *You* control the meeting so that it ends on schedule. The participants will appreciate this; they have their own schedules to maintain. Set a time limit beforehand on discussion of less important items on the agenda.

  If meetings have gone on too long in the past, try scheduling them one hour before lunch or one hour before the end of the day. Everyone will develop a strong motivation to see them end.

- **Limit the number of meetings within a certain period.**

  Don't schedule several meetings consecutively. People need mental breaks, time to deal with their own pressing issues and return important phone calls. If possible, limit your normal meetings to one hour.

  Check the meeting schedules of your key managers. Holding too many meetings in a short time makes it difficult for them to prepare and may disrupt their own work patterns.

- **Never leave a meeting without writing a list that defines all actions agreed upon.**

  Send it to all attendees, asking for additions or corrections. This way, everyone essentially signs off on the list and acknowledges the actions and deadlines.

- **All potential interruptions should be eliminated.**

  Telephone calls to participants, papers to be signed, or people walking in with questions should only be allowed if the situation absolutely cannot wait until the end of the meeting.

- **Use breakfast and lunch for meetings with people in your firm.**

  Breakfast meetings have a built-in deadline, as most people are anxious to get back to their offices. Since it's the first meeting of the day, people are fresh and focused. I've found breakfasts seem to be more oriented to specific business problems, while lunches seem to focus on more general topics and building personal and social relationships. In both cases, the no-interruption rule must hold.

Our boardroom often functions as a lunch-meeting room. My own office has a table and chairs that accommodate lunch for four. Lunch meetings there eliminate travel time and waiting in restaurants.

- **Schedule a meeting with yourself.**
Create "discretionary" or "disposable" free time. This allows you to sit down and *think.* Management consultants McKinsey & Company, in a recent study titled "Leveraging CEO Time," recommended blocking out at least two "CEO Time Alone" sessions a week, each two hours long.

A Stitch in Time

———————— TeamThink ————————
Devote 80 percent of your time to the top 20 percent of your priorities.

Tackle your hardest job first. Usually when we are faced with a number of projects to work on, we take the easiest or the most rewarding one first. Start with a job you really don't want to do. Once you get it out of the way, everything else will seem easy.

Red Auerbach

Stop telling yourself you work better under pressure. Nobody works better under pressure for any sustained period. Often we create needless pressure for ourselves because we spend too much time on low-priority items. It is essential to identify and isolate the most important projects in the workload. To help you set priorities and focus, I suggest the following:

- **List your major projects for the year.**

  I list no more than twelve major projects in any one year—if I'm doing more than twelve, I'm probably not doing them well. After I put them in order of importance, I divide the year into quarters and place the projects' completion targets in the appropriate quarters. I try to divide the twelve major projects equally among the quarters.

- **Identify your major projects for the month.**

  John Katzman, founder and president of *Princeton Review* (a study guide for aptitude tests), based in New York City, published a week-by-week desk diary for all employees and franchise owners. The diary included important company deadlines, cartoons, people's birthdays, and a list of commitments for branch managers. This is pretty ambitious for most organizations, but it does show an innovative method of reviewing time management.

  Every month I list in order of importance the major projects that I want to see accomplished that month and set specific dates for their completion. I don't expect to hit all the target dates, as other projects or emergencies may come up, but at least I will know why and where I am refocusing my energies. A monthly calendar shows you "the big picture" and allows you to plan and manage large blocks of time.

  I share this list with my senior managers so that they know where my energies are directed for the month and how my list may affect their own priorities. I also find that by constantly reviewing this list, I learn whether or not I have accomplished anything meaningful that month.

- **Identify your major projects for the week.**

  Every Thursday I spend one hour reviewing my schedule for the following week. I determine what appointments may need to be made and whether priorities need to be rearranged. It's a way of making sure my schedule is balanced and geared to accomplish what I want.

  Consider using a weekly briefing report prepared by your

management team. This report could alert you to any problems, update you on special reports, or highlight the goals of each unit for the week. Not only does this give you a capsule report showing where you need to focus; it also reaffirms for your team what the important issues are for that week.

———— TeamThink ————
Effective control of your time will be governed more by your habits than by outside forces.

You can take command of your time through a series of simple steps. Here are some that have worked for me:

- **Cut down on your reading material.**
  Half the material that we look at isn't worth reading. Determine in advance which publications are important. In my firm, reading lists are disseminated by the person assigned to cover each publication. We only look at materials that the person has highlighted.

- **Have your mail screened by an administrative assistant.**
  Usually, your assistant can write routine letters for your approval and signature. You should only look at mail that absolutely must be handled or seen by you.
  Make a decision about each piece of paper that crosses your desk. Either pass it on or handle it, but try to handle it only once.

- **Inform your managers that you want no memo to run longer than one page.**
  This forces them to be concise and organized. Set a date for replies on all memos you send or answer.

- **Have your secretary reconfirm every appointment.**
  Your secretary should reconfirm the day before and again two hours in advance so that no meeting is canceled at the last minute, disrupting your schedule.

- **Control your open-door policy.**
  The only drawback of an open door is that employees' problems may not be immediate and do interrupt your schedule. You don't have to solve such problems on the spot; there's nothing wrong with scheduling a meeting time to deal with the issue.

  James Treybig, CEO of Tandem Computers, keeps a calendar outside his door so that any employee can sign up for an appointment.

- **Make your telephone calls more productive.**
  Leave an action message instead of just your name. For example, you could say, "Fax your answer to me today."

  Group your phone calls at one time during the day. You get into a rhythm and tend to be better focused.

  Jot down a short agenda so that you can cover all the issues and know exactly what to accomplish with each call.

- **If your budget allows it, travel first-class on all flights longer than two hours.**
  It costs more, but it keeps you rested and helps you think or work efficiently.

If Shakespeare had been in pro basketball, he never would have had time to write his soliloquies. He would have always been on a plane between Phoenix and Kansas City.

Paul Westhead,
former coach,
Denver Nuggets

- **Develop a method of capturing your thoughts.**
  I keep a small portable dictation machine in my car, in my briefcase, and at home; then I don't spend the rest of my day trying to remember my brilliant ideas.

I keep a pad and pencil behind my bed and I'll get up in the middle of the night and jot down notes for things I will bring up in a meeting.

Buck Rodgers

- **Create "quiet time" sanctuaries.**

  I've found that I can get tremendous amounts of work done on airplanes and have finally figured out it's because I have no interruptions. I now work at home one day a week and accomplish the same thing. I am fortunate enough to have a fully equipped office at home with a fax machine and a separate telephone line.

  I also create quiet time at the office by having all telephone calls held and allowing no interruptions for certain periods of the day. In the past I have even rented a hotel room near the office for a day. Such "quiet time" enables me to reestablish control of my perspective and deal with tough issues that need undisturbed contemplation.

- **Avoid guilt work.**

  I used to load up my briefcase for the weekend with too much work; I'd feel pressure all weekend if I didn't get to it. Now I take home *only* what I intend to do that weekend.

- **Consider management by exception.**

  Delegate problem-solving and decision-making to others whenever possible and save yourself for the issues that absolutely must be handled and guided by you.

- **Focus on your biorhythms.**

  It's best to tackle your toughest problems during your peak periods. We all operate on certain biorhythms. I happen to function better in the morning than I do at night.

Space-age Time-savers

————————— TeamThink —————————
The answer to time constraints is not to work harder, but to work smarter by taking advantage of new technology.

What we've done in this business is to take a nine-month-a-year job of ten or twelve hours a day and turn it into a fifteen-month-a-year job of fifteen hours a day— and that's what gets us. I could do this job right now with a fax machine on the beach in Florida and probably not (bleep) it up.

Bill Parcells

Improvements in communication are so dramatic and fast-moving these days that we need to constantly reexamine the way we view our offices and the way we function in them. The office of the 1980s is obsolete. The office of the 1990s can function wherever we are. The following discussion represents an update on where the changes are happening today. My purpose in presenting this is to help you pick out the technological marvels that fit your own operational style.

To counter the wasted time and stress of his daily two-hour round-trip commute to and from the office, the CEO of Sunclipse Industries makes the trip in a van with a driver. Inside the van is a typewriter, a fax machine, and a desk with all the materials he needs to conduct his work. Not only does the CEO begin functioning as soon as he gets into the van, but he avoids the agitation of driving. He has redirected a previously wasted ten hours in his week.

A transportation company in Los Angeles has recently constructed a rolling office in a van. Set up to accommodate as many as ten people traveling to and from their offices, the van enables each passenger to conduct business using the telephones, telex, and fax machines. The idea is that while you may not be able to create more hours in your day, you can maximize the hours you have.

Hotels in the 1980s competed for business customers by providing certain amenities such as French soaps and designer shampoos. Today they compete with computer modems in the rooms, voice mail, and paging systems.

MGM Grand Airlines has a series of private compartments on its airplanes that accommodate four people, enabling groups to conduct business meetings during the five-hour trip from California to New York. What a great way to secure hours of high-quality management time!

The Golden State Warriors basketball team now uses a private plane to transport its players to out-of-town games. This saves time, keeps the players together, and gets them places on their own schedule, not that of an available airline.

As they pace the sidelines watching their teams on the field, the NFL coaches wear headsets that keep them in constant communication with their offensive and defensive coordinators, seated in the team booths high above the stadium. These up-to-the-second reports create such an advantage that if the telephone system of one of the teams fails, the other team must also cut off its communication with its coaches upstairs.

Car telephones are becoming more and more popular, although many holdouts still scoff at the idea and see their use as affected or status-seeking. But a 1992 study by the Gallup Organization indicated that seven out of ten cellular-phone users reported that their business and personal lives had dramatically improved with the new tool. More than half of the users reported increased business revenues; more importantly, they said that they'd added an hour or two to their day by increasing business productivity.

I have found my car telephone invaluable. Not only can I now use formerly wasted daily commute time (two hours a day in my case), but if I'm driving to an appointment or a lunch, my staff and clients can reach me with important calls or messages. I've even installed call waiting on my car line and an answering machine for the car phone.

Recently, I was being driven to O'Hare Airport in Chicago to return home from a business meeting. My staff called me from Los Angeles on my portable telephone, which occupies a small compartment in my briefcase, to inform me that my flight to L.A. via Dallas had been canceled because of poor weather. My secretary had rearranged my flight and was calling to give me details of the alternate route. The phone call enabled me to save time on my connections to L.A.

At many airports you can now rent portable cellular phones for your business stay, and many hotels offer beepers that enable you to be contacted when you're in a meeting elsewhere in the city.

I've put a headset unit on the telephone in my office. It's light and not in the least uncomfortable. It frees both my hands, allowing me to make notes, file, and organize my desk while carrying on a phone conversation. It's worked so well, I now have one on my car phone too. I have my staff prepare a daily list of people I want to reach from my car. The list stays within easy reach while I'm driving.

With skyphones on airplanes and telephones on trains, I don't understand why more car rental agencies have not yet offered rental cars with phones for traveling businesspeople. I'd rent one every time.

More companies are making use of teleconferencing. In 1992, United Way had a major crisis involving its CEO and the use of headquarters funds. Some of its local chapters were withholding funds and questioning the leadership. Within one week, United Way had organized a national teleconference with all its chapters. Through this instant communication, they helped defuse the crisis.

Sending memos, too, is now almost easier done than said. Thanks to electronic mail, memos can be sent to you while you're traveling and be waiting for you when you arrive. You can send memos through any telephone into your computer from wherever you are so that your managers, anywhere in the world, can tap into the phone system and receive them. Some systems have voice mail, allowing you to call a telephone number and get the entire message verbatim through an international taping system.

Microsoft uses electronic mail as a conveyor belt for ideas. Virtually all Microsoft employees worldwide send a variety of memos, notes, comments, and brainstorms back and forth twenty-four hours a day. It doesn't take a technical genius to use the system, either. The message is typed on the computer screen and sent by pressing a few buttons, and the person on the other end sees a flashing signal. The fact that the system is unstructured encourages frequent use and spontaneity.

Roger Ailes, the Republican image consultant in George Bush's 1988 presidential campaign, was able to coordinate a national strategy across all fifty states by using electronic mail and overnight delivery services. He could make script changes for political advertisements within minutes and send copies of completed spots for videotape viewing daily. This flexibility allowed the campaign to respond immediately to current polls as no previous campaign had.

A fax machine in my house not only enables me to receive office correspondence when I'm working at home; it also enables my officers or managers traveling in different time zones to send me messages anytime on crucial matters. I can then get back to them at a time that's convenient for both me and them.

Many traveling reps, who practically live in their cars, have had fax machines installed in their autos. If they're in some small town, a fax machine may not be readily available. A car fax means they're always reachable by the home office, too. (There's now even a service in Los Angeles that sends customers up-to-the-minute faxes that show the traffic flow on the freeways.)

Player draft days for the NBA and NFL are filled with incredible tension for team management. Close to a hundred athletes are in consideration, and although each participating team knows its order in the draft, there is no way to determine in advance which players will still be available when it's a particular team's turn. Especially stressful is the relatively short time allowed a team for its selection.

To alleviate the confusion of those intense minutes and facilitate informed decisions, teams now use computers programmed with all the pertinent statistics on each draft candidate.

Nobody has ever stolen second without starting at first base. But Otis Nixon may be the first to start at a database. Like many successful base stealers, the Atlanta Braves' outfielder has kept a notebook on opposing pitchers for years. But now he is attempting to take an even bigger lead on the opposition by going high-tech. Nixon has entered the material from his notebook into a personal computer, setting up the "Otis Nixon Pitcher Database."

Nixon explained: "I want to be the best base-stealer in the league, and this gives me an edge on the competition. I think all this research means ten, maybe fifteen stolen bases a year." He has stolen 277 in his career.

Nixon has data on how long a pitcher takes from delivery to the plate, his move to first, his variations in the throw to first, and his fielding ability. "I also have a special notes section on each pitcher, what type of pitch they throw in steal situations and how hard they throw," he said. He would not reveal any of his information on current pitchers, but did allow a look at the data on former pitcher John Tudor, a left-hander with the Dodgers and the St. Louis Cardinals. The entry read: "Very high leg kick, but different from most left-handers. Throws over to first 3–4 times. Can steal third base easily because of his big leg kick and doesn't have spin move." Nixon said: "Some guys rely on their memory. This is better than relying on your memory."

A Hughes Network Systems unit has started operating a digital phone service on airlines which enables passengers to link their laptop computers to a telephone system to send and receive computer data and faxes. Alaska Airlines and Northwest Airlines will offer the service, with other major carriers sure to follow.

Lou Kwiker, a highly successful venture capitalist, was involved in a complex merger. He took his financial analyst with him to New York and by using his laptop on the airplane during the five-hour flight was able to unravel some of the more intricate problems. By the time they met with legal counsel in New York, the financial aspects of the deal were already worked out.

Hand-held computers are becoming more prevalent. At Avis, garage staffs use them to print customer receipts to speed up rental returns; at Federal Express, drivers report parcel deliveries with electronic scanners. At Otis Elevator Company, service personnel respond to emergency calls using hand-held computers to query service files. A number of police departments, including that of Newark, New Jersey, give their officers hand-held computers to enter license numbers and detect stolen cars.

PHYSICAL CONDITIONING

We stress conditioning, believing that a better-conditioned athlete can whip a superior athlete who isn't in top shape.

Bear Bryant

In sports, the success of an athlete depends in part on his physical condition and his ability to avoid injuries. It's no different in business. The better we feel, the better we can function. Athletes devote a fair amount of time to physical conditioning—shouldn't we do the same in business?

Eleven years ago, the noted financier T. Boone Pickens badly lost a game of racquetball. Recognizing that he had been beaten by his own poor conditioning, he responded by launching a comprehensive wellness program for his 400 employees at Mesa Limited Partners, and built a $2.5-million, 30,000-square-foot facility open to all employees and their families. The center offers exercise equipment, an indoor running track, a basketball court, and classes in tae kwon do.

Employees earn small cash bonuses for good habits, ranging from $6 per month for not smoking to $700 a year for a combination of perfect work attendance, regular exercise, and other positive life-style habits. Those who use the exercise facility get perks such as free gym clothes and laundry service.

The results of Pickens's wellness program are impressive:

1. Per-employee health-care costs declined to 41 percent of the national average, after rising only 4.8 percent during a period when the national average rose 105 percent.

2. Absenteeism declined by more than 50 percent from an initial rate that was close to the national average.

3. Morale has improved and productivity has increased.

4. Follow-up studies have shown that employees who regularly use the program incur only half the medical expenses incurred by those who don't.

Most of us don't have businesses that can afford to emulate T. Boone Pickens's, but we can implement some sort of wellness program. It could be as simple as disseminating information or establishing a bonus award system based on results.

The majority of businesspeople with whom I'm involved do not take good care of themselves. The standard line is "I'm too busy." I've lost too many friends prematurely and I've seen too many people retire sooner than necessary. These items are not news bulletins; you've heard them all before. But let me reiterate them to try to raise your awareness once again:

- **Develop some type of exercise program.**
  Studies show that a physical workout of thirty minutes four times a week is a very good exercise program. At one time I did not exercise at all. Eight years ago, when I started to walk on a treadmill, I could only walk one mile in fifteen minutes. I now run fifteen nine-minute miles a week. The improvements in my stamina and my physical well-being show up in my annual EKG—and the difference is staggering.

  Whether it's running, swimming, stair-climbing, or bicycling, there are so many ways to exercise that are not costly and not time-consuming that you owe it to yourself, your company, and your family to get involved in some program.

- **Get regular physical checkups.**
  Through my annual running EKG treadmill test, my doctor charts my progress and spots any potential problems. I get a

blood workup, checking out important items such as my cholesterol count, twice a year.

- **Watch your diet.**
I maintain my weight (the running helps), but a lot of travel and business dinners don't make it easy.

Game Time

────────────── **TeamThink** ──────────────

No one is going to measure you by the number of hours you work: people (including you) measure you by what you accomplish.

Vince Lombardi said, "I never lost a game, I just ran out of time." We will all eventually run out of time. Let's try to maximize the time we have.

8

Filling
the Stands

I'm the chief executive officer of an entertainment company.

David Stern,
commissioner,
National Basketball Association

When the Los Angeles Lakers first arrived in L.A. from Minnesota, they had trouble selling enough tickets to cover their expenses. They were glad to see 5,000 fans at a game. Eventually, they moved to their own building (the Forum), developed their signature fast-paced game style, which they called "Showtime," added the popular Laker Girls to perform during time-outs, offered membership in a private dining club inside the Forum, and enticed Hollywood stars to attend the games. All these attractions worked; they now fill the stands with about 17,500 fans every night. They realized that *entertainment* was what their fans (customers) were really buying.

Harry Dalton, general manager of baseball's Milwaukee Brewers, says, "We're in the entertainment business. We have a pennant race every year and the professional part of us wants to win the pennant, but the practical part of us wants to be an entertaining item that draws people who want to spend their money here. We can't guarantee a pennant every year, but you do want to be able to guarantee the entertainment. When you lose, people should go out of here saying, 'We had a good time tonight.' "

Basketball commissioner David Stern, the Brewers' Harry Dalton, and Lakers owner Jerry Buss all realize that although technically they oversee, manage, or own sports teams, the product they sell is entertainment.

Cal-Surance is in the insurance *business*, but I make sure all of our people know and understand that what we are really selling is *service*. That is why our motto is "Insurance is our business, but service is our product."

Identify the product you are really selling. Is it entertainment? Is it service? Is it security? Then make sure your marketing and sales effort centers around your real product. There is no doubt about the product in the mind of Philip J. Riese, executive vice-president of American Express Consumer Card Group, when he emphatically states, "American Express is a service company first, a financial company second."

Thor Egelmann, vice-president of personnel of Disneyland, says, "We consider ourselves to be in show business, not the hotel or restaurant business. When our people are at work, they are on stage."

SERVICE ABOVE ALL

Claire Rothman, president of the California Forum, says, "Part of my role as team leader is to make sure all of our employees know how their role fits into our service concept. Even if they aren't in a creative position, their actions can destroy what everyone else is fighting for; from the operator who answers the phone, to the usher when he takes your ticket, and most of all the parking lot attendant who can make the client miserable for the whole night. They are all a part of our service team."

———————— TEAMTHINK ————————
Service must become more than just a philosophy or a department in your business—it must be a focus and a reality.

Service has become the element that determines the success of most businesses. Customers or clients respond favorably or unfavorably to your organization primarily based on the service they receive or don't receive. They will stay with you or leave you depending on how they perceive your service. Successful service starts when senior management adopts a philosophy of service and then consciously converts that philosophy into a reality. To achieve this requires completing a number of steps which I discuss in this section—the service mission, service objectives, and service training.

Renn Zaphiropoulos, president of Versatec, Inc., a manufacturer of computer printers in the Silicon Valley, defines business as providing a service for profit. "If you provide the service and make no profit," he says, "it's philanthropy. If you make a profit and provide no service, it's thievery."

Karen Wegmann, executive vice-president of Wells Fargo Bank in California, says, "To a customer, everybody at Wells *is* Wells. Saying 'It's not my department' doesn't work here. Ours is a fix-it culture."

The Service Mission

———————— TEAMTHINK ————————
The first step is to develop a service mission that employees can understand and support with an action plan.

As a brand-new basketball franchise, the Charlotte Hornets faced some handicaps. Because a new franchise builds its team largely from other teams' lesser players, a new team is not as competitive in its early years and consequently has a hard time winning fans. To offset this disadvantage, Hornets owner George Shin decided to focus on customer service to make the games enjoyable for the fans even if the Hornets lost.

The Hornets established a service mission to "provide top-flight service to their season-ticket holders." Their mission incorporated a five-step service strategy: "The season-ticket holder is the most important person to us; we depend on the season-ticket holder, not the other way around; we should never think of the season-ticket holder as interrupting the work that we have to get done; we should never argue with a season-ticket holder, and we should do everything within our power to meet the wants and desires of the season-ticket holder."

McDonald's motto, "Quality, service, cleanliness, and value," actually articulates the corporation's service mission. McDonald's focuses on delivering what it promises, and because it does, it's successful. McDonald's service is fast, friendly, and efficient. Parents feel comfortable having their kids eat there because cleanliness is evident. McDonald's quality can be seen and tasted, and value is evidenced at the cash register. McDonald's employees demonstrate an understanding of and commitment to their service mission.

The service mission of Stew Leonard's store in Norwalk, Connecticut, is reflected in his "Rule Number One—The customer is always right. Rule Number Two—If the customer is ever wrong, reread rule Number One." These words are chiseled into a 6,000-pound rock that rests just outside the front door of the world's largest (and most profitable) dairy store.

Midwest Express airlines advertises its service mission: "The best care in the air." The company strives to provide luxury service at coach fares or less with wide leather seats and gourmet meals including complimentary wine or champagne.

Service Objectives

While your service mission is a broad general declaration of what you want to achieve, your service objectives become your action plan, which is very specific. For example: "We will answer every telephone within three rings; we will return every call within twenty-four hours."

Some of the service objectives adopted by the Charlotte Hornets to satisfy their season-ticket holders included paying extra careful attention to simple yet important items such as providing good and ample parking, super-clean rest rooms, and dazzling entertainment at halftime. George Shin was also determined to have everyone in the Hornet organization participate in service activities for the Charlotte community, from neighborhood parties to the YMCA and Rotary Club meetings.

Does it make a difference? Even though the Hornets represent the second-smallest market among the NBA's twenty-seven teams, in their first season their service mission propelled them to set NBA records for attendance, averaging 23,000 fans per home game. With their tremendous support from the community, the Hornets had the largest profit in the 1989–90 season of any NBA team.

Federal Express Corporation's ongoing objective since the company delivered its first package in 1973 is "100 percent customer satisfaction." To achieve that objective, FedEx constantly makes changes that keep pace with new technology and customer needs. Last year, the corporation implemented 1,500 alterations that were as simple as a wording change in their procedure manual or as major as a change in service.

Fidelity Investments, based in Boston, serves over 6 million individual and corporate customers. Through Fidelity's four telephone service centers, the company has established a service objective of answering every telephone call by the third ring, with a real live person—not a recording. Fidelity even tracks its performance through its own auditors.

The AutoZone auto parts stores have a special rule called "Drop/Stop-30/30." This reminds AutoZoners of their service objective, which is to serve customers immediately. When a customer enters an AutoZone store, employees are to drop whatever is in their hands, stop whatever they are doing, and help that customer before he is thirty feet or thirty seconds into the store.

Two of my organization's service objectives get heavy emphasis. All telephone calls are returned within twenty-four hours, no matter where the caller is from and no matter where our employee may be. I've often returned calls from airports, cabs, and doctor's offices. Also, we try to reply to every letter within forty-eight hours of receipt—even if the answer is that we don't have an answer yet but will get one as soon as possible.

Some organizations even attach a service guarantee to their service objective. Domino's Pizza, for example, promises delivery within thirty minutes or the pizza costs $3 less. At Satisfaction Guaranteed Eateries, any guest who has to wait more than twenty minutes gets a free meal.

The Hampton Inn chain offers guests a guarantee. "If you're not completely satisfied for whatever reason, you are not expected to pay. Every staffer from room cleaner to desk clerk is empowered to grant the guarantee." Holiday Inn proclaims, "If it's not right, it's on us." Neiman Marcus, the department store, has a "no questions asked" refund policy.

Service Training

"I am a believer in training," says J. Willard Marriott, Jr., president and chairman of Marriott Hotels. "Our hotels have a checklist of sixty-six steps to make sure that a room is made up precisely the right way. If each maid made up her room differently, you would just have a hodgepodge. Consistency in the service business is vital and training is essential to achieve this consistency."

The role of service is redefining almost every industry because providing excellent service is becoming a requirement for survival. But how do you define service? Clearly service is an intangible. The only way it can be measured is by a customer's level of satisfaction.

In a real sense, every employee in your organization has a customer. Consequently, each of those employees has some basic responsibility for quality of service and customer satisfaction. The employees who must greet, meet, or deal directly with your customers or clients need training that adequately reflects the degree of difficulty of customer contact built into their job. Competent companies provide that kind of training when their employees start their jobs and on a continuing basis.

What gets taught in the training depends on the job's requirements. However, first and foremost is the necessity for product knowledge.

Street sweepers at Disney World go through four days of training—not because it takes that long to learn trash pickup, but because Disney expects their street sweepers to answer questions about the park.

The service representatives who man the phone at Procter and Gamble's telephone answer center have been out to the manufacturing plants to see how the company's products are made.

L. L. Bean, the tremendously successful sales catalog organization, trains all its customer service reps to be so knowledgeable about the products in the catalogs that they can help the customer make informed purchase decisions whether the product is mountain-climbing boots or a complete outfit for a white-water-rafting excursion.

Federal Express believes it can't support a customer-oriented service objective without a strong emphasis on training. President and CEO Frederick W. Smith views training as one of the three most important events that take place at the company.

Before a Federal Express courier ever delivers a package, he will have gone through three weeks of service training. Before a customer service agent ever answers a phone call, he will have gone through five weeks of training. The training doesn't stop there; every six months employees are expected to pass a job-knowledge test. Those employees who don't are sent back to training. Those who meet or exceed the test standards are eligible for merit increases or proficiency pay.

Service Beyond Expectations

———————— TeamThink ————————

Every customer or client in today's business environment expects some service, but you can make a significant impression by offering service beyond expectations.

"Exceed your customers' expectations," said Sam Walton, chairman of Wal-Mart Stores, who died in 1992. "If you do that, they'll come back over and over. Give them what they want—and a little more. Let them know you appreciate them. Make good on all your mistakes, and don't make excuses—apologize, stand behind everything you do."

It may take some creative thinking, innovation, or brainstorming sessions to create superb service, but the rewards in customer satisfaction, customer loyalty, and increased business will be well worth the effort. The idea is to offer a service that others are not yet offering, don't want to offer, or think can't be offered.

Stew Leonard's has a bus that picks up senior citizens and brings them to his store. And notes left in his suggestion box are followed up by a call to the customer within twenty-four hours.

Don Buyer Volvo of Falls Church, Virginia, has night-shift mechanics who make repairs until 3:00 A.M., so that if something is left unfinished by the day mechanic, the customer doesn't have to wait an extra day to get the car back. More than half a dozen people stay on duty until 8 P.M., so daytime commuters can get their cars without having to leave work early.

Melinda McIntyre-Kolpin, CEO of First Professional Bank in Santa Monica, California, created a courier service system that makes from 400 to 800 pickups a day from clients' offices, avoiding the necessity for clients to come to the bank. While other banks offer this service on a limited basis, First Professional offers it to all its customers at no charge. While other banks use outside messenger services, the couriers from First Professional are bank employees; not only is their attitude different, but they can often answer clients' questions on the spot.

First Professional is open seven days a week, and it has a twenty-four-hour answering service to take customer calls and relay them to one of four bank officers, including the CEO, who are on call at all times. One middle-of-the-night call came from a client whose child was in jail; the client needed cash for the bail bondsman. Another late-night call came from a frantic customer who was leaving early the next morning for Australia and had forgotten to stop by the bank to get cash for the trip.

Zimbrick Car Dealerships in Madison, Wisconsin, offers free cab rides to work for customers who drop their cars off for servicing. Zimbrick's managers make it a point to have dinners with the cab company's drivers to get feedback on how the customers really feel about the quality of service at the dealership. Information received from the cabdrivers has motivated Zimbrick to install a children's play area and cubicles with desks and telephones for customers so that they can work while waiting for their cars.

Last year Cal-Surance inaugurated a new service that has impressed the hell out of our customers. We distributed a list of the home telephone numbers of every one of our senior executives and officers, including mine, to *every* client. Our message is clear: If you have a problem at any time, evenings or weekends, we are available.

Correcting Service Problems

"Customers don't expect you to be perfect," says Donald Porter, senior vice president of British Airways. "They do expect you to fix things when they go wrong."

──────── TEAMTHINK ────────
Anticipate problems with service delivery to your customers and have a program in place to deal with them quickly and efficiently.

You don't want your employees to say things to your customers like "I'll have to check—it's not in the computer." "Someone will get back to you." "Those guys are always messing up." "I'm too busy to get to this at the moment." "It's not my job." Establish a procedure that enables the customer to complain easily if he wants to. The complaint process should be visible and accessible. Because most people resist confrontation and are intimidated by even the thought of it, it is sometimes easier for them to voice their complaints through an inanimate object such as a questionnaire or a suggestion box. But if you have an individual whose job it is to receive complaints, it is extremely important that he be receptive, friendly, and empathetic to the complainer.

Remember that suggestion box at Stew Leonard's dairy store? One evening after six o'clock, Stew Leonard, Jr., found a crisply worded complaint written by a customer half an hour earlier, indicating that she had wanted chicken breasts for dinner, but the store was sold out. It so happened that a Perdue chicken truck pulled up at that moment to the loading dock. Within minutes, Leonard had someone heading off to the frustrated customer's house with a complimentary two-pound package of fresh chicken breasts.

British Airways has installed video booths at Heathrow Airport in London so that travelers can tape their reactions upon arrival. Customer-service representatives view the tapes and respond.

Claire Rothman of the California Forum personally handles every complaint. "With a building that seats 17,505 people, the complaints range from 'Why can't I get 500 tickets to the hot concert?' to 'I was the third person in line for tickets and I'm in the last row.' Rothman has all complaint calls transferred directly to her.

There is a great story about Club Med–Cancún. On a flight from New York to Mexico, the plane was en route ten hours longer than scheduled and ran out of food and drinks. It finally arrived at two in the morning, with a landing so rough that oxygen masks and luggage dropped from overhead. The passengers were hungry and unhappy and felt that their vacations had been ruined before they even started. An attorney on board collected names and addresses for a class-action lawsuit.

When Silvio DeBortoli, the general manager of the resort, was told of the horrendous flight, he took half his staff to the airport, where they laid out a table of snacks and drinks and set up a stereo system to play music. As the guests filed through the gate, they received personal greetings, help with their bags, and a chauffeured ride to the resort. When they arrived at the resort they found a lavish banquet, complete with mariachi band and champagne. Moreover, the staff had convinced other guests to meet and greet the newcomers and the partying continued until sunrise. In the end, most of those vacationers felt they had wound up having a better vacation than if their flight had gone like clockwork.

It is essential to take care of the customer's problem to the customer's satisfaction. Many businesses believe that means going to whatever lengths are necessary. No matter what goes wrong, if you make it easy for your customers to complain, give them a name and a number to call, communicate with them on every complaint, and show that you care, your chances of having them as repeat customers are high.

Here are some easy ways for customers to voice their complaints:

- **Establish an 800 number for customer questions and problems.**
  Put this number on every piece of paper your customer receives. Monitor the number of calls and their origins, and it will help you identify your own service problems.

- **Create a customer-service executive.**
  Publicize this person's name and position on all your literature, and make certain this person has the authority to solve the problem.

- **Set up a fax number specifically for complaints.**
  The faster you can identify the problem the faster you can resolve it.

- **Include a "problem-alert" form in all correspondence.**
  This enables the customer to complain immediately and also conveys the message that you are open to any complaints.

The quality of your service represents the strongest motivator for customers to return and for them to recommend you to others. In a very real sense, your service is also your primary sales product. However, until someone becomes your customer or client, you don't have the opportunity to show how good your service is—so, the selling of your service becomes an integral part of your sales strategy.

"If you're not serving the customer, your job is to be serving someone who is," says Jan Carlzon, CEO of the Scandinavian Airline System.

THE SALES TEAM

TEAMTHINK
Selling should not become the exclusive responsibility of your sales force; it must become part of the job description of everyone in the entire organization.

"At Harvard Business School, there are over a dozen courses on marketing, and not a single one on selling," the late industrialist and publisher Malcolm Forbes once said. "The day anyone in any business thinks he's too important to sell, he ceases to be important to his business."

For many companies, selling has changed dramatically. Traditionally, it was seen as the vocation of a single individual skilled and persuasive in the art of selling. Now, in many organizations including my own, selling is conceived as a team effort put forward by a number of individuals who coordinate their efforts toward the customer.

People within an organization may be team players, but they

can only be molded into part of the sales team with the organization's encouragement and support. Sales teamwork is a by-product of the organization and has to come from the top down. You cannot legislate teamwork. It is an attitude that develops over a long term, and it is essential in a well-run sales organization.

You need to develop a new culture in your company in which the responsibility for sales becomes part of everyone's job. There must be an overlap in job descriptions so that they all come together in this area, and you need to constantly reinforce that overlap.

You want to create an attitude of shared responsibility. You can't have everyone off doing his own thing, doing his job only and leaving the rest for everyone else. Everyone has to believe that he is part of the sales team.

In a "team sell," it should be impossible to tell where one person's responsibility stops and another's starts. In a real team environment, positive energy is created by collaboration—the company supports open discussion and develops respect for different points of view. Communication among sales, service, and technical personnel must be encouraged.

The Chrysler Corporation recognized the need for greater employee involvement in sales and service, so in 1992 the corporation announced plans to spend $30 million to reeducate the more than 100,000 employees in its dealerships, from sales managers to switchboard operators. Chrysler calls this new program "Customer One." The program includes meetings in small groups at which employees act out such roles as guides at Disney World or bellhops at a Ritz-Carlton Hotel to improve the way they respond to customers. Chrysler is using customer handling techniques from other nonautomotive businesses as models for the kind of service they want their employees to provide in order to improve sales. The corporation has also announced cash incentives for dealers with high customer satisfaction scores.

Uniroyal Chemical developed an "Adopt-a-Customer" program designed to give customers more personalized service while making sales and production employees more familiar with specific customer needs. The Adopt-A-Customer teams are composed of people from sales and manufacturing, including line operators, shipping lab people, and raw material suppliers. The teams partner with specific customers. Rick Fonte, manager of employee involvement and development, says, "This program has led to improved quality and cost savings at our customers' plants." This collaborative result has to translate into better sales for Uniroyal.

Traits of a Successful Salesperson

Over the past thirty years, I have had the opportunity to closely observe many direct-sales people in my own organization. Every one who has done well possesses similar traits that I believe contributed to his success.

- **He establishes credibility and trust with the customer.** Only if someone trusts you will he buy from you. If he doesn't trust you, he won't buy no matter how much he needs your product or service. Honesty creates credibility and credibility leads to trust.

- **He can distinguish a "prospect" from a "suspect."** A successful salesperson can quickly and accurately tell the difference between a true potential buyer and a mere shopper or looker. Too many salespeople spend 90 percent of their time with non-buyers and only 10 percent with strong potential buyers, which means the majority of their time and effort is wasted. If a salesperson spent 90 percent of his time with true potential customers, he would substantially increase his effectiveness.

- **He recognizes the client's real need.** A prospective customer may say he is looking for a burglar alarm system. If the salesperson identifies that the client's need is to feel safe, instead of focusing on all the bells and whistles of the system, he will focus on the security the system offers. While the need in a product like this is pretty obvious, there is always a need, perhaps much more subtle, that a successful salesperson must uncover.

Jamie Lowe, general manager of the Orlando Twins, recognizes that what their fans (customers) need was "something extra" besides watching a baseball game. He explains his strategy: "Our goal is to fill each date with a promotional night, group night, or some kind of special event. A giveaway costs about four thousand dollars per night. The greatest thing we've done right now is we're giving away a car each month; it will be the fan-of-the-month drawing."

- **He really listens.**

Many salesmen are so eager to hear themselves talk, they only pretend to listen while they are really concentrating on what they are going to say next. It's important that a salesperson listens not only to what is being said, but also to what is not being said.

The best salesperson is the one who listens to the client's needs, understands them, and develops a method of meeting them.

- **He loves to win and hates to lose.**

"I want people who are smart, tough, self-reliant, who love to win," Ross Perot, chairman of Perot Services, once said. "If you run out of people who love to win, look for people who hate to lose."

- **He works hard at his job.**

There are certain qualities that you look for in people, whether you are on a football team or in business. You look for people who are committed, devoted, and doing the best job. Talent isn't going to matter, either. I'll take the guy who is out breaking his butt over a guy with talent in a close situation every time. I may get my butt beat a few times, but in the long run, I'll win because I'll have a guy with more character.

Mike Ditka,
former coach,
Chicago Bears

- **He deals with the fear of failure and rejection.**

People talk about being under a lot of pressure. What it seems to me they're talking about is a fear of failure. You can see it in a batter's eyes when Roger Clemens is pitching.

Whitey Herzog

- **He is well prepared.**

The will to prepare to win is infinitely more important than the will to win. A team that is really willing to prepare is the team that has the best chance to win and wants to win.

Bobby Knight,
head basketball coach,
University of Indiana

SALES NEGOTIATING STRATEGIES

"I'm a very firm believer that both parties to an agreement have an opportunity for it to be good," says Claire Rothman, president of the California Forum, "and for it to be good, both parties have to feel that they got most of what they wanted."

_____ **TEAMTHINK** _____
The most successful negotiations occur when both parties come out with some needs satisfied.

In 1980, manager Whitey Herzog decided he desperately needed a good backup catcher for the St. Louis Cardinals. He wanted Darrell Porter, then playing for Kansas City. Herzog was planning to offer a trade to Kansas City when he found out that Porter had become a free agent and could negotiate with other teams.

Porter lived in Kansas City and reportedly loved the area. Although Porter's agent had been in touch, it was obvious to Herzog that he was being used to force the Kansas City Royals to make a counteroffer. With that in mind, Herzog devised a strategy. He called Porter's agent with an extraordinary offer for that time, $200,000 up front as a signing bonus, $500,000 for the first year, and $700,000 for the four years after that, on one condition—the offer was to be accepted that afternoon or the deal was off. Herzog didn't want to give Kansas City time to make its own offer. Although Porter was on his honeymoon on a cruise ship, his agent reached him by ship-to-shore telephone and the deal was clinched.

By putting a deadline on the deal, Herzog didn't allow himself to be used as a pawn in someone else's game. By design, he preempted other offers by his exceptionally strong first offer. By planning his negotiating strategy *before* opening negotiations with Porter, Herzog was able to guide the direction of the negotiation. The negotiation succeeded because both parties got a good deal—Herzog got the catcher he wanted and Porter got a terrific contract.

You negotiate in business all the time, whether it's for something you want as an individual (a promotion, a raise, time off, a bonus, more staff) or something you want for the company (better pricing, higher commissions, better terms, financing terms). Successful sales are always contingent upon successful negotiating. Most businesses have begun to recognize the broad scope and importance of effective negotiating techniques.

Successful negotiation necessitates good preparation and effective strategy. Here for your consideration are twenty of my negotiating strategies.

1. Create a conducive atmosphere.

The setting and your attitude are almost as important as the issues to be discussed. If possible, I always try to have a meeting at the other person's office—normally he will feel more comfortable in his own setting. Otherwise, I try for a neutral setting.

Bob Woolf, top negotiator for Larry Bird, Larry King, and

others, says, "I once negotiated a contract on behalf of Sidney Green, with Jonathan Kovler, then co-owner of the Chicago Bulls, while floating atop rubber rafts on Horse Pond near my home on Cape Cod. I'll do everything in my power to create the kind of atmosphere where my negotiating partner enters the talks with an attitude favorable to making a deal. It will make my job easier."

2. Negotiate in person whenever possible.

The problem with telephone discussions is that you can't observe facial expressions and body language. It's also easier for the other party to say no.

Herb Cohen, professional negotiator and consultant to some of the largest corporations in America, says, "Any time an idea, proposal, or request calls for a change in the current handling of affairs, it requires a personal oral presentation. Documents, letters, and phone calls may precede or follow such a meeting, but they are not persuasive in themselves. The message is simple—if you are serious about getting something you want, present it yourself—in person."

3. Only negotiate with the person who will make the decision.

If you talk with someone who is just a messenger or a middleman for the real decision-maker, you can't make meaningful trade-offs or close the deal because he doesn't have the authority to do so. Find out as early as possible who does have the authority and try to meet with that person.

4. The person who makes the first offer in a negotiation normally will take less.

Unless, like Whitey Herzog, you are making an offer that doesn't allow for a counteroffer, do not make the first offer. Seldom does the other party accept a first offer, and he will use it only as the starting point for the negotiations.

Bob Woolf points out, "I've found that I never want to make the first offer. You always want to be in the position of getting information before you give it. If you can get them to go first, you may find that you've made some false assumptions about what you thought they'd offer. The opportunity is there to gain valuable information that may cause you to alter your counteroffer."

5. Try to avoid confrontational demands.

Most people see a demand as a line drawn in the sand and a dare to cross it. This causes many of them to want to go to war. At that point, all negotiations cease.

The discussion will go better if you can make proposals, suggestions, or recommendations, give alternatives, or suggest possibilities.

6. Don't assume too much.

Assumptions are a vital part of the negotiating process. However, they are not always subject to rational verification. The key is to be willing to change your preconceived notions as more facts come to light. Very often a great deal of time is wasted because both parties misunderstood the facts.

Gerald Nierenberg, president of the Negotiation Institute, says, "There is nothing wrong with making assumptions. The problem arises when we act and think as if the assumption is the absolute fact."

7. Ask questions and more questions.

The more questions you can ask the other person, the more you will understand his position. Questions also direct the flow of the meeting.

It helps to have your questions worked out in advance; a poorly worded question will not elicit a clear answer. Most people fail to ask enough *why* questions.

8. Think about the other person's position. What are his wants and needs?

If you really try to understand what he wants and needs, you can better determine how far you can satisfy him and still get what *you* want.

9. Listen carefully to the other person.

Listening may be the most important skill in developing good strategies. Always listen with your third ear. What is he not saying? What does he really mean?

"Effective listening requires more than hearing the words transmitted," says Herb Cohen, "It demands that you find meaning and understanding in what is being said. After all, meanings are not in words, but in people."

10. Try to see what lies below the surface in the negotiation so that you deal with the real issues.

The most important issues may be hidden by smokescreen discussions that mean nothing.

11. Do your homework.

You must fully understand your situation, the other person's situation, and the options open to both. To accomplish this, do as much advance research as possible.

Ask yourself these questions: What are the areas of common ground that you share with the other party? What does the other party need or want—is he tight for cash or does he need a quick deal? What is the nature of the negotiation— friendly or hostile?

As Herb Cohen says, "If you fail to plan, you are planning to fail."

12. Think of negotiations as a combination of power, information, and timing.

The strategic use of these factors will determine the success of the negotiations. Who has the power to do what in the meeting? How much information should be divulged? When should you raise which issues at what time in the meeting? What time constraints, if any, do you or the other party face?

The kick I get out of baseball is in the back-scene, front-office maneuvering; the trading and the dealing. The one way I can put myself on the field, if only vicariously, is by assembling a team that represents my ability as a scout, a trader, and a psychologist. Building a ball team is like dealing yourself a poker hand. You have all winter to rummage around through the deck for the best possible combination of cards. The season itself becomes little more than the laydown of the hand you've dealt yourself—with one exception. You still have that brief period between mid-April and June fifteenth to try to pick up that one key player or make that one key trade that will plug your most glaring weakness.

> Bill Veeck,
> former owner,
> Chicago White Sox

13. Approach every meeting as a negotiating meeting.

There is no such thing as a social lunch or dinner meeting during a negotiation. The participants normally have some points they want to make, and they operate with a hidden agenda.

In 1930, Babe Ruth was negotiating a new contract with the Yankees. It was the peak of the Depression and well before agents negotiated contracts for the players. For his prodigious services, Ruth asked for $80,000 from the Yankees—a momentous sum for 1930. Ruth called a meeting with the news media as a means of negotiating with the Yankees. At that new conference, he said what he wanted. A reporter objected that Ruth was asking for too much, reminding the slugger that if he got the $80,000, he would be making more than President Herbert Hoover. Ruth's response: "I had a better year than Hoover." The Yankees paid the $80,000.

14. Remain cordial with the other party.

Bob Woolf tells of a time when the other party was unusually considerate and the impact that had on the negotiations: "When I was negotiating a contract for Gerald Wilkins with the New York Knicks, I was paired with the general manager of the basketball team, Al Bianchi. Gerald [was] the young, exciting guard whose brother, Dominique, is the Atlanta Hawks' spectacular forward. Gerald was improving every year and was a vital part of the Knicks' resurgence in 1988 and 1989.

"Al and I met for several hours, but we were still far apart on terms for Gerald's new contract. We were both tired and a little discouraged as the meeting came to a close. However, a small extra gesture of politeness on Al's part breathed new life into my attitude. Al took the trouble to leave his office and walk me a considerable distance to the elevator doors down the hall from his office in Madison Square Garden. I felt that he was trying to let me know that even though we hadn't made much progress that day, he did want to come to an agreement. By extending that small courtesy, he was saying, let's keep working at it. His extra gesture eased my apprehensions about his determination to make a deal. We did eventually come to terms on an excellent contract for Gerald, which was achieved through extra efforts, both large and small."

15. Concentrate first on areas of agreement, rather than disagreement.

There are always areas where both parties agree, so start with them. This establishes the right atmosphere for the rest of the discussions and may help avoid confrontation.

16. Discuss the issues you know will be difficult in the early part of the negotiations.

Introduce them after you have reached some areas of agreement. Don't save the toughest for last—if you do, these issues linger in the background all through the meeting and can sour the negotiations.

17. Always have alternatives and a range of issues.

Don't get stuck with no options or one issue only. You always need a fallback position. What happens if the other party says no to your issue? What's Plan B—or C or D? Most issues have alternatives. As an example, if the amount can't be changed, perhaps the payment terms can, or other benefits can be added to the deal.

18. Avoid weak arguments.

You generally know which ones they are—eliminate them. Otherwise the other party will tend to focus on them to dispute your stronger arguments.

19. Package the compromises.

You normally allow concessions in a fair negotiating meeting. Try to avoid making a series of individual compromises. If you review your compromises as a group, you can put them in better perspective and perhaps avoid giving up too much.

20. Hold back your solutions.

If you propose your solutions too early, you may not have included all of the important issues that might come up during the meeting. Also, you don't want early solutions to become the start of the negotiations.

Strategies are helpful, but at the end of the negotiations, all parties need to feel good about the results. Here's what three top negotiators say about this:

I think a negotiation settlement should be like a trade— if it doesn't help both sides, it's no good.

Red Auerbach

You can get what you want if you recognize that each person is unique and needs can be reconciled. Mutual satisfaction should be your goal—collaborative win-win negotiations.

Herb Cohen

The mature negotiator will have an understanding of the cooperative pattern. He will try to achieve agreement and will remember that in a successful negotiation, everyone wins.

Gerald Nierenberg

Sales, negotiating, and service are intertwined; if you're not a decent negotiator, you will not sell as well. If you're not a service organization, your sales will be hurt dramatically. And if you can't sell, the other two won't matter.

9

Good Guys Finish First

If the rules are broken in football, you receive a penalty, or might even be thrown out of the game. It is high time we define clearly the rules of playing the game in the U.S.A., and it's high time we had the intestinal fortitude to make them stick.

Tom Landry

In 1947 there wasn't one black baseball player in the major leagues. Branch Rickey, general manager of the Brooklyn Dodgers, knew this was wrong. The invisible barrier that had kept blacks from playing organized baseball had become a moral issue for Rickey and he decided to do something about it.

Rickey selected Jackie Robinson to play for the Dodgers and thus to become the first black player in the majors. Robinson was carefully chosen because of his extraordinary talent, but also because Rickey believed Robinson had the character to withstand the abuse he was sure to receive from other teams and the fans, and that he had the courage *not* to fight back.

After Rickey announced that he had signed Robinson, the reaction was immediate, volatile, and, from within the baseball establishment, virtually all negative. Several of Robinson's teammates, led by a Southern clique that included Dixie Walker, openly expressed their hostility, calling for a player boycott if Robinson was allowed to play.

Leo Durocher, the Dodgers' manager, heard that the players were drawing up a petition. Late one night when the team was on the road, Durocher called all his coaches and players together for a team meeting. It was two o'clock in the morning, and most of them were in their pajamas or underwear.

Durocher said, "I hear some of you fellows don't want to play with Robinson and that you have a petition drawn up that you are going to sign. Well, boys, you know what you can do with that petition . . . Mr. Rickey is on his way down here and all you have to do is tell him about it. I'm sure he'll be happy to make other arrangements for you.

"I heard Dixie Walker is going to send Mr. Rickey a letter asking to be traded. Just hand him the letter, Dixie, and you're gone. Gone! If this fellow is good enough to play on this [blank] team, and from what I've seen and heard he is [blank] going to play on this ballclub and he is going to play for me. I don't want to see your petition and I don't want to hear anything more about it. The meeting is over; go back to bed."

Durocher had delivered his message loud and clear. Nothing more was said about it, and the Dodger players eventually accepted Robinson as part of the team. To show their support, the team refused to stay in hotels that wouldn't admit blacks.

Jackie Robinson led the league in stolen bases, batted .297, played a nearly flawless first base, and was named baseball's first Rookie of the Year. Robinson went on to become a Hall of Famer and paved the way for other blacks to enter major-league baseball.

It took tremendous courage for the Dodgers to be the first to hire a black player and to do what they believed was right. By adding Robinson to their team, not only did they do the right thing, they made a shrewd organizational move. With Robinson on their team, the Dodgers went on to win multiple pennants and a World Series in 1955.

THE SPORTS ETHIC

Recruiting is the worst part of college football. The need to win is so great now that certain coaches swallow their

*pride, certain administrators look the other way, certain
payoffs are given—I'm sick of it.*

Bo Schembechler

In 1989, Hart Lee Dykes received immunity from the NCAA
for revealing the unethical recruiting practices of the University of
Illinois, Texas A&M, Oklahoma, and Oklahoma State. Oklahoma
State was found guilty of more than forty rules violations, including providing cash payments in excess of $5,000 and a sports car to
an unnamed player (reported to be Dykes).

College athletics have very specific rules governing recruiting,
but a number of schools have had difficulty following them. As
Marianne Stanley, women's basketball coach of Old Dominion, has
said, "What good are rules if you don't enforce them?" Although
certain schools go out of their way to treat athletes differently from
their other students, such as ignoring their grades, requesting favors from their professors, and offering easier courses, most institutions avoid such tactics.

A debate has been raised over the past few years questioning
the apparent disregard of some colleges and universities for the
quality of education received by their athletes. No league rules
address an athlete's class or grade requirements. Of major concern
is the recent disclosure of the low graduation ratio of many athletes. Only 22 percent of the basketball players who entered North
Carolina's state universities in 1986 graduated; and to date, North
Carolina State, North Carolina A&T, Carolina Central, Western
Carolina, the University of North Carolina at Charlotte, and
Winston-Salem State have all failed to graduate *any* of the basketball players who enrolled in 1986.

Duke University, on the other hand, exemplifies a real commitment to excellence in the classroom. The reason Duke has yet
to suspend a banner from the rafters of its home arena honoring the
Blue Devils' 1990 Final Four Team is that one of the players hasn't
earned his degree. In reference to that starting guard, Duke coach
Mike Krzyzewski said, "For us to hang a banner when one of our
guys didn't graduate would be a disgrace." Coach K. went even
further. In June 1992, he informed star center Christian Laettner,

the only college basketball player selected to participate in the 1992 Olympics, that if he didn't get his degree by the end of the first summer session, his retired jersey and Duke's 1992 National Championship banner would come down. Laettner was missing one unit needed to graduate, which he completed before the start of the Olympics.

Notre Dame, a leading football and basketball power, brags about what it didn't do to get back to the top. It has no athletic dorms, no training table, no breaks from professors for athletes, no special courses, no taking five years to get your degree, and almost no social life for players during the season. "We do not alter the philosophy of the university for athletics." says executive vice-president Reverend William Beauchamp.

If someone had told me in my youth that the following events would happen in the United States over the next few decades, I'd have wondered if he was talking about the same country: A U.S. President forced to resign because of the coverup of a criminal action; an arms-for-hostages scandal; the creation of a special prosecutor in Washington because we no longer trusted the integrity of the Justice Department; an "insider trading" scandal on Wall Street with some of our financial leaders under prosecution and in jail; Commodities Exchange members under indictment for illegal dealings; a major investment banking house "plea bargaining" in order to keep its senior management out of jail; several colleges placed on probation because of illegal recruiting; and a national sports hero banned from baseball because of illegal betting.

A few years ago, the Manville Corporation was one of the giants of American business. Today Manville is in Chapter 11 bankruptcy because of the liability suits brought against it in connection with asbestos. A California court found that Manville had hidden the asbestos danger from its employees, rather than looking for safer ways to deal with it. A New Jersey court was even harsher, finding that Manville had made a conscious, coldblooded business decision to take no protective or remedial action, disregarding the rights of others for "over forty years." For all practical purposes, this company was placed in jeopardy by a failure of corporate ethics.

In 1985, E. F. Hutton and Company pleaded guilty to 2,000

counts of mail and wire fraud. Hutton had engaged in a form of check kiting, intentionally overdrawing checking accounts for a day or two to gain interest. At the time, Hutton was the second-largest independent broker in the country. The firm never recovered from the damage to its reputation and was purchased by Shearson Lehman a year later.

What happened to these organizations? How could so many executives condone such behavior? Could it be that because the activity helped the company, they considered it acceptable? Did they believe they would never be found out? What message did their actions send to their employees? I strongly agree with Jack Miller, president of the Quill Corporation, who said, "Management must reenforce the reality of a living code of ethics by setting the example."

THE MANAGEMENT OF ETHICS

TEAMTHINK

It is the responsibility of management to establish and communicate a clear set of business ethics for employees to follow and to create an environment that encourages employees to uphold those ethics.

In 1990, in their off season, three Georgia Tech football players, apparently drunk, verbally abused two young women at a pizza parlor near campus. One of the players punched one of the women in the face, breaking her nose. Two of the players pleaded guilty to disorderly conduct. Three months later, these players violated their university-imposed probation, had their scholarships revoked, and left school.

At that point, it seemed that Georgia Tech had taken appropriate actions with those players. Astonishingly, however, not one of the players missed a game once the football season began; their scholarships were reinstated and they were told they had a clean slate. Georgia Tech had clearly abandoned the principle of its first response.

By contrast, defending national champion Notre Dame barred three of its top athletes from playing the entire season. One was dropped for disciplinary reasons, one was academically ineligible, and one was suspended for having a hit-and-run accident when he was intoxicated. When objections were voiced within the university to the harshness of the school's actions, coach Lou Holtz said, "If you cannot support the university, you need not be employed here. Notre Dame has a philosophy and I trust that philosophy."

The first step in establishing your company's ethics is to articulate what is ethical and what is not in a published code of ethics.

Too many business leaders think that establishing a written ethics policy is all that is needed; however, the true test of their ethics lies with leaders' actions in dealing with the practical realities of day-to-day business. Developing a code of ethics for your organization is a good start, but it's not enough.

More and more corporate executives are realizing that if employees are to take ethics policies seriously, companies have to come down hard when transgressions occur. "If one doesn't severely sanction ethical transgressions, word spreads that the boss is not really interested in ethics," says Harvard Business School professor John P. Kotter.

If ethics are to be taken seriously, a company ultimately has to fire people, but firing isn't the only solution. Unethical actions should have consequences, and these consequences should be serious, visible, and negative. In some circumstances, for instance, a demotion may be sufficient to make the point. In other cases, it is necessary to demonstrate that a certain type of misbehavior will not be tolerated in the company.

Firing someone for unethical conduct sends a strong message through the company. When an individual is fired, his peer group is severely affected. But firings should not be done for public relations purposes—in effect throwing an employee to the proverbial wolves. You cannot punish one person and allow others to escape moral accountability. You must be consistent.

Ethics are also important for practical reasons. If one person on the team doesn't keep the standard of the game high, suspicion will fall on the entire team. The team will be regarded throughout the department, the corporation, and the industry as not to be trusted. The team will have a tarnished reputation, and everyone on it will suffer.

Reputation is fundamental. It represents the future of any organization, and an executive shouldn't hesitate to take the necessary steps to maintain it. Everyone understands an error. But ethical transgressions are not errors.

Charles T. Munger, vice-chairman of Berkshire Hathaway, Inc., says, "There is no better way to communicate ethics than to have ethical imperatives dominate the life of the CEO." And I might add, the lives of the company's officers. It is essential for them to create a culture that doesn't put up with ethical misconduct—not one that merely holds a one-day program on ethics for the sake of public relations. "The ethical standards of a company are judged by its actions—not by pious statements of intent put out in its name," says Sir Adrian Cadbury, chairman of Cadbury Schweppes.

In developing a code of ethics for Cal-Surance, we followed certain guidelines:

- **Make it clear and practical.**
  Use clear, straightforward language and cover practical situations that your employees are likely to face. For example, may your employees accept gifts from clients or suppliers, or give them?

- **Effectively communicate the code to your employees.**
  Some companies, ours among them, include the code in their employee handbook; others hold seminars, and some communicate on a regular basis through the company newsletter.

  The St. Paul Insurance Companies named their code "In Good Conscience." At annual meetings, they discuss the impact of ethics on day-to-day situations. They highlight issues such as insider information, gifts and entertainment, contact with legislators, and employee privacy.

Chemical Bank has an extensive ethics education program. All new employees attend an orientation in which they read and sign off on Chemical's code of ethics. They even have a course called "Decision-Making in Corporate Values," a two-day seminar away from the bank that deals with ethical issues.

- **Consider written acknowledgment.**
   Think about having each employee sign a copy of the code and place a copy in his personnel file.

   William A. Dimma, deputy chairman of Royal Le Page, a major Toronto real estate and development corporation, recalls the time his company developed a clear policy against a practice referred to as "flipping properties." When they discovered that a branch manager and seven of his agents were engaging in the practice, the company fired them all. Dimma explained, "One of the agents sued the company because she said no one had explained the policy to her. We had—we had posted the policy on a bulletin board in the branch office." But Royal Le Page could not produce a form with the woman's signature attesting she had actually read the policy. The company lost the lawsuit.

- **Tailor additional codes to apply to the different areas of the company.**
   You could have a supplemental code of ethics for your finance department and a different supplemental code for the sales department. Because their needs, functions, and client contacts differ, the areas that will test their ethics vary also.

- **Design a code that also protects your clients.**
   In a recent study of 200 codes, it was found that most were designed primarily to protect the company against its own employees and made no mention of protecting customers.

- **Spell out the actions you deem clearly unacceptable. Examples are:**
   giving out false financial information about the company;

lying to employees, customers, or suppliers; submitting false or padded expense accounts; withholding information that is of material importance to another party.

- **Develop a method for reporting violations.**
  Create a path of reporting such that no manager can block the report. Also watch for retaliation against a whistleblower. This is a danger for the employee with the courage to make the report. Some organizations have created an ethics reporting officer, an ethics committee, or even a private post-office box to receive complaints.

- **Develop a consistent method of enforcement.**
  Every other employee will be aware of the way the violator of the code is treated. That will signal just how serious management is about following the code.

Here are some directives from our code of ethics:

Do not give false or misleading representation of our products or services.
Do not use improper methods of gathering information from our competitors.
Give honest responses to customer inquiries.
Avoid any conflict of interest involving the marketing of products and services.
Do not give excessive gifts to clients or underwriters without company approval.
Do not accept excessive gifts without approval of the management of the company.
Do not make untruthful remarks about competitors, their products, or their employees.

The Anixier Brothers in Evanston, Illinois, a distributor of electrical wire and cable worldwide with 2,500 employees, has a very straightforward ethics code called "Truth." Here is one section:

*We tell the truth to each other and to our customers and
    suppliers.*
*The cold, hard unvarnished, uncomfortable kind of
    truth.*
The whole story, not just part of it.
We don't stretch it, bend it, or avoid it.
And if someone raises hell about the truth . . . let them.
Just say it like it is.

Citicorp developed a clever way of getting its ethical message
across: a board game called "The Work Ethic," complete with
question cards and Parcheesi-like markers. Citicorp says it's been
played in forty-five countries by as many as 40,000 of its employees, from clerks to top executives. For example, there's a question
that deals with a customer who offers you theater tickets in exchange for a new backdated IRA at 9:00 A.M. the day after tax
returns were due. (If you accept, you're fired and out of the game.)

QUESTIONS OF ETHICS

TEAMTHINK
**It's not easy to come up with what is ethical to
you. You must reflect and question yourself to
come to terms with your own answers.**

Sometimes it's hard to see the thin line between what is
ethical and what isn't. It often depends on the perspective from
which you're viewing it. This story about "Pop" Warner, who
coached at Carlisle Institute and later at Stanford University, is a
good example.

In 1908 Warner's Carlisle team was scheduled to play Harvard. The week before the Harvard game, Warner had used a clever
trick to help defeat a strong Syracuse team. Carlisle players had
pads sewn to their pants and jerseys. The pads were the same size,
shape, and color as a football, making it very difficult to tell which
player had the ball and which were only pretending. When Carlisle

started to practice on Harvard's field the day before the game, Percy Haughton, Harvard's coach, saw the football-like pads.

"That's not fair," said Haughton mildly. Warner said, "It's not against the rules. I can put anything I like on my players' jerseys."

But Haughton had a few tricks up his sleeve. Just before kickoff, Warner and Haughton met on the field to pick out the game football. Warner reached into the bag of balls Haughton had brought and pulled one out. It was red! Haughton had dyed all the balls crimson, the color of Harvard's jerseys. "It's not against the rules," Haughton said, smiling. "A football doesn't have to be brown, does it?" Warner walked back to the sidelines muttering to himself. Harvard won the game, 17–0.

When baseball manager Leo Durocher got thrown out of a game (a fairly regular event), he would circumvent the penalty by going up to the press box and relaying his signals to the team through a sportswriter friend.

Chuck Dressen found a simple way to continue managing the Dodgers after getting thrown out of a game. He would put on a fake mustache and glasses and join the groundskeeping crew for the rest of the afternoon.

When Bill Veeck owned the Cleveland Indians, he would actually have the fences moved back when the New York Yankees and their power hitters were in town. When St. Louis came to town, he moved the left-field fence in as far as he could and kept the right-field fence as deep as possible; St. Louis had no right-handed power, but they did have a couple of left-handers who could hit. As Veeck liked to say, "It was a most obliging and adaptable fence."

All of these acts were pretty blatant, but the men involved probably just shrugged them off as gamesmanship.

As manager Maury Wills said after being suspended for having the batter's boxes in the Seattle King Dome drawn a foot too long, "That's not cheating. Just a little gamesmanship." But calling such actions gamesmanship is just a smokescreen. Cheating or breaking the rules is *always* a breach of ethics.

Here are some questions that might help you think about your own ethical posture:

- If I know what is going on, can I live with it?

- If it affects the bottom line, will I still do it?

- If it's not expressly forbidden, will I permit it?

- Is it right to make a profit when someone's survival is involved?

- How will I feel about myself at the end of the day if I do something that my conscience tells me is unethical?

- Do I condone or ignore unethical behavior in my company as long as I don't do it personally?

- How well does my firm honor agreements and covenants both internally and externally?

- Does the importance of an individual to my organization determine how I will deal with an unethical act he commits?

You cannot mandate or dictate the ethical standards of others, only of yourself. Sir Adrian Cadbury has observed, "Ethical signposts do not always point in the same direction. The real difficulties arise when we have to make decisions which affect the interests of others."

In 1982, New England Patriots coach Ron Meyer buried the spirit of fair play during a blinding blizzard in Foxboro, Massachusetts, where the Dolphins and Patriots were locked in a scoreless standstill. Because of the snowstorm, neither team had even remotely threatened to score a touchdown. Each attempted a field goal that failed because of the weather.

However, with four minutes and forty-five seconds remaining, New England ground out a drive that stalled out at the Miami sixteen-yard line. The Patriots then called time to let kicker John Smith clear away a spot on the slick, snow-covered field for an attempt at a field goal that could win the game.

Suddenly a light bulb lit up in Coach Meyer's mind. "I saw

John Smith on his hands and knees trying to get the snow cleared, and all of a sudden it hit me," recalled Meyer. "Why not send a snowplow out there?" He raced down the sideline looking for the operator of the John Deere plow that had been clearing the yard lines during time-outs. He told the driver to clear off a spot on the field for the kicker.

The driver made a beautiful initial fake with the snowplow by retracing his previous path along the twenty-yard line. Then, catching officials and Dolphins off guard, he swerved to his left, sweeping snow ahead of him and leaving a perfect swath of green AstroTurf between the twenty-three- and twenty-five-yard lines. It was the best sweep the Patriots fans had seen in years. The Dolphins cursed and threatened the snowplow driver, but no one stopped him. Explained defensive tackle Bob Baumhower, "I saw him coming, but what was I supposed to do? No way I'm going to take on a plow."

When play resumed, Smith planted his foot squarely in the path cleared by Henderson and kicked a game-winning thirty-three-yard field goal. The Dolphins cried foul, insisting the snowplow play was illegal. But the officials did nothing and New England won the game.

This story illustrates the dilemma that arises when conflicting interests are at stake. If you were to ask the Patriot fans and players whether using the snowplow to clear the field for the kicker was an unethical action, chances are they would not only contest the charge, but would acclaim it as a darn good idea. The Dolphins and their fans, however, rated the action a deed most foul. No judge or jury is available to render a decision in these types of situations.

No matter how the Patriots sugar-coated their action to the public, and even though no written rules were violated, the players, coaches, and fans had to know they'd gotten away with something. If we excuse our actions just because we can legally get away with it, we have our consciences to answer to.

Conflicts of Interest

————————— TeamThink —————————
You can't engage in a situation that raises a conflict of interest. To ignore the conflict, or to pretend it doesn't exist, damages your ethical posture and that of your company.

Tommy Lasorda was asked to appear on a television show. He arrived from a prior engagement wearing a dinner jacket and was informed that his TV hosts wanted him in a Dodger uniform. Fortunately, he had one in the trunk of his car. While he was changing, the script was brought to him by the producer. It turned out that the script called for a barrage of insults, the humor was somewhat blue, and the dialogue was in poor taste. Lasorda changed back into his street clothes. "I won't do it," he told the producer, "I don't like it, it's not me and this is bad for baseball." He walked out of the studio, forfeiting the easy fee he would have been paid for the short routine. His agent said to him, "You've got class, Tommy, and you've got principle and I love you for it."

What would your organization do if you faced a conflict of interest regarding a client? I remember the advertising agency that created the no-smoking advertisement for Northwest Airlines. The same agency also represented a major tobacco company, whose executives became incensed when they saw the advertisement and canceled their account with the agency. There was a clear conflict of interest between the agency and two clients with opposing views. How could the agency have expected to handle both accounts and ignore the ethics of the situation?

Our organization has a major program with the Transamerica Insurance Company to insure agents for malpractice. Because of the size of the program, our relationship with Transamerica is a very close and important one. Another major insurance company approached us and asked us to become its lead agent nationwide to attack another major program that Transamerica was currently writing. Though this was a very lucrative opportunity, I informed the other company that we were not willing to take on the program. How could I possibly sit down with Transamerica in the morning on our program and then go back to my office in the afternoon and devise a strategy for attacking its other program?

Favors—Who's Getting and Who's Giving

What is your company's position on giving gifts and favors to ingratiate the company with your key clients? Which are acceptable? Are tickets to sporting events, theater tickets, or free cabins in the mountains each year acceptable? An insurance sales organization I know provides a new car to the insurance buyer of one of its clients every year. How would you feel if that was your insurance buyer?

A survey conducted in 1991 by the National Association of Purchasing Management, the accounting firm of Ernst & Young, and the Center for Advanced Purchasing Studies in Tempe, Arizona, found that only 3 percent of purchasing agents surveyed said they would not accept any favors.

Sir Adrian Cadbury raised some interesting issues when he said, "How far should you go in buying business? What payments are legitimate for companies to make to win orders; and the reverse side of that coin, when do gifts to employees become bribes? I use two rules of thumb to test whether a payment is acceptable from a company's point of view: Is the payment on the face of the invoice? Would it embarrass the recipient to have the gift mentioned in the company newspaper? The first test ensures that all payments, however unusual they may seem, are recorded and go through the books. The second is aimed at distinguishing bribes from gifts; a definition which depends on the size of the gift and the influence it is likely to have on the recipient."

One of the things I suggest to our clients is that they require from all of the people in their organization who are purchasers a record of whatever gifts or perks they receive. Nonreporting of any gifts could be a reason for dismissal.

In my organization, we require that an employee report any gift that exceeds $500 in value. I am comfortable with giving clients small gifts, such as calendars, flowers, plants, or a bottle of wine. I would be very uncomfortable with extravagant gifts to clients. If a client is given tickets to a sporting or concert event, he is to be accompanied by people of our firm; the purpose of the event is not favor-buying but relationship-building.

Stealing the Signals

——————————— **TeamThink** ———————————
If you don't want your employees to give out confidential information, you can't ask them to secure confidential information about your competition.

Al Worthington, who pitched for the Giants in 1959, was asked to use binoculars so that he could interpret the instructions that the opposition's coach was signaling to his players on the field. Worthington refused, saying he would not play for a team that cheated. San Francisco obligingly traded him to Boston, perhaps a more law-abiding environment. No dice. Boston traded him to Chicago, who traded him to Cincinnati, who traded him to Minnesota. Four teams in four years. It was tough to find a town that welcomed a guy with a conscience that was better than his curveball.

How do you feel about your employees' securing confidential information from employees in another organization? Once Cal-Surance was bidding for a national account. Our competitor called our office pretending to be with the legal department of the prospect and asked several important questions, including our pricing on the account. Our employee accepted the questions at face value and gave the caller the information he requested. Upon learning of the call, we became suspicious and called our contact at the prospect, who stated that he had never made the call. It was obvious to us who had—our competitor. We went back to our insurance underwriters and told them the story. They were so incensed at the unethical act that they reduced the original quoted price for the client and we were able to secure the account. Score one for the good guys.

I recently interviewed a prospective employee who knew I was in competition with a particular unit in his current company. Without my asking him, he gave me information about that company that I should not have been told. I didn't hire him; my belief was that while he was still on the payroll of the other company, he had no right to take its money and tell me its secrets just because he wanted to buy my favor during the interview.

THE ETHICAL TRAIN

────────── TEAMTHINK ──────────
Ethical guidelines, procedures, or practices will not make bad people good or good people better, but they may influence most people, bad or good, to behave themselves most of the time.

In sports, the rules make everything fair. They become the boundaries, the frame of reference. To violate the rules is in essence to jeopardize the game. Ethics become part of the business rules of the game. As managers, we want everyone to know the rules and to play by them.

More and more companies are realizing how important it is to deal with the subject of ethics as a positive item in their corporate culture. Ethics must be managed. If we reward the good guys for being good guys, and if we increase the probability that anyone who violates the code will be exposed and dealt with, we will have in effect ethical procedures.

Recently a major insurance company gave Cal-Surance an exclusive arrangement for a new program on a national basis. I asked the company managers why they selected us. Their answer was because of our professionalism and our ethical reputation. This is why I think that if there is no better reason to be ethical, it's simply good business. By the way, you feel better too. Nice guys—good guys—do finish first.

You play a game, naturally, to win. I really feel you should win with honor. In other words, win without cheating.

Don Coryell,
former head coach,
San Diego Chargers

10

Winning the Game

In my whole life, I never played in a losing football game. It taught me to expect to win. Later on in life, I think K mart, or whatever competition we were facing, just became Jeff City High School, the team we played for the state championship in 1935.

Sam Walton,
late chairman and CEO,
Wal-Mart Stores

When Los Angeles Raiders owner Al Davis was inducted into the Pro Football Hall of Fame in 1992, one of his best friends, former Raider coach and CBS sports announcer John Madden, said, "Al doesn't fish, hunt, or play golf. He has just one commitment—winning." In a play on Davis's oft-quoted last-minute locker-room instruction to one of his Super Bowl teams—"Just win, baby"—Madden turned toward the life-sized bust of Davis that had just been installed in the Hall of Fame and said, "Al Davis just won, baby."

TEAMTHINK

People who expect to win consciously adopt a winning attitude. This attitude is transmitted to the people around them.

Right now, I'm preparing myself to go to spring training. I want to get the team prepared mentally and physically to meet our competitors head on. I want them to believe that by the end of this year, the pennant flag will be flying over Dodger Stadium. If I can get those twenty-five players believing that, along with the preparation it takes to get physically prepared, there is no question that we will win the pennant this year. I believe that and I want them to believe that.

Tommy Lasorda

Ever since I started watching sports, I have been aware of the impact a winning attitude has on actually winning. As a result, I *expect* to win every time I am at bat on a new account or in any major negotiation meeting. Sports taught me the following precepts:

- **Winning's more fun than losing, so always plan to win.** Although I've never met anyone who takes any joy in losing, I've seen too many business people actually forecast failure in their company with remarks such as "We don't expect to show a profit this year" or "We don't stand a very good chance of getting this account," and citing various excuses such as the economic climate, the strength of the competitors, etc.

  I have had people on my own team *plan* for poor results and rationalize the plan. On the other hand, I have taken those same projections, reworked them with that team, convinced them we could improve the situation, and ended up with a winning year.

  All of my business strategies center around winning. Why would anyone set up an operational plan that creates losses by design?

Winning isn't everything, but it beats anything that comes in second.

Bear Bryant

- **Most of us hate to lose.**

  Once in a while I you hear the old saw, "Winning isn't important; it's how you play the game." I have never agreed with that statement; I would rather play the game well *and* win.

  As closely as I follow football, I can never remember which team came in second at any of the Super Bowls. Even though the runner-up in the Super Bowl was better than the twenty-six other teams that never reached the finals that year, after the loss that team usually felt like a loser.

  In 1992, Eric Dickerson, one of the best running backs in the NFL, took a pay cut of $1.1 million so he could be traded from the Indianapolis Colts (who lost fifteen of sixteen games in 1991) to the Los Angeles Raiders. Dickerson wanted to end his career with a winning team; he said, "I hate losing."

Show me a good loser in professional sports, and I'll show you an idiot.

> Leo Durocher,
> former manager,
> Brooklyn Dodgers,
> New York Giants,
> Chicago Cubs

- **Accept that we operate in a competitive environment and that sometimes loss is inevitable.**

  As youngsters, one of the first competitions most of us experience (with the exception of sibling rivalry) is in sports. Sports are competitive and place us in adversarial relationships; we can learn that competition is stimulating and can be fun—and that it is impossible to win all the time.

  Now a San Francisco lawyer, Linda Stoic played professional basketball in the early 1980s with the San Francisco Pioneers. Stoic says, "Many women in law or business become devastated when they lose. Their whole self-esteem is wrapped up in being competent and thorough. It's important to learn that winning and losing are all part of the system."

  We all might do well to take to heart the motto of the

Special Olympics: "Let me win, but if I cannot win, let me be brave in the attempt."

- **Learn from a loss so that you can win the next time.**
  A truly winning team learns from defeat. A loss is treated as a signal to practice longer and harder, to make adjustments, to do whatever is necessary to win the next time.
  Basketball coach Mike Krzyzewski's philosophy about losing has a lot to do with leading the Duke University Blue Devils to back-to-back NCAA Championships:
  "Never forget a defeat, because that is the key to victory.
  "The best way to succeed is by failing. You learn how to use failure.
  "Losing doesn't make you a loser . . . it's a reminder that we have to work hard to win."

- **Every game, including business, has rules.**
  An attractive aspect of sports is that all sports have very specific rules on how to play the game. You have no choice but to play by the rules; if you don't, other people won't play with you. From childhood, therefore, I learned the importance of playing by the rules, and this has carried over into my business life. I always want to have the rules defined before I embark on any new venture, deal, or opportunity.
  "Negotiating has often been compared to a game," says professional negotiator Gerald I. Nierenberg. "A game has definite rules and a known set of values. Each player is limited in the moves he can make, the things he can and cannot do. True, some games have a greater element of chance than others, but in every game, a set of rules governs the behavior of the players and enumerates their gains and losses."

THE IMPORTANCE OF TEAMWORK

"In sports and business you work with different people," says Deborah Slaner Anderson, executive director of the Women's Sports Foundation. "You may know the people, but that doesn't matter. You have to learn how to work together. You have to learn to play on each other's strengths because that will make the team stronger. You have to learn to pick up the ball when someone makes a mistake or someone flounders. It's no coincidence that in business schools now they have you work in teams. You're given projects and you work on them in teams. This is what works in real life. I don't think it's a mistake that we use sports terminology when we are talking about business terms."

——— TEAMTHINK ———
Teamwork results when interrelated elements meld a group of individuals into a cohesive functioning unit that works toward mutually satisfying goals.

The one thing I've decided after looking at baseball from top to bottom is that unless the whole organization is working together for one common purpose and under one common philosophy, the club isn't going to win and it isn't going to make money, and you're not going to keep your job. The scouts have to find good players; the coaches have to teach; the minor-league staff has to keep the pipeline full of young players; the manager and the general manager and the front office have to keep the players happy and the budget in line; and the owner has to find good people and let them do their jobs. It sounds easy, but it's not.

Whitey Herzog

Teamwork is the sum of all of the parts that have been discussed in the preceding chapters. If any one of the major elements isn't working well, whether it's leading, building, keeping, or motivating your team, there's a good chance that teamwork will not happen. It takes constant attention to and management of all of these elements to achieve a consistently high degree of teamwork throughout your organization.

Modern business has moved away from the traditional military organizational scheme with the general sitting on top of the pyramid and the troops many levels away from the apex. In an era that requires quick action, innovation, and synergistic management, it takes too long for the general to tell the colonel, the colonel to tell the captain, the captain to tell the lieutenant, the lieutenant to tell the sergeant, and the sergeant to pass the message to the troops. In fact, combat troops never did operate this way. The company unit was provided with an objective and used the most effective means to complete its mission successfully. In essence, the unit operated as a combat team.

In the past, many companies were set up as very separate units defined by product, customer, or territory. Today, many organizations are in a state of flux, and the twenty-first-century organization will have more self-managing teams, special task forces, ad hoc committees, and other devices to better address today's needs. With the new emphasis on managing processes rather than functional departments, the role of the manager is changing and the need for true teamwork functions is increasing.

The San Diego Zoo with its Wild Animal Park has done more than most businesses to transform itself into a twenty-first-century organization. Besides its spectacular collection of animals and birds, it deserves to be seen for its management as well. Not only does the zoo face stiff competition from nearby Disneyland and Sea World, but as a world-renowned scientific and conservationist organization, the zoo must maintain high technical standards and a strong record on environmental issues.

The old zoo was managed through its fifty departments—animal keeping, horticulture, maintenance, food service, fundraising, education, and others. It had all the traits of functional management. But these departments are now invisible in the redesigned parts of the zoo. Tiger River, for example, is run by a team whose members are jointly responsible for the display. Team members include mammal and bird specialists, horticulturists, and maintenance and construction workers, but it's hard now to tell who comes from which department.

Seven people run Tiger River; when it started there were eleven, but as team members learned one another's skills, they decided they didn't need to replace workers who left. Freed from managerial chores now handled by the teams, executives can go out and drum up more interest in the zoo.

Has this had any effect on business? Southern California tourism took some hits in 1991 and 1992—first from the Gulf War, then from the recession—but the San Diego Zoo enjoyed a 20 percent increase in attendance. Part of the reason is probably price: at $12, it costs less than half as much to enter the zoo as it does to get into Disneyland.

Zoo director Douglas Myers credits employees' new sense of ownership. "I told them recession is coming; we're going to target our marketing on the local area alone, and we're going to ask our visitors to come back five times—so each time they'd better have more fun than the time before. The employees came through."

Peter Drucker predicted in his 1989 book *The New Realities*, "The emphasis in companies will be on building teams and the valued managers will be those who are flexible enough to shift from one group to another, performing a variety of tasks."

While companies have tried for a long time to develop a feeling of teamwork among their employees, there is a new movement in corporate America that puts emphasis on team-building. This team concept is spreading rapidly in industries such as automaking, aerospace, electrical equipment, electronics, food processing, paper, steel, and even financial services. The corporate air now reverberates with the language of teamwork . . . Team Xerox, Team Pontiac, Team Nabisco, etc.

Companies must learn to make teams out of the people they already have, and the quality of the team will determine how well the work gets done. A willingness to work with others does not in itself guarantee a good team. People must acquire skills for working with one another toward common goals.

This is not easy. Alfie Kohn writes in his 1986 book *No Contest* that people are taught from early childhood to be competitive, to do their best to come out ahead of others. They are *not* taught to share ideas or credit with others; they are *not* taught to work with others toward a common goal; they have *not* learned how to feel good about the success of a team effort.

To change this, more and more companies are turning to

consultants who specialize in team-building. These consultants are brought in to set up new teams, to help teams in trouble resolve their problems, and to fine-tune a smoothly working team to ensure that it continues to succeed.

The purpose of team-building is not to get people to like one another, but to teach them how to work with one another. Team-builders go about their task in a variety of ways. Most begin by gathering information about the team through interviewing and a variety of psychological tests. In the next phase, the team usually meets off-site in a two- or three-day retreat for feedback and team-building exercises. While the experts believe that trust and friendship are desirable, the emphasis is on communication.

Even the best team-building sessions, however, will be of little value if the company does not create an environment conducive to teamwork. This may mean structural changes in the organization (such as the ones initiated at the San Diego Zoo). For most companies, adopting the team approach is no small matter; it means wiping out tiers of managers and tearing down bureaucratic barriers between departments.

DePalma Hotel Corp., a hotel management firm based in Dallas, uses self-directed teams of executives to improve operations at each of the fifteen hotels it manages nationwide. The managers of sales, food service, customer service, and housekeeping all meet to trade ideas for improving service. "No one is boss on that committee," says CEO Joseph DePalma. "It's a meeting where people come to look forward to participating instead of coming just to listen to the general manager."

In many companies, teams now establish their own work standards, their sequence of work, the production process, the tools that will be used, and their own schedules. Advocates of team organization say these practices avoid duplication of effort, increase cooperation, spur new ideas, improve product quality, and—not incidentally—increase profits.

One organization discarded time clocks and eliminated special parking spots for management. Gencorp's automotive plant in Shelbyville, Indiana, has gone even further. All employees, including managers, are called "associates," wear blue shirts and blue slacks or skirts, and receive the same company benefits. Gencorp has all but erased the inequality that can erode team solidarity.

Some team-building experts recommend incentives based upon the performance of the team as a whole, and there is good reason to believe that group incentives teamed with individual incentives can produce substantial benefits. The Boston Celtics are not paid on the basis of individual statistics (as are the players of some clubs). Robert Keidel, author of *Corporate Players: Designs for Working and Winning Together*, suggests this may be why the Celtics have never had the league's highest-scoring player, but it may also be why they've won sixteen championships.

Whether a business that adopts team organization and provides team-building experiences and the proper work environment will do as well as the Celtics is uncertain. But team organization is certainly one of the inspired business experiments of our time.

WINNING AT HOME

Sustain a family life for a long period of time and you can sustain success for a long period of time. First things first. If your life is in order, you can do whatever you want.

Pat Riley,
head coach,
New York Knicks

—————— TEAMTHINK ——————
Too often when building a career, we become so absorbed in our work that our lives get out of balance and the quality of our personal life and our family's suffers.

Ray Meyer, the retired coach of the DePaul University basketball team, still remembers coaching against Adolph Rupp, the famous Kentucky Wildcats basketball coach, over forty years ago. Kentucky was one of the top teams in the country, and this was the first major potential win for young Coach Meyer. As his wife,

Marge, watched from the stands, Meyer was constantly shouting instructions. The score was tied; DePaul had the ball with a few seconds left in the game, but a Kentucky player stole the ball and scored a basket, and the game was over.

Meyer was bitterly disappointed at missing such a great opportunity. Still, he tried to console the young player who had lost the ball, and he was able to talk with reporters. After that, emotionally drained, he finally drove home, telling himself he had handled the disappointment as well as possible. At midnight, he was startled by the ringing of the telephone. It was his wife, Marge; it seems he had left her at the stadium.

After forty-two years of coaching, Meyer decided that this wasn't the way to live. His son is now the coach at DePaul. What does Meyer senior advise his son? "Enjoy life. Hug your wife. Cherish your son. Quit thinking the world revolves around DePaul basketball. Ten years from now, who will care? Do this and sleep will come easier. The craving for antacid tablets will lessen."

Ara Parseghian was one of the most successful coaches in the history of Notre Dame football. His best year was 1966, when Notre Dame was undefeated and won the National Championship. In order to achieve that, Parseghian started his day at 5:00 A.M., and he rarely got home before 10:00 P.M. One year he counted only seventeen nights that he had spent at home during the entire season. He had become coach in 1964 at age forty, and he retired eleven years later because of the adverse effects of the pressure and because he wanted to improve the quality of his life with his family. He now works as a television sports announcer and has sworn that he would never consider returning to coaching.

These men had to come to grips with the question many business people ask themselves: Can you build a successful business career, sustain your health, and maintain a successful personal and family life all at the same time?

WHAT'S THE SCORE?

──────────── **TEAMTHINK** ────────────
Life is similar to sports in that if we don't establish goals for ourselves, we will lack direction and purpose.

Imagine being on a golf course, hitting a great drive onto the green and finding out that there's no cup to putt the ball into. How can you finish the hole and determine your score? What about having a tennis game in which all you and your partner do is volley back and forth for two hours? How do you know when the game's over, or whether you've won? In any *sport*, or in *life*, we would lose interest quickly if there was no way of keeping score or achieving some goal.

How are you *keeping score?* When the dust settles and it's the end of the day, what is it you really want? Have you ever really asked yourself and come to grips with the answers? If you've identified what you want, are you close to getting it? If not, can you do something about it? Does your family get what they need or want from you? What have you not had time to do because of your business?

In 1989 Bill Walsh was coach of the San Francisco 49ers, one of the most successful professional football teams of the decade. He had just won his second Super Bowl in a row and had a team that looked unbeatable for the next year. Yet after thirty years in the game, and at the peak of his career, he made the decision to retire. He left coaching and became a respected announcer for NBC. In 1992, he surprised the sports world by becoming head football coach at Stanford University, saying he wanted to work with young people again.

"My career has been fulfilled in every sense," Walsh said. "At some point, you do what your heart tells you. You do those things that you prefer to do when you have the freedom. I haven't always had that freedom. Most of us don't during our early years. The idea that you would purely choose to do whatever satisfies you is where bliss is. To be able to live life according to your personal needs, related to satisfaction and gratification—what a break that is for people."

Receiving Your Awards

Imagine yourself sitting at a table at your retirement dinner. You're being introduced by the chairman of the board.

"We're here to honor John Smith," the chairman says. "He's served this company faithfully for over thirty years. During that period, our company has tripled in size, mainly due to his consistently unswerving efforts. John accomplished this at great sacrifice to himself. His golf game is nonexistent because of time constraints, he's canceled numerous vacations whenever a business problem arose, and he didn't complain about moving five times in five years, even when he had to live apart from his family for nine months."

If this is the type of presentation you would be comfortable hearing, there's no need for you to read the rest of this chapter. On the other hand, if statements such as "I never knew John personally"—from your working associates, "I missed the closeness and the intimacy"—from your spouse, and "He never had much time for me"—from your kids would bother you, then this section may be the most important one in the book for you.

Why not write your own retirement speech now, while you can still make some changes in your life? I'm serious about this. Take some quiet time when you can't be interrupted and list what you would want someone to say about you.

Start with your own wish list first, naming what you really want. Try not to limit yourself based on the way things are or on what might constrain your ability to do these things. Here are some of the things I wish for:

From my Family:
Love.
Attention—notice me as a person.

Encouragement—to help me with my quest.
Respect—for what I am and what I stand for.
Understanding—of my need to achieve.
From the Business:
Challenge—to keep me motivated.
Rewards—for what I do.
Recognition—acknowledgment of my accomplishments.
Income—to achieve my financial goals.
Time Off—for me and my family.
Less Stress—for quality of life.

Here's an intense exercise to help you really get in touch with your most important goals:

- Imagine learning that you have one year to live. List three things you'd like to do during this last year.

- Assume eleven months have passed and you have one month left. List three things you would like to do.

- Make a new list assuming you have one week left, and another assuming you have only forty-eight hours left.

- Examine what you've written. If your list includes activities you're not currently pursuing, what's stopping you from pursuing them now?

How do these lists fit your current life-style and work-style? If you could change certain things, would you and could you? To have it all may not be possible. If you can achieve 70 percent of your goals, you are a fortunate person.

"Success follows doing what you want to do," Malcolm Forbes said. "There is no other way to be successful."

AVOIDING TURNOVER AT HOME

I believe there must be room in everyone's life for things besides his profession—his family, for example. My wife

*goes with me on road trips and when I go home to her,
I leave football behind me, and I go home every evening.
I turn to other things besides football every evening.*
> Tommy Prothro,
> former head football coach,
> UCLA

———————— **TeamThink** ————————
If you trade off business success for family problems, it is only a question of time before the family breaks down.

Joe Gibbs, head coach of the 1992 Super Bowl Champion Washington Redskins, was so involved with the team in 1989 that he felt he couldn't take two days off to go to his father's funeral. In my opinion, that's being way out of balance.

While many people achieve success in their business lives, that success often eludes them in their personal and family lives. Fifty-five percent of all marriages that began since the mid-1970s are likely to end in divorce. For second marriages, the estimated divorce rate is 60 percent. And of course these statistics don't include the number of couples who are merely existing together.

In his book *Thank God It's Monday*, Dr. Pierre Mornell explains that the traits men bring to their business life, which account in large part for their success, they fail to bring to their personal lives. As an example, if you were to list the qualities that contribute to business success, your list would probably include energy, creativity, enthusiasm, commitment, and assertiveness. Yet when these businessmen come home, Mornell asserts, they usually leave these qualities at the office. They don't expend the same energy or effort at home because it feels too much like work. It's like saying, "I gave at the office." Then these men often wonder why their personal lives aren't working.

Sometimes I get out of balance, consumed by the business. If this lasts very long, I eventually have problems at home. My wife often uses a metaphor, likening my total available time to a pie. She says she doesn't require the whole pie but does need a slice large enough to feel satisfied. When, on top of my commitment to my company, I decided to write this book, all she asked was that it didn't cut into her piece of the pie.

It's important that everyone get a fair share of the pie, including yourself. But before you take away a bite or more from someone else's slice, you'd better check with that person first to see if it's okay. It isn't always easy, but if you become so busy with your business that your spouse and family are left with the crumbs, you will be a good candidate to become a divorce statistic.

If you want your family life to be successful, you need to devote the same type of energy, thought, attention, and commitment to it that you have to your business. This may not guarantee success, but it will be the best you can do.

AFTERWORD

As I stated in the introduction, *TeamThink* is a collection of concepts and principles that I have taken from sports and modified to fit today's business environment, which recognizes the importance of having a first-rate team.

The objective of *TeamThink* is to help you foster teamwork in your company, and to help you let your employees know who you are, what you stand for, and where you want to go. It's also important that they accept your goals and make a commitment to help the team achieve them.

My objective in writing this book has been to provide you with at least two new ideas per chapter which will trigger new thoughts and directions. I hope you've enjoyed my playbook. I've certainly enjoyed sharing my plays with you.

Let me close with these words:

If I can get those guys to believe in themselves, if I can get those guys to put forth all the effort that they have, if I can get those guys to play the game with an unselfish attitude and put the winning of the team ahead of their own individual accomplishments, if I can get those guys to be proud of the uniform that they're wearing, if I can get those guys when they're at home with their family and they look up at that clock to say, "I can't wait—another fifteen minutes and I'm headed for the ball-park"—that's the responsibility of the manager.

Tommy Lasorda

BIOGRAPHIES
___OF SPORTS PERSONALITIES___

ALLEN, GEORGE
George Allen led the Los Angeles Rams from 1966–70, with a record of 49 wins, 19 losses, and 4 ties. From 1971–77, he coached the Washington Redskins (67 wins, 30 losses, and 1 tie). In 1972 he led the Redskins to their first Super Bowl. He died December 31, 1990.
   Source: *Sports Illustrated 1992 Sports Almanac*

ALSTON, WALTER
Walter Alston managed the Dodgers in Brooklyn and Los Angeles from 1954–76. Alston's Dodgers won four World Championships and seven pennants and had eight second-place finishes. He was elected to the Baseball Hall of Fame in 1983.
   Source: *Total Baseball*, Second Edition

ANDERSON, SPARKY
Sparky Anderson is the only manager to win a World Series in both leagues, to win 100 games in both leagues, and to be Manager of the Year in both leagues. The "Big Red Machine" won the pennant in 1972, 1973, 1975, and 1976. In 1975 and 1976 the Reds won the World Championship. In 1984, Anderson led the Detroit Tigers to a World Championship.
   Source: *Total Baseball*, Second Edition

AUERBACH, RED

Red Auerbach is the winningest coach in NBA history. He led the Boston Celtics to the NBA Championship in 1957, 1959, 1960, 1961, 1962, 1963, 1965, and 1966. Auerbach was elected to the Naismith Memorial Basketball Hall of Fame in 1968.

As president of the Celtics, he was named NBA Executive of the Year in 1980.

Sources: *The Sporting News NBA Register 1991–92; The Encyclopedia of North American Sports History* (1992)

BLAIK, RED

Earl Blaik coached the Dartmouth football team from 1934–40. In 1941 he returned to West Point, where he remained as coach through 1958, leading the team to the national championship in 1944 and 1945. He was named Coach of the Year in 1946 and was elected to the Hall of Fame. Blaik died in May 1989.

Source: *NCAA Football's Finest*

BROWN, PAUL E.

Brown was founder and head coach of the Cleveland Browns 1946–62. Although he had only one losing season in those seventeen years, he was fired after the 1962 season. He founded and was head coach of the Cincinnati Bengals 1968–75 and was the principal owner, vice-president and general manager. He was inducted into the Pro Football Hall of Fame in 1967. Brown died August 5, 1991.

Source: *Who's Who in America 1990–91; The Encyclopedia of North American Sports History* (1992)

BRYANT, BEAR

Bear Bryant was named Coach of the Year in 1961, 1971, and 1973 and was named SEC Coach of the Year four times, as well as being named the All-Time SEC Coach. He was voted Coach of the Decade by the Football Coaches Association of America. In his thirty-eight-year career he had 323 wins (the most of any coach in college football), 85 losses, and 17 ties. He led his teams to four National Championships as well as eight Conference Championships. He was head coach at Alabama from 1958–73. Bryant died January 26, 1983.

Sources: Bear Bryant biography; *NCAA Football's Finest; Saturday Afternoon: College Football and the Men Who Made the Day*

CORYELL, DON

Don Coryell coached the San Diego State Aztecs for 12 years (1961–72), where his teams posted an overall record of 104 wins, 19 losses, and 2 ties. The Aztecs were unbeaten in 1966, 1968, and 1969, winning 25 games in a row from 1965–67, then going on to win 31 more games without a defeat.

Coryell was head coach in the NFL for fourteen years—1973–77 with the St. Louis Cardinals and 1978–86 with the San Diego Chargers. He won five division championships, including AFC West Championships for the Chargers in 1979, 1980, and 1981. He won NFL Coach of the Year honors in 1979. Coryell is the only coach, as of the end of 1986, to win 100 games on both collegiate and professional levels. In 1986, Coryell resigned after eight games.

Source: *San Diego Chargers Media Guide,* 1986

DAVIS, AL

From 1963–66 Davis was head coach of the Oakland Raiders (now the Los Angeles Raiders) and in 1966 became owner and managing general partner. In 1982 he moved the Oakland Raiders to Los Angeles. The Raiders have won the World Championship three times in Super Bowls XI, XV, and XVIII.

Sources: *Who's Who in America 1990–91; Current Biography Yearbook 1985; Sports Illustrated 1992 Sports Almanac*

DAY, CLARENCE HENRY ("HAP")

A Hall of Famer, Clarence Day played fourteen years with NHL teams. After refereeing for two years, he coached the Maple Leafs from 1940 to 1950, winning five Stanley Cups (three of them in a row). He became general manager of the Leafs in 1950, retiring in 1957.

Source: *Who's Who in Hockey*

DE BARTOLO, EDWARD J., JR.,

After attending Notre Dame University 1964–68, Ed De Bartolo joined De Bartolo Corp. in San Francisco in 1960, becoming executive vice-president in 1975 and president and chief administrative officer in 1979. De Bartolo became the owner of the San Francisco 49ers in 1977.

Source: *Who's Who in America 1990–91*

DITKA, MIKE

After playing football in the NFL for twelve years (1961–72), Mike Ditka became assistant coach with the Dallas Cowboys 1973–81. In 1982 he became head coach of the Chicago Bears and as of the end of the 1991 season was still with the Bears. In 1985 the Bears won the NFC Championship and Super Bowl XX. Ditka was named *The Sporting News* Coach of the Year in 1985. Ditka was named to the Hall of Fame in 1988, as well as being named Coach of the Year by the NFL.

Source: *The Sporting News Football Register 1991; Who's Who in America 1990–91*

DRESSEN, CHARLES W.

Chuck Dressen played in the National League for Cincinnati 1925–31 and New York in 1933. After a number of managing jobs, including the Brooklyn Dodgers, Dressen coached the Yankees in 1947–48. He became manager at Oakland, in the Pacific Coast League, 1949–50. Dressen returned to the Dodgers as manager in 1951. In 1952 and 1953 the Dodgers won the pennant but lost the series to the Yankees.

Source: *Who's Who in Professional Baseball; Who Was Who in American Sports*

DUROCHER, LEO

Durocher was an outfielder for the New York Yankees, Cincinnati Reds, St. Louis Cardinals, and Brooklyn Dodgers, batting .247 in seventeen seasons and playing on teams that won three pennants and two World Series. Durocher managed the 1941 Brooklyn Dodgers and the '51 and '54 New York Giants into the World Series; in 1954 the Giants won. In twenty-four seasons with the Dodgers, Giants, Chicago Cubs, and Houston Astros, Durocher's teams won

2,008 games, sixth on the all-time list. Durocher died in October 1991.

Source: *Sports Illustrated 1992 Sports Almanac*

FINANNE, DAN

Dan Finnane in 1992 marked his seventh season as president and part owner of the Golden State Warriors. He is in charge of the day-to-day operation of the franchise. Since purchasing the team along with Warriors chairman Jim Fitzgerald in May 1986, Finanne has helped mold the organization into one of the most progressive in the NBA.

Source: Biography of Dan Finanne

FITZSIMMONS, COTTON

Former coach of the Phoenix Suns, Cotton Fitzsimmons coached for nineteen seasons starting in 1970 and had over 800 victories. He started in a small school in Missouri as a teacher and coached for thirty-four years.

GIBBS, JOE

Since 1981 Gibbs has been head coach of the Washington Redskins. In 1982, the Redskins won the NFC Championship game from Dallas and won Super Bowl XVII from Miami. In 1983, the team won the NFC Championship game from San Francisco, but lost Super Bowl XVIII to the Los Angeles Raiders. In 1987, Washington again won the NFC Championship, from Minnesota, and won Super Bowl XXII from Denver. Gibbs was named *The Sporting News* NFL Coach of the Year in 1982 and 1983.

Source: *The Sporting News 1991 Football Register*

GILLMAN, SID

Under his leadership, the Los Angeles/San Diego Chargers won five division titles and one AFL championship (1963). Gillman coached the Los Angeles Rams in 1955–59, the Los Angeles Chargers 1960, the San Diego Chargers 1961–69, and then Houston 1973–74. He has a lifetime record of 124 wins, 101 losses, and 7 ties. Gillman also served as general manager in San Diego and Houston.

Source: *Sports Illustrated 1992 Sports Almanac*

GLANVILLE, JERRY

In 1974–76 Glanville was an assistant coach of the NFL Detroit Lions. From 1977 to 1982, he was an assistant coach of the Atlanta Falcons, then spent 1983 as assistant coach of the Buffalo Bills. In 1984–85 he was assistant coach with the Houston Oilers, replacing Hugh Campbell as head coach in 1985. Glanville was with Houston through 1989 and became head coach of the Atlanta Falcons in 1990.

Source: *The Sporting News 1991 Football Register*

GRIMM, CHARLES "JOLLY CHOLLY"

In August 1932, first baseman Grimm became manager of the second-place Chicago Cubs. Nine days later the team was in first place, winning the pennant but losing the World Series to the New York Yankees. Grimm managed Dallas (Texas League) in 1950, then went back to Milwaukee (AA) in 1951, until he was named manager of the Boston Braves in May of 1952. The Braves moved to Milwaukee in 1953, where Grimm remained until June 17, 1953. He was vice-president of the Cubs 1957–59 and field manager until 1961, when he returned to broadcasting.

Source: *Who's Who in Professional Baseball*

HEISMAN, JOHN WILLIAM

John Heisman's coaching career stretched from 1892 to 1927; he coached at Oberlin College, Akron, Auburn, Clemson, Georgia Tech, Pennsylvania, Washington & Jefferson, and Rice. A major force for change in football in his time, he invented the center snap, the double pass, the spin buck, and the Heisman shift, among others. He won 185 games, lost 68, and tied 18. Heisman was named to the Hall of Fame in 1954.

Source: *College Football USA 1869–1971*

HERZOG, WHITEY

Herzog became a scout for the Kansas City Athletics in 1964 and coach for one year (1965). He coached the New York Mets in 1966 before becoming director of player development (1967–72). Herzog managed the Texas Rangers in 1973 and the California Angels 1974–75, becoming manager of the Kansas City Royals mid-1975 and leading the team to a second-place finish, followed by three consecutive division titles. When Kansas City finished second in 1979, Herzog was fired. His St. Louis Cardinals won the World Championship in 1982 and pennants in 1985 and 1987. In 1985, he was named Manager of the Year. Herzog is now California Angels senior vice president for player personnel.

Sources: *Total Baseball*, Second Edition; *Who's Who in America 1990–91*

HOLTZ, LOU

In 1969 Holtz became head coach at the College of William and Mary. In 1972 he accepted the position of head coach at North Carolina State, where he coached for four seasons. In early 1976, Holtz was named head coach of the New York Jets, but after eleven months he returned to college football as head coach of the University of Arkansas Razorbacks. Holtz resigned to become head coach at the University of Minnesota. At the end of the 1985 season, Holtz was hired by Notre Dame as head coach. They were generally considered one of the best teams in the country with a losing record. In 1987, Notre Dame faced another tough schedule, but won eight of its first nine games and went on to finish the season with eight wins, three losses, and a top-ten ranking, squaring off against Texas A & M in the Cotton Bowl. Although the Irish lost the game 35–10, it was their first appearance in a major bowl game since 1981. In 1988 they had their first undefeated season since 1973, winning their first championship in eleven years. Holtz was named National Coach of the Year in 1977 by *The Sporting News* and Southwest Conference Coach of the Year in 1979 by the Associated Press and United Press International. In 1991, the Irish had ten wins and three losses and beat Florida in the Sugar Bowl. As of the beginning of the 1992 season, Holtz was still coach at Notre Dame.

Source: *Current Biography Yearbook 1989; Contemporary*

Newsmakers 1986; The Sporting News College Football 1992 Year-book

HOLZMAN, RED

Red Holzman began his NBA coaching career with Milwaukee. In 1955–57 he coached at St. Louis. For the rest of his coaching career, 1967–82, he was head coach of the New York Knicks. Holzman was named coach of the Year in 1970 and elected to the Naismith Memorial Basketball Hall of Fame in 1985. His New York Knicks won the NBA Championship in 1970 and 1973.

Source: *The Sporting News NBA Register 1991–92*

JACKSON, PHIL

Phil Jackson played with the New York Knicks from 1967–1978, when he was traded to New Jersey. Jackson was one of the 1973 NBA Championship Knicks. He played with New Jersey through 1980. Jackson began his coaching career at Albany in 1982, where he stayed for five seasons with a record of 115 wins, 107 losses. He was named CBA Coach of the Year in 1985 and was coach of the CBA Championship team in 1984. In 1987 he became assistant coach of the Chicago Bulls, becoming coach in 1989. The Bulls won the NBA Championship in 1991 and 1992.

Source: *The Sporting News Official 1991–92 NBA Register*

KNIGHT, BOBBY

Bobby Knight began coaching the University of Indiana in the spring of 1971; after twenty years at Indiana, his win/loss ratio was 3 to 1, 459 wins to 153 losses. Knight has won three NCAA titles (1976, 1981, and 1987). He also holds "The Amateur Triple Crown," having won the 1984 Olympic gold medal and 1979 NIT title in addition to the NCAA titles. Knight was Big Ten Coach of the Year in 1973, 1975, 1976, 1981, and 1989, and was named to the Hall of Fame in 1989. Entering the 1991–92 season, Knight had a career record of 532 wins.

Source: *Blue Ribbon College Basketball Yearbook 1991–92; Who's Who in America 1990–91; Sports Illustrated 1992 Sports Almanac*

KRZYZEWSKI, MIKE

In taking Duke to its first NCAA Championship at Indianapolis, Krzyzewski became the only man since John Wooden to take a team to four straight Final Fours. Krzyzewski played for Bobby Knight at the U.S. Military Academy and was head coach there for five years beginning in 1975. Krzyzewski was hired to replace Bill Foster at Duke University in 1980. He was the coach of the U.S. team at the Goodwill Games in 1990, and was assistant coach under the Detroit Pistons' Chuck Daly at the 1992 Olympics.

Source: *College Basketball Yearbook 1991–92*

LANDRY, TOM

In 1949 Tom Landry began playing professional football with the New York Yankees of the American Football Conference, which merged with the New York Giants of the NFL, where he played cornerback for six years. He assisted in coaching during his final playing years and in 1956 was named the Giants' full-time defense coach. During those four years, the Giants had a 33–14–1 record and won the division title twice and the World Championship once. Landry became coach of the Dallas Cowboys in the year of their formation (1960) and stayed until 1988, enjoying consecutive winning seasons from 1966–88. Under Landry's leadership, the Cowboys went to the Super Bowl five times in the 1970s (1971, 1972, 1976, 1978, and 1979), winning in 1972 and 1978. Landry's record with the Cowboys was 270 wins, 178 losses, and 6 ties. Landry was dismissed by the Cowboys in early 1989. In 1989 he was named head of the Dallas International Sports Commission.

Sources: *Current Biography Yearbook 1972; USA Today,* Tuesday, Nov. 29, 1989

LaRUSSA, TONY

In August 1979 Tony LaRussa took over as manager of the White Sox. He was with the Sox for the next seven years and in 1983 was named Manager of the Year by *The Sporting News,* the Associated Press, and the Baseball Writers Association of America. He left the White Sox in June 1986 and became manager of the Oakland Athletics in July. LaRussa is the fortieth manager in major-league history to win 1,000 games. No manager has led the A's for more games or more victories. From 1988–90, the A's led the major leagues in victories, winning three consecutive American League pennants. The Athletics under LaRussa's leadership, won the World Series in 1989, and he was named Manager of the Year again by *The Sporting News* and the Baseball Writers Association of America.

Source: *American League 1992 Red Book*

LASORDA, TOMMY

In 1992, Tommy Lasorda entered his sixteenth season as manager of the Los Angeles Dodgers. At the end of the 1991 season he had a 1,276–1,100 record. Lasorda led the Dodgers to the World Championship in 1981 and 1988 and won the National League Pennant in 1977, 1978, 1981, and 1988. The Dodgers won the Western Division Title in 1977, 1978, 1981, 1983, 1985, and 1988. In 1980 the division title was lost to Houston in a one-game playoff. Lasorda was named Manager of the Year by the Baseball Writers Association of America in 1983 and 1988, by the Associated Press in 1977, 1981, and 1983, and by United Press International in 1977, 1983, and 1988. He was the second National League manager to win the pennant in his first two years.

Sources: *National League 1992 National Green Book; Who's Who in America 1990–91*

LEAHY, FRANK

Frank Leahy played for the legendary Knute Rockne as a tackle until his playing career was ended by a knee injury in 1930. Leahy coached at Notre Dame from 1941–53. In his fifteen years as coach (he led Boston College 1939–40), he had a record of 107 wins, 13 losses, and 9 ties. 1946–49, Notre Dame went thirty-nine games without a loss. Leahy fielded seven unbeaten teams and had a win-loss percentage of .864. In his early career he led Boston College to two bowl games (the 1939 Cotton Bowl and the 1940 Sugar Bowl). Leahy was named Coach of the Year in 1941. He was named to the Hall of Fame in 1970.

Sources: *College Football USA 1869–1971; NCAA Football's Finest; Saturday Afternoon: College Football and the Men Who Made the Day*

LOMBARDI, VINCE

In 1959, Vince Lombardi became general manager and head coach of the Green Bay Packers. After missing the playoffs in 1963 and 1964, the Packers won three consecutive championship games. Lombardi led the team in the first two Super Bowls, 1967 and 1968. In his last seven years with the Packers, they won more than 75 percent of their games and five NFL championships. After his second Super Bowl victory, Lombardi retired as head coach, remaining as general manager. In 1969, he went to the Washington Redskins and began turning that team around, but in 1970 he was diagnosed as having cancer and died shortly after the season started.

Sources: *War of the Words; The Encyclopedia of North American Sports History*

MADDEN, JOHN

Madden joined the Raiders as linebacker coach in 1967, compiling a 13–1 record, the best in AFL history, and winning the league's championship. Madden was named head coach in February 1969. He coached the Raiders from 1969–78, leading his team to seven division championships, an American Football Conference Championship, and a World Championship in Super Bowl XI in 1977. He had a career record of 103 wins, 32 losses, and 7 ties, a percentage of .763. He was the second coach in forty years with 100 or more victories in ten seasons. Hired by CBS in 1979 as an analyst, he became their top analyst and color commentator three years later. He received Emmy awards in 1981 and 1982 in the sports personality analyst category. He has written several books.

Source: *Current Biography Yearbook 1985*

MARTIN, BILLY

Billy Martin's first stint as a major-league manager was with the Minnesota Twins in 1969; the Twins won their division title that year. The season with Minnesota was followed by three in Detroit, two in Texas, and three in Oakland. Martin was hired and fired five times by the New York Yankees. In his first year with the Yankees, 1976, he led the team to the pennant; a World Championship followed in 1977. He was fired in 1978 after ninety-four games, rehired in 1979 for the last two-thirds of the season, then fired again. After three years in Oakland, he was back with the Yankees for all of 1983, most of 1985, and part of 1988. He died in 1989.

Source: *Total Baseball*, Second Edition

McCARTHY, JOE

Though Joe McCarthy never had the chance to play in the big leagues, he was named manager of the New York Yankees in 1931. The Yankees won eight American League pennants for him and seven World Series. He was the first manager to win pennants in both leagues (Chicago of the National League in 1929 and New York of the American League in 1932.) From 1926–50 his teams won seven World Series and nine pennants. His is the all-time highest winning percentage among managers for a regular season (.615) and World Series (.698). McCarthy died in 1978.

Sources: *Who's Who in Professional Baseball; Sports Illustrated 1992 Sports Almanac*

McCARVER, TIM

After graduating from Memphis State University, Tim McCarver was catcher with the St. Louis Cardinals (1959–69, 1973, 1974), Philadelphia Phillies (1970–72, 1975–79, part of 1980), Montreal Expos (June–November 1972), and Boston Red Sox (1974–75). He was sportscaster for the Philadelphia Phillies 1980–82 and has been a sportscaster for the New York Mets since 1983. He is also a sportscaster for ABC. He received Emmy awards for local baseball broadcasting in 1986 and 1987.

Source: *Who's Who in America 1990–91*

McCRACKEN, BRANCH

After eight years (1931–38) at Ball State, Branch McCracken became head basketball coach at the University of Indiana; he led Indiana from 1939–65. Indiana made the NCAA tournament four times, winning the championship in 1940 and 1953. McCracken was named to the Naismith Memorial Basketball Hall of Fame. Through the 1991 NCAA tournament, he held the Final Four career record for the highest winning percentage—100 percent (4–0).

Source: *NCAA Basketball's Finest*

McGUIRE, AL

Al McGuire was basketball coach at Belmont Abbey 1958–64, then coached at Marquette 1965–77. He led Marquette to the NCAA Tournament in nine years, winning the championship in 1977. McGuire was named Coach of the Year by the Associated Press, United Press International, and the U.S. Basketball Writers Association in 1971. He coached the team to the NIT title in 1970.

Source: *NCAA Basketball's Finest*

McKAY, JOHN

John McKay was head football coach at the University of Southern California 1960–75. He led the Trojans to three national championships and nine Pacific-Eight championships and played in eight bowl games. McKay was 127–40–8 in his years at USC. He was named Coach of the Year in 1962 and 1972 and inducted into the Hall of Fame. In 1976 he became coach of the Tampa Bay Buccaneers, coaching until the end of the 1984 season. He served as club president through 1985. In recent years he has been a consultant to Tampa Bay.

Sources: *NCAA Football's Finest; Los Angeles Times* Nov. 6, 1984; *Official 1985 National Football League Record & Fact Book*

MEYER, RAY

Ray Meyer coached at DePaul University his entire coaching career (1943–84). DePaul went to the NCAA Tournament thirteen years under his leadership. Through the 1991 season, Meyer was tied for the NCAA career record for most years coached at one school. Meyer was named Coach of the Year by the Associated Press and United Press International in 1980 and 1984, by the USBWA in 1978 and 1980, and by the NABC in 1979. He was named to the Naismith Memorial Basketball Hall of Fame. He coached the team to the NIT title in 1945.

Source: *NCAA Basketball's Finest*

MEYER, RON

Before becoming a head coach in the NFL, Meyer was assistant coach at Purdue University (1965–70) and a scout for the Dallas Cowboys (1971–72). From 1973–75 he was head coach at the University of Nevada at Las Vegas, with three winning seasons. From 1976–81, Meyer was head coach at Southern Methodist University, leading the team to the Holiday Bowl in 1980. In his nine-year collegiate coaching career, he had 60 wins, 38 losses, and 1 tie. From 1982–84 he was head coach for the New England Patriots. In December 1986 he became head coach for the Indianapolis Colts. His NFL record as of the end of 1990 was 54 wins, 45 losses, and no ties.

Source: *The Sporting News Football Register 1991*

NEALE, HARRY

Harry Neale coached in the National Hockey League and World Hockey League 1973–82. From 1973–76, he was coach for Minnesota in the WHL, losing in the 1973–74 and 1974–75 semifinals. He finished the 1974–75 season with New England, again losing in the semifinals. He stayed with New England through the 1977–78 season, losing in the league finals. He became coach for the Vancouver Canucks of the NHL in 1978–79, coaching through part of the 1981–82 season. Neale coached the Detroit Red Wings for part of the 1985–86 season.

Sources: *The Complete Record of Professional Ice Hockey* (1982); *NHL Official Guide & Record Book 1988–89*

NEWELL, PETE

Pete Newell coached basketball at three universities during his fourteen-year collegiate career: San Francisco (1947–50), Michigan State (1951–54), and the University of California at Berkeley (1955–60). The University of California made the NCAA Tournament for four straight years (1957–60), winning the championship in 1959. Newell coached San Francisco to the NIT title in 1949. He was named Coach of the Year by United Press International and the U.S. Basketball Writers Association in 1960 and has been named to the Naismith Memorial Basketball Hall of Fame. In 1960 he was the Olympic team coach.

Source: *NCAA Basketball's Finest*

PARCELLS, BILL

Bill Parcells was an assistant coach in the NCAA at Hastings College (1964), Wichita State (1965), Army (1966–69), Florida State (1970–72), Vanderbilt (1973 and 1974), and Texas Tech (1975–77). In 1978, Parcells was head coach at the Air Force Academy. He moved to the NFL as an assistant coach with the New England Patriots (1980) and the New York Giants (1981 and 1982). In 1983–90 Parcells was head coach with the New York Giants, with a record of seventy-seven wins, forty-nine losses, and one tie. In 1986 he led the Giants to the NFC Championship and won Super Bowl XXI from Denver. Again in 1990, the Giants won the NFC Championship and Super Bowl XXV from Buffalo. In 1986, Parcells was named *The Sporting News* Coach of the Year. He retired after the 1990 season, but returned in 1993 as head coach of the New England Patriots.

Source: *The Sporting News Football Register 1991*

PARSEGHIAN, ARA

Ara Parseghian's football coaching career spanned twenty-four years (1951–55 at Miami in Ohio, 1956–63 at Northwestern, and 1964–74 at Notre Dame). At Notre Dame he lead the team to three National Championships and to five bowl games (1969, 1970, 1972, 1973, and 1974), winning three. In his career his teams won 170 games, lost 58, and tied 6. Parseghian was named Co-Coach of the Year in 1964 and was inducted into the Hall of Fame. Parseghian retired in 1974 at the age of fifty-one.

Sources: *NCAA Football's Finest; Saturday Afternoon: College Football and the Men Who Made the Day*

PATERNO, JOE

Joe Paterno has spent his head coach career at Pennsylvania State University (1966 to present). At the end of the 1989 football season, he had led Penn State to two National Championships and his teams had played in twenty bowl games in twenty-four years

(1966–89). Paterno was named Coach of the Year in 1968, 1978, 1982, and 1986. As of the beginning of the 1992 season, Paterno was still coaching at Penn State.

Sources: *NCAA Football's Finest; The Sporting News College Football 1992 Yearbook*

PITINO, RICK

University of Hawaii coach Bruce O'Neil hired Rick Pitino as a graduate assistant upon his graduation from the University of Massachusetts and he became a full-time assistant in 1975–76 and served as the interim head coach late in the season when O'Neil resigned. Pitino then took an assistant coaching position at Syracuse, spending two years there before getting his first head coaching position at Boston University. He stayed at Boston University for five years. He was twice named New England Coach of the Year and in his final year at Boston led the Terriers to their first NCAA tournament appearance in twenty-four years. Pitino moved to the New York Knicks as an assistant coach before becoming head coach at Providence in 1985. He was named the John Wooden National Coach of the Year and *The Sporting News* Coach of the Year. In 1987, Pitino returned to the Knicks, as head coach. In 1989 he undertook leadership of the troubled University of Kentucky team.

Source: *College Basketball Yearbook 1991–92*

PROTHRO, TOMMY

Tommy Prothro was head football coach at UCLA 1965–70. From 1965–70 he had a record of 41 wins, 18 losses, and 3 ties, winning one conference title and one Rose Bowl championship. He was named National Coach of the Year in 1965.

Source: *College Football Almanac (1984)*

RICKEY, W. BRANCH

Famous for integrating major-league baseball in 1947 by signing Jackie Robinson to the Brooklyn Dodgers, Branch Rickey also conceived the minor-league farm system in 1919 in St. Louis and instituted the batting cage and sliding pit. Rickey managed the St. Louis Browns 1913–15 and was named vice-president in 1916. He was manager of the St. Louis Cardinals 1919–25, serving as vice-president 1917–20 and 1925–42. He was president and general manager of the Brooklyn Dodgers 1942–50. From 1951–55 Rickey was general manager of the Pittsburgh Pirates, becoming a member of the Pirates' board of directors 1956–59. From 1963–65 he was an adviser to the St. Louis Cardinals.

Sources: *Who's Who in Professional Baseball; Sports Illustrated 1992 Sports Almanac*

RILEY, PAT

From 1981 to 1990 Pat Riley was head coach of the Los Angeles Lakers, winning the Pacific Division Championship every year and winning the NBA Championship in 1982, 1985, 1987, and 1988. He was named Coach of the Year in 1990. After the 1989–90 season, he temporarily retired from basketball to become a sports announcer. At the end of the 1990–91 season, he returned to the NBA and joined the New York Knicks.

Source: *The Sporting News NBA Register 1991–92*

ROBINSON, FRANK

Managing the Cleveland Indians to two fourth-place finishes and a fifth, 1975–77, Frank Robinson was the first black to lead a big-league team. He also managed the San Francisco Giants 1981–84 and the Baltimore Orioles 1988–91. Robinson is the first man to win MVP's in both leagues as a player (1961 with the Reds and 1966 with the Orioles). In 1966, his first in the American League, he also won the Triple Crown and World Series MVP. He was named to the Baseball Hall of Fame in 1982.

Sources: *Total Baseball*, Second Edition; *Sports Illustrated 1992 Sports Almanac*

RODGERS, BUCK

Buck Rodgers had been in professional baseball for thirty-four years as of the beginning of the 1992 season. Rodgers was one of the original Los Angeles Angels (later the California Angels) and stayed with that club through 1969. He still holds the American League record for games caught by a rookie. He first began coaching with the Milwaukee Brewers in 1981 and led them to a second-half title, their first postseason experience. He managed the Montreal Expos for six years, but was fired in June of his seventh year, 1991. In 1987 he led Montreal to a third-place finish, for which he was named Manager of the Year in six different polls. In August 1991, he was hired by the California Angels.

Source: *American League 1992 Red Book*

RUPP, ADOLPH

Adolph Rupp coached basketball at the University of Kentucky 1931–72. Through the 1991 season, Rupp held the NCAA career record for most victories. He led Kentucky to the NCAA Tournament twenty times, taking the championship four times. He coached the team to the NIT title in 1946. He was named Coach of the Year by United Press International in 1959 and 1966, and by the U.S. Basketball Writers Association in 1966. He was named to the Naismith Memorial Basketball Hall of Fame. In 1948, he was the Olympic team coach.

Source: *NCAA Basketball's Finest*

SCHEMBECHLER, BO

Bo Schembechler coached football at Miami University in Ohio 1963–68 and the University of Michigan 1969–89, a total of twenty-seven years, with a record of 234 wins, 65 losses, and 8 ties. At Michigan, he led his teams to seventeen bowl games (winning five).

Source: *NCAA Football's Finest*

SHARMAN, BILL

Bill Sharman was part of the Boston NBA Championship teams 1957, 1959, 1960 and 1961. In 1961 he was signed as a player coach by the Los Angeles Jets (American Basketball League). The team folded mid-season and he then guided the Cleveland Pipers to the ABL Championship. In 1966–68, Bill Sharman coached San Francisco in the NBA. From 1968–70, he coached the ABA Los Angeles team and then coached the Utah Jazz 1970–71 to win the ABA Championship. 1971 found him back in the NBA as head coach of the Los Angeles Lakers, winning the NBA Championship. He coached the Lakers for seven seasons, through 1976; his record was 333 wins and 240 losses. Sharman was named to the Naismith Memorial Basketball Hall of Fame in 1974. In 1970 he was named to the NBA Twenty-fourth-Anniversary All-Time Team. He was named ABA Co-Coach of the Year in 1970.

Sources: *The Sporting News NBA Register 1991–92*

SHULA, DON

From 1963–69, Don Shula was head coach of the Baltimore Colts. In 1968 the Colts won the NFL Championship and played in Super Bowl III, losing to the New York Jets. In 1970 Shula joined the Miami Dolphins, where he was still head coach at the beginning of the 1992 season. He led the Dolphins to the Super Bowl in 1972, 1973, 1974, 1983, and 1985, winning in 1973 and 1974. His Dolphins won the AFC Championship 1971, 1972, 1973, 1982, and 1984. Shula is the only head coach to take more than one team to the Super Bowl. He was named *The Sporting News* Coach of the Year in 1964, 1968, 1970, and 1972. In 1991, the Dolphins had eight wins and eight losses and were tied for second place in the AFC East.

Sources: *War of the Words; The Sporting News Football Register 1991; Athlon Pro Football 1992*

SMITH, DEAN

Dean Smith has been coach at the University of North Carolina for thirty-one years and has led the team to the NCAA Tournament twenty-one times, the tournament record for most appearances and most consecutive appearances, as well as being tied for record for most victories, through 1991. North Carolina is the nation's all-time winningest program, almost half of the victories led by Dean Smith. There are more Smith graduates in the pro ranks than any other school. Smith was named Coach of the Year by the NABC in 1977 and by the U.S. Basketball Writers Association in 1979 and has been named to the Naismith Memorial Basketball Hall of Fame. He coached the 1976 Olympic team to a gold medal. North Carolina won the NIT title in 1971.

Source: *NCAA Basketball's Finest; Blue Ribbon College Basketball Yearbook 1991–92*

SMYTHE, CONN

Conn Smythe assembled the New York Rangers that won the 1928 Stanley Cup. Released before the playoffs, he bought the Toronto St. Pats, changing the name to the Maple Leafs. With Smythe as general manager from 1929–61, the team won seven Stanley Cups (1932, 1942, 1945, 1947, 1948, 1949, and 1951). The award for the Most Valuable Player (MVP) is named after him. The guiding force in building the Maple Leaf Gardens, Smythe served as managing director and president until his retirement in 1961. A builder of the Hall of Fame, he resigned from the Hall of Fame committee in June 1971.

Source: *Who's Who in Hockey; Sports Illustrated 1992 Sports Almanac*

STENGEL, CASEY

Casey Stengel won ten pennants in twelve years. On the last day of the season in 1949, Stengel's first year with the Yankees, the team caught the Red Sox for the pennant, then beat the Dodgers in the World Series. This was the first in a string of five straight World Championships, 1949–53. From 1955–58, the Yankees won four pennants in a row under Stengel's leadership and two more World Championships. In 1960 he won his final pennant. Fired by the Yankees because of his age, he took on the Mets in their first four seasons; although the team finished last each year, they showed improvement each season. Stengel was named to the Hall of Fame in 1966.

Source: *Total Baseball*, Second Edition

SWITZER, BARRY

Barry Switzer coached the Oklahoma Sooners football team 1973–88. In those sixteen years, the Sooners had a record of 157 wins, 29 losses, and 4 ties. The Sooners won two National Championships (1974 and 1985) under Switzer's leadership and went to bowl games in thirteen of those sixteen years. The Sooner bowl record for those thirteen games is eight wins and five losses.

Source: *NCAA Football's Finest*

TARKENTON, FRAN

Fran Tarkenton's playing career as quarterback ran from 1961 to 1978 with Minnesota and the New York Giants. He is the all-time leader in touchdown passes (342), yards passing (47,003), pass attempts (6,467), and pass completions (3,686). Tarkenton was named Player of the Year in 1975.

Source: *Sports Illustrated 1992 Sports Almanac*

TURNER, TED

Educated at Brown University, Ted Turner joined Turner Advertising in 1963. From 1963–70, he was CEO of various Turner companies, then becoming chairman of the board and president of Turner Broadcasting Systems, Inc. He has been president of the Atlanta Braves since 1976 and chairman of the board of the Atlanta Hawks since 1977. He was sponsor and creator of the Goodwill Games in Moscow in 1986. Turner won the America's Cup in his yacht *Courageous* in 1977 and has been named Yachtsman of the Year four times.

Source: *Who's Who in America 1990–91*

VEECK, BILL

Bill Veeck owned three baseball teams, the Cleveland Indians (1946–49), the St. Louis Browns (1951–53) and the Chicago White Sox (1958–61 and 1975–80), all in the American League. Veeck integrated the American League, put players' names on their uniforms, and gave baseball its first two-million-attendance team, the 1948 Cleveland Indians. In 1948 Cleveland won the pennant. Veeck brought in Larry Doby, the American League's first black player, and Satchel Paige. Veeck died in 1986.

Source: *Contemporary Newsmakers 1986*

WALSH, BILL

Bill Walsh's 49ers were named the Football Team of the Decade when the team won its third Super Bowl in eight seasons in January 1989. Walsh was the head coach of the 49ers from 1979 until his retirement after the 1989 Super Bowl. In 1966, Walsh joined the Oakland Raiders of the American Football League as an offensive backfield coach. After one year in the pros, he enrolled in Stanford's graduate school of business and became head coach of the San Jose Apaches of the Continental Football League. When the Apache franchise folded, Walsh returned to pro football as offensive coordinator and quarterback coach for the new Cincinnati Bengals, where he stayed eight seasons. Walsh spent one season with the San Diego Chargers in 1976 before accepting the head coaching position at Stanford University in 1977. In early 1979, Ed De Bartolo, Jr., named Walsh head coach of the 49ers. In three seasons he turned the 49ers around and led them to their first Super Bowl victory in 1981. Walsh retired in 1989 but returned to coaching at the college level at Stanford University.

Source: *Current Biography Yearbook 1989*

WARNER, POP

Pop Warner's Carlisle Indians were football's first to wear headgear and the first to use the huddle. Warner invented the double-wing formation. From 1895–1938, his teams (Georgia, Cornell, Carlisle, Pittsburgh, Stanford, and Temple) won a total of 313 games, lost 106, and tied 32. His teams won three National Championships (Pittsburgh in 1916 and 1918 and Stanford in 1926). He led Stanford to three Rose Bowl games and Temple to one, for a record of one win, two losses, and one tie. He placed forty-seven men on All-American teams, including Jim Thorpe. Warner was elected to the Helms Hall of Fame and the National Football Foundation Hall of Fame.

Sources: *College Football USA 1869–1971; NCAA Football's Finest; Who Was Who in American Sports*

WEST, JERRY ALAN

Jerry West played with the Los Angeles Lakers his entire NBA career, 1960–73. He was named the NBA Playoff MVP in 1969. He was a member of the 1972 NBA Championship Lakers. He coached the Los Angeles Lakers from 1976 to 1979 and became general manager in 1982. He was named to the Naismith Memorial Basketball Hall of Fame in 1979 and the NBA Hall of Fame in 1980. In 1980 he was named to the NBA Thirty-Fifth-Anniversary All-Time Team.

Sources: *The Sporting News NBA Register 1991–92; Who's Who in America 1990–91*

WESTHEAD, PAUL

From 1970–79, Paul Westhead was head coach at La Salle University. In 1979, he moved to the NBA, leading the Los Angeles Lakers to the NBA Championship in his first year. He coached the Lakers for three years. The 1982–83 season found him coaching the Chicago Bulls. In 1985 he returned to the NCAA as head coach at Loyola Marymount, staying through the 1989–90 season. In 1990 he returned to the NBA as head coach of the Denver Nuggets.

Source: *The Sporting News NBA Register 1991–92*

WOODEN, JOHN

John Wooden was head basketball coach at UCLA 1949–75. In those twenty-six years, the Bruins never had a losing season. Wooden led the team to the NCAA tournament sixteen times, winning the championship ten times. Through the 1991 NCAA tournament, he was tied for the most tournament career victories and held the Final Four career record for the most championships, most appearances, most consecutive appearances, and most victories. Wooden's record at UCLA was 620 wins and 147 defeats, a winning percentage of .808. His forty-year career total was 885 wins and 203 losses, for a percentage of .813. He was named Coach of the Year by the Associated Press in 1967, 1969, 1970, 1972, and 1973; by United Press International in 1964, 1967, 1969, 1970, 1972, and 1973; by the U.S. Basketball Writers Association in 1964, 1967, 1970, 1972, and 1973, and by the NABC in 1969, 1970, and 1972. He was named to the Naismith Memorial Basketball Hall of Fame, the only man honored there both as a player and as a coach.

Sources: *NCAA Basketball's Finest; Current Biography Yearbook 1976; Who's Who in America 1990–91*

NOTES

INTRODUCTION

Page

1 **Warren:** *Baseball's Greatest Quotations,* compiled by Paul Dickson, (HarperCollins Publishers, 1991) p. 463.

7 **Lasorda:** *The Artful Dodger* by Tommy Lasorda and David Fisher (Arbor House, 1985) p. 252.

CHAPTER 1: LEARNING THE NAME OF THE GAME

9 **Holtz:** "Energized Irish Quicken Beat with Holtz Magic" by Paul Attner, *National Sports Daily,* November 28, 1988.

10 **Pieper:** "Are Values Baloney," *Executive Edge,* vol. 23, no. 3: 1.

Eilers: *The Fighting Spirit: A Championship Season at Notre Dame* by Lou Holtz, with John Heisler (Pocket Books, 1989) p. 4.

Herzog on mission of Angels: "The Wit and Wisdom of the White Rat" by Pat Jordan, *Los Angeles Times Magazine,* May 10, 1992: 14.

Shell Oil's mission: *Agency Operations and Sales Management, Volume II* by Carol A. Hammes, Peter R. Kensicki, E. J. Leverett, Jr., Ronald T. Anderson (Insurance Institute of America, 1986) p. 140 (reprinted from *Marketing Management,* 3d ed., by Philip Kotler [Prentice-Hall, 1976]).

Page

10 **Volkswagen's mission:** Ibid.

11 **AT&T's mission:** Ibid.

 I.M.M.C.'s mission: Ibid.

 Mrs. Gooch's mission: Bag from Mrs. Gooch's.

 Pizza Hut's mission: Response to questionnaire by Steven Reinemund, CEO.

 Burson-Marsteller's mission: *What Works for Me: 16 CEOs Talk About Their Careers and Commitments* by Thomas R. Horton (AMACOM, 1986) p. 190.

12 **Holtz:** *The Fighting Spirit: A Championship Season at Notre Dame* by Lou Holtz, with John Heisler (Pocket Books, 1989) p. 60–65; "Energized Irish Quicken Beat with Holtz Magic" by Paul Attner, *National Sports Daily*, November 28, 1988.

13 **Herzog chastises and suspends Templeton:** *Baseball Inside Out: Winning the Games Within the Games* by Bruce Shlain (Viking Books, 1992) p. 76.

15 **Philosophy of Anixier Brothers:** *Up the Organization* by Bob Townsend (Knopf, 1970) [addendum to paperback edition].

 Haas of Levi Strauss on values: "Value Driven Management" by Lee Ginsburg and Neil Miller, *Business Horizons*, May–June 1992: 23.

15–16 **G.E. value statement:** "Speed, Simplicity, Self-Confidence: An Interview with Jack Welch" by Noel Tichy and Ram Charan in *Managers As Leaders* (Harvard Business Review, 1991) p. 100.

17 **Riley's guarantees:** *Showtime: Running Away with the 1987 World Championship* by Pat Riley (Warner, 1988) pp. xi–xii.

17–18 **Landry sends letter to players:** *Tom Landry* by Tom Landry and Gregg Lewis (HarperCollins, 1991) p. 283.

19 **Tunney:** *Impartial Judgment: The "Dean of NFL Referees" Calls Pro Football as He Sees It* by Jim Tunney, Ed.D., with Glenn Dickey (Franklin Watts, 1988) p. 178.

Page

19   **Schembechler's goal:** *BO* by Bo Schembechler and Mitch Albom (Warner, 1989) p. 55.

19–20   **Tarkenton on "pinpointing":** *How to Motivate People: The Team Strategy for Success* by Fran Tarkenton, with Tad Tuleja (Harper & Row, 1986) p. 33.

20   **Auerbach:** *MBA: Management by Auerbach,* Red Auerbach, with Ken Dooley (Macmillan, 1991) p. 37.

   Coleman of Apple: "Five Future No. 1s" by Carol Hymowitz, *The Wall Street Journal,* March 20, 1987: 18D (Special Report on Executive Style).

21   **Holtz asks team, "Who . . . wants to be great?":** *The Fighting Spirit: A Championship Season at Notre Dame* by Lou Holtz, with John Heisler (Pocket Books, 1989) p. 4.

   Glanville: *Elvis Don't Like Football* by Jerry Glanville and J. David Miller (Macmillan, 1990) p. 179.

22   **Auerbach referring to Walton:** "Red Auerbach on Management," *Harvard Business Review,* March–April, 1987: 117.

22–23   **The best companies are FUN places to work:** "Unhealthy Business" by Morty Lefkoe, *Across the Board,* June 1992: 30.

23   **Gore:** Ibid.: 27.

23–25   **Delta employees buy plane for the company:** *Barbarians to Bureaucrats: Corporate Life Cycle Strategies* by Lawrence M. Miller (Ballantine, 1989) p. 161.

26   **Johnsonville CEO encourages employees "to be independent thinkers":** "Unhealthy Business" by Morty Lefkoe, *Across the Board,* June 1992: 28.

   Madkins: "UCLA Not Ready for Swan Song" by Jerry Crowe, *Los Angeles Times,* March 26, 1992: C1.

   Nettles: *Sports Quotes: The Insiders' View of the Sports World* by Bob Abel and Michael Valenti (Facts on File Publications, 1983) p. 90; *The*

Page

Greatest Stories Ever Told About Baseball by Kevin Nelson (Perigee, 1986) p. 215.

27 **Baylor:** *Baseball's Greatest Quotations,* compiled by Paul Dickson (HarperCollins, 1991) p. 36.

Negative corporate culture and psychonueroimmunology: "Unhealthy Business" by Morty Lefkoe, *Across the Board,* June 1992: 29.

Few employees answer yes to "Do you enjoy your work?": Ibid.

Johnson & Higgins survey: Ibid.

27–28 **Many CEO's are unaware of negative corporate culture in their own companies:** Ibid.: 31.

28 **Lombardi:** *Sports Quotes: The Insiders' View of the Sports World* by Bob Abel and Michael Valenti; "The Toughest Man in Pro Football" by Leonard Shecter (reprinted from *Esquire,* 1967), in *Thirty Years of Best Sports Stories,* ed. by Irving T. Marsh & Edward Ehre, p. 238.

Blaik: *You Have to Pay the Price: The Red Blaik Story* by Earl H. Blaik, with Tim Cohane.

Leonard: "Stew Leonard's Fact Sheet" by Stew Leonard (provided by Stew Leonard).

29 **Schembechler never lets up:** *BO: Life, Laughs and Lessons of A College Football Legend* by Bo Schembechler and Mitch Albom (Warner, 1989) p. 54.

Slogans posted at Stew Leonard's: "Stew Leonard's Fact Sheet" by Stew Leonard (provided by Stew Leonard).

30 **Allen:** *Sports in America* by James Michener, p. 421.

Lombardi: *Lombardi: Winning is the Only Thing,* ed. by Jerry Kramer (World 1971) pp. ix–x.

Lombardi complains about knee: "The Toughest Man in Pro Football" by Leonard Shecter (reprinted from *Esquire,* 1967) in *Thirty Years of Best Sports Stories,* ed. by Irving T. Marsh and Edward Ehre, p. 238.

31 **Nordstom legend:** Personal communication, June 1992.

Page

"People remember stories better than written policies": "The Parables of Corporate Culture" by Claudia H. Deutsch, *New York Times,* October 13, 1991.

32 **Enterprise Rent-A-Car company legend of "Icepick Killion"**: Personal communication, June 1992.

Cy Young's nickname: *The Greatest Stories Ever Told About Baseball* by Kevin Nelson (Perigee, 1986) p. 116.

33 **Sparrow flies out from under Stengel's cap:** Ibid., pp. 48–49.

DePree: *The Healthy Company: Eight Strategies to Develop People, Productivity and Profits* by Robert H. Rosen, Ph.D., with Lisa Berger (J. P. Tarcher, 1991) p. 2.

CHAPTER 2: LEADING THE TEAM

34 **Anderson:** "Turnaround in Tigertown", *The Sporting News,* July 13, 1987: 12–13.

"People don't want to be managed. . . .": Ad placed by United Technologies in the *Wall Street Journal.*

35 **Kotter:** "What Leaders Really Do" by John P. Kotter, *Harvard Business Review,* May–June 1990: 3.

36 **Leahy:** *The Coaches* by Bill Libby (Henry Regnery, 1972) p. 241.

37 **Welch:** "Speed, Simplicity, Self-Confidence: An Interview with Jack Welch," in "Managers as Leaders," *Harvard Business Review,* September–October 1989.

Cleveland Browns innovations: "Coach of Coaches" by Steve Wulf, *Sports Illustrated,* August 12, 1991: 7.

37–38 **How Koplovitz shaped USA Network:** "Five Future No. 1s", Carol Hymowitz, *The Wall Street Journal,* March 20, 1987: 18D (Special Report on Executive Style)

38 **Fitzsimmons:** Interview with Bob Costas on NBC-TV.

Page

39 **Buffett:** *1991 Annual Report*, Berkshire Hathaway.

Peters: *Baseball's Greatest Quotations* compiled by Paul Dickson (HarperCollins, 1991) p. 340.

Hayes relieved as coach: "Buckeye Legend Hayes Dead at 74" by Ben Henkey, *The Sporting News*, March 23, 1987: 42.

Landry: *Sports Quotes: The Insiders' View of the Sports World* by Bob Abel and Michael Valenti, p. 11.

39–40 **McKay:** *McKay: A Coach's Story* by John McKay, with Jim Perry (Atheneum, 1974) p. 5.

Krzyzewski: "Looking for Advice in Unusual Places," *Working Smart*, vol. 17, no. 13 (July 1991): 1.

40 **McKay quote:** *McKay: A Coach's Story* by John McKay, with Jim Perry (Atheneum, 1974) p. 7.

McKay and the three letters: Ibid.

41 **Van Derveer:** "Sidelined" by Frances Munnings, *Women's Sports & Fitness* September 1990: 42.

McCracken: *The Coaches* by Bill Libby (Henry Regnery, 1972) p. 45.

Tarkenton's "participative huddle": *How to Motivate People: The Team Strategy for Success* by Fran Tarkenton, with Tad Tuleja (Harper & Row, 1986) pp. 68–69.

41–42 **Bryant suspends Namath:** *Speaker's Treasury of Sports Anecdotes, Stories and Humor* by Gerald Tomlinson (Prentice Hall, 1990) pp. 52–53.

42 **Knight kicks son off team:** "Knight Kicks Son Off Team," Associated Press, *Los Angeles Times*.

43 **Burson on the importance of long-range strategy:** *What Works for Me: 16 CEOs Talk About Their Careers and Commitments* by Thomas R. Horton (AMACOM, 1986) p. 188.

46 **Winter on Jackson:** *USA Today*, June 10, 1992.

Page

DePree: *Leadership Is an Art* by Max DePree (Michigan State University Press, 1987) pp. 24–25.

47 **Finanne:** Personal interview.

48 **Rodgers:** *Baseball Lives: Men and Women of the Game Talk About Their Jobs, Their Lives and the National Pastime* by Mike Bryant (Pantheon, 1989) p. 205.

Davis: *Football's Greatest Quotes* by Bob Chieger and Pat Sullivan (Simon & Schuster, 1990) p. 183.

49 **Rothman:** Personal interview.

Hesburgh: *What Works for Me: 16 CEOS Talk About Their Careers and Commitments* by Thomas R. Horton (AMACOM, 1986) p. 172.

50 **Rodgers:** *Football's Greatest Quotes* by Bob Chieger and Pat Sullivan (Simon & Schuster, 1990) p. 32. (from *San Francisco Examiner*, 1983)

Parseghian: *The Fighting Spirit: A Championship Season at Notre Dame* by Lou Holtz, with John Heisler (Pocket Books, 1989) p. 129.

Holtz: Ibid., p. 271.

51 **Martin:** *What Works for Me: 16 CEOs Talk About Their Careers and Commitments* by Thomas R. Horton (AMACOM, 1986) p. 118.

51–52 **Newell's brain picked by Taylor:** *Fifty Years of the Final Four* (NCAA) by Billy Packer (Taylor Publishing, 1987).

52 **Pitino:** "Win! A Master Motivator Teaches You to Create Superstars" by Michael Maren, *Success*, April 1992: 40.

52–53 **Lasorda's "heaven" metaphor:** *The Artful Dodger* by Tommy Lasorda and David Fisher (Arbor House, 1985) p. 167.

54 **Ault runs out:** *The Football Hall of Shame* by Bruce Nash and Allan Zullo (Pocket Books, 1986) p. 112.

54–55 **Fan sends note to Durocher:** *Dodgers! The First 100 Years* by Stanley Cohen (Carol, 1990) pp. 73–74 (recounting anecdote from *Bums*, told by Pete Reiser to Peter Golenbock).

Page

55 **Rupp:** *The Coaches* by Bill Libby (Henry Regnery, 1972) p. 186.

Holtz: *The Fighting Spirit: A Championship Season at Notre Dame* by Lou Holtz, with John Heisler (Pocket Books, 1989) p. 20.

56 **Lombardi:** *Lombardi: Winning is the Only Thing*, ed. by Jerry Kramer (World, 1970) p. x.

CHAPTER 3: BUILDING THE TEAM

57 **Auerbach:** *MBA: Management by Auerbach* by Red Auerbach, with Ken Dooley (Macmillan, 1991) p. 28.

58 **Dodgers scouts:** "The Most Valuable Exec in Either League," *Forbes*, April 12, 1982: 132.

Bragan: *The All Time Greatest Sports Quotes*, by Great Quotations, Inc., p. S15.

Wilken's success picking drafts: *Baseball Lives: Men and Women of the Game Talk About Their Jobs, Their Lives and the National Pastime* by Mike Bryant (Pantheon Books, 1989) p. 196.

Three teams pass over Rodman: *Los Angeles Times.*

59 **Finanne:** Personal interview.

Riley becoming coach of Lakers: "A Big Winner From the First" by Sam McManis, *Los Angeles Times*, January 21, 1990; *Winnin' Times: The Magical Journey of the Los Angeles Lakers* by Scott Ostler and Steve Springer (Macmillan, 1988) p. 177; "A Big Winner from the First" by Sam McManis, *Los Angeles Times*, January 21, 1990: C3.

60 **Meyer:** *Coach* by Ray Meyer, with Ray Sons (Contemporary Books, 1987) pp. 6, 94.

61 **Turman:** *Business Rules of Thumb* by Seth Godin and Chip Conley (Warner, 1987) p. 164.

Wooden: *They Call Me Coach* by John Wooden, as told to Jack Tobin (Word Books, 1972; 1973) p. 124.

Page

Finanne: Personal interview.

62   **Mornell:** Interview of Pierre Mornell, M.D., author of *Thank God It's Monday or How to Prevent Success from Ruining Your Marriage* (Bantam, 1985).

Spencer: Personal interview.

West: *Auerbach: An Autobiography* by Arnold "Red" Auerbach and Joe Fitzgerald (G. P. Putnam's Sons, 1977) p. 156.

63   **Fagiano:** "Interviewing for Style" by David Fagiano, *AMA Management Review,* November, 1990: 4.

63–64   **Herzog:** *White Rat: A Life in Baseball* by Whitey Herzog and Kevin Horrigan (Harper & Row, 1987) p. 2.

64   **Presidents' Five Biggest Headaches:** "Resourceful Recruiting" by Catherine D. Fyock, *Small Business Reports,* April, 1992: 49.

65   **Arrington:** "The $90 Million Man," reprint from article in *ASTA Agency Management* (publication of American Society of Travel Agents [provided by Michael Arrington in response to questionnaire]).

66   **Pipp looks up Gehrig:** *The Giant Book of Strange But True Stories* by Howard Liss (Random Books, 1976).

69   **Parcells:** *Parcells: Autobiography of the Biggest Giant of Them All* by Bill Parcells, with Mike Lupica (Bonus Books, 1987) pp. 247–48.

70   **Spencer:** Personal interview.

71   **Finanne:** Personal interview.

Studies confirm what people say: "The Secret of Making A Good Hire" by Anita Gates, *Working Woman,* February, 1992: 72.

72   **Johnsonville employees' . . . replacements:** *Inc.* Magazine, interview with Ralph Stayer, CEO of Johnsonville Foods, Inc., quoted in *Boardroom Reports,* October 15, 1990: 15.

Ducks: Dan Kuzio, COO, Cal-Surance Cos.

Page

73 **Sugar:** *Baseball's Greatest Quotations*, compiled by Paul Dickson (HarperCollins, 1991) p. 208.

Drucker: *The Frontiers of Management: Where Tomorrow's Decisions Are Being Shaped Today* by Peter F. Drucker (Harper & Row, 1986) p. 125.

74 **Swtizer:** *The Bootlegger's Boy* by Barry Switzer and Bud Shrake (Jove, 1991) pp. 81–82.

75 **McGuire:** *The Third and Possibly the Best 637 Best Things Anybody Ever Said*, compiled by Robert Byrne (Fawcett-Crest, 1986) #339.

Turner: *Speaker's Treasury of Sports Anecdotes, Stories, and Humor* by Gerald Tomlinson (Prentice Hall, 1990) p. 230.

McCarthy: *Baseball's Greatest Managers* by Harvey Frommer (Franklin Watts, 1985) p. 158.

76 **Auerbach recalls blunder:** *MBA: Management by Auerbach* by Red Auerbach with Ken Dooley (Macmillan, 1991) pp. 188–89.

77 **Neale:** *Commitment to Excellence* by Great Quotations, Inc., p. S23.

"You have to improve your club . . .": *Baseball's Greatest Quotations*, compiled by Paul Dickson (HarperCollins, 1991) p. 281.

80 **Gaffney:** *301 Great Management Ideas* by Sara P. Noble (Goldhirsh Group, 1991) p. 9.

Corning employees hire replacements: "How to Help New Managers Be Effective More Quickly" by Dr. Leonard R. Sayles, *Boardroom Reports*, November 1, 1990: 12.

80–81 **Schwartz:** "Welcome to the Company," *HR Focus*, November 1991: 19.

82 **White:** *Business Rules of Thumb* by Seth Godin and Chip Conley (Warner, 1987) p. 71.

Page

Sloan picked every executive: "How to Make People Decisions" by Peter F. Drucker, *Harvard Business Review*, January, 1985: 45.

82–83 **Drucker:** Ibid., p. 48.

CHAPTER 4: KEEPING THE TEAM

84 **Auerbach:** *MBA: Management by Auerbach* by Red Auerbach with Ken Dooley (Macmillan, 1991) p. 13.

Joyner leaves Angels: "Joyner Goes to Royals," *Los Angeles Times*, December 10, 1991: C1.

84–85 **Havlicek:** *Speaker's Treasury of Sports Anecdotes, Stories, and Humor*, by Gerald Tomlinson (Prentice Hall; 1990) p. 121.

85 **Eight out of ten workers would change jobs:** "Are You Hiring the Right People?" by Donald D. DeCamp, *AMA Management Review*, May 1992: 44.

Mullen decision to sign contract: "A Warrior's Faith" by Peter Korn, *Inside Sports*.

86 **Average worker has eight employers by 40:** "Did You Know That . . . ," *Boardroom Reports*, June 1, 1990: 15.

88 **Davis hires from within, except for Shanahan:** *Slick: The Silver and Black Life of Al Davis* by Mark Ribowsky (Macmillan, 1991) pp. 328–29.

DeBartolo buys train passes: "The Hand That Feeds Them" by Rick Reilly, *Sports Illustrated*, September 10, 1990: 126.

88–89 **Davis injured:** *MBA: Management by Auerbach* by Red Auerbach, with Ken Dooley (Macmillan, 1991) p. 141.

89–90 **Shula loses Super Bowl:** *The Winning Edge* by Don Shula, with Lou Sahedi (E. P. Dutton, 1973) pp. 109–12.

91 **Lasorda manages turnstile:** "Lasorda Manages to Keep the Wives Happy," *Los Angeles Times*, October 21, 1987.

Page

91–92   **DeBartolo sends flowers:** "The Hand that Feeds Them" by Rick Reilly, *Sports Illustrated*, September 10, 1990: 124.

92   **Veeck:** *Veeck . . . As in Wreck* by Bill Veeck, with Ed Linn (Bantam, 1962) p. 15.

Rothman: Personal interview.

93–94   **Harbor Sweets employee schedule:** "Managing the New Work Force", M. E. Mangelsdorf, *Inc.*, January 1990: 82.

94   **Dodgertown:** "The Town O'Malley Built" by Frederick C. Klein, *Wall Street Journal*, March 6, 1987.

96   **Meyer:** *Coach* by Ray Meyer, with Ray Sons (Contemporary Books, 1987) p. 235.

Herzog: *White Rat: A Life in Baseball* by Whitey Herzog and Kevin Horrigan (Harper & Row, 1987) p. 15.

Bear Bryant reprimands player: *The Legend of Bear Bryant* by Mickey Herskowitz (McGraw-Hill, 1987) pp. 95–96.

97   **Phillips:** *Playboy*, 1981; quoted in *Football's Greatest Quotes* by Bob Chieger and Pat Sullivan (Simon & Schuster, 1990) page 27

97–98   **Donuts:** *Parcells: Autobiography of the Biggest Giant of Them All* by Bill Parcells, with Mike Lupica (Bonus Books, 1987) p. 184.

98   **Clemson tradition:** "Traditions Set Tone," *USA Today*, September 27, 1991: 2C; "PAWS!" by Curry Kirkpatrick, *Sports Illustrated*, October 23, 1989: 109.

Heisman: Ibid.

Warriors picnic: Interview with Dan Finanne.

98–99   **Cherry Tire vacations:** *301 Great Management Ideas* by Sara P. Noble (Goldhirsh Group, 1991) p. 14.

100   **Grimm asks Veeck what he wants for birthday:** *The Best, Worst and Most Unusual in Sports* by Stan and Shirley Fischler (Crowell, 1977) p. 31.

Page

Pee Wee Reese's birthday: Ibid., pp. 14–15.

101   **Lotus, Maytag . . . anniversary gifts:** "Not Exactly A Gold Watch" by Catherine Fredman and Alexandra Siegel, *Working Woman*, March 1992: 65.

102   **Mets honor Stengel:** "Mets Left Polo Grounds for Shea Stadium," *Sports Illustrated*, May 18, 1992: 95.

103–104   **Vermiel and "burn out":** "A New Life" by Gary Smith, *Sports Illustrated*, March 28, 1983: 65–67.

104   **Potter:** *Secrets of Executive Success: How Anyone Can Handle the Human Side of Work and Grow Their Career* by Mark Golin, Mark Bricklin, David Diamond, and Rodale Center for Executive Development (Rodale Press, 1991).

104–105   **Signs of burnout:** *Coping with the Fast Track Blues* by Robert M. Bramson, Ph.D. (Doubleday, 1990); *Is It Worth Dying For?* by Dr. Robert S. Eliot and Dennis L. Breo (Bantam, 1989).

105   **Madden:** *No Medals for Trying: A Week in the Life of a Pro Football Team* by Jerry Izenberg, (McMillan, 1990) p. 187.

Drucker: *The Frontiers of Management: Where Tomorrow's Decisions Are Being Shaped Today* by Peter F. Drucker (E. P. Dutton, 1986) p. 269.

108   **Schembechler:** *BO: Life, Laughs and Lessons of a College Football Legend* by Bo Schembechler and Mitch Albom (Warner, 1989) p. 147.

108–109   **DePree:** *Leadership Is an Art* by Max DePree (Michigan State University Press, 1987) p. 23.

CHAPTER 5: MOTIVATING THE TEAM THROUGH RECOGNITION AND REWARD

110   **Robinson:** Interview with Frank Robinson by Tracy Ringolsby, *Inside Sports*, April, 1990: 23–26.

Jordan: "Pippen Loses Punch" by Chris Baker, *Los Angeles Times*, May 26, 1992: C4.

Page

110–111   **Kotter:** "What Leaders Really Do" by John P. Kotter, in *Managers as Leaders* (Harvard Business School Publishing Division, 1991) p. 7.

111–112   **Gibson plays injured in World Series:** "A Big Blast in L.A." by Peter Gammons, *Sports Illustrated*, October 24, 1988: 36.

112   **Sharman:** *That Championship Feeling: The Story of the Boston Celtics* by Joe Fitzgerald (Charles Scribner's Sons, 1975) p. 73.

113   **Martin:** "Love, Hate and Billy Martin" by Frank Deford, *Sports Illustrated*, June 2, 1975.

Lasorda hugs player: "Business Secrets of Tommy Lasorda" by Brian Dumaine, Lasorda interview, *Fortune*, July 3, 1989: 131; *The Artful Dodger*, Tommy Lasorda and David Fisher (Arbor House, 1985) p. 127.

Martin: *Billyball* by Billy Martin, with Phil Pepe (Doubleday, 1987) p. 33.

Nettles: Ibid.

113–114   **Bryant:** *Bear: The Legend of Bear Bryant* by Mickey Herskowitz (McGraw-Hill, 1987) pp. 149–50

114   **Xerox "You Deserve an X Today" Program:** *The Healthy Company* by Robert H. Rosen, Ph.D., with Lisa Berger, (Tarcher, 1991) p. 40.

115   **Lasorda's 111% Club:** *The Artful Dodger* by Tommy Lasorda and David Fisher (Arbor House, 1985) p. 174.

117   **Burroughs "Brag Sheet":** *The Healthy Company* by Robert H. Rosen, Ph.D., with Lisa Berger (Tarcher, 1991) p. 40.

Stew Leonard's "Stew's News" touts employees: *The Service Edge: 101 Companies That Profit From Customer Care* by Ron Zemke, with Dick Schaaf (NAL Dutton, 1989) p. 319.

118   **Bryant removes hat in honor of players:** "The Mastery of the Bear" by Peter Axthelm, *Newsweek*

118–119   **Grant praises everyone but Tarkenton:** *How To Motivate People: The Team Strategy for Success* by Fran Tarkenton, with Tad Tuleja (Harper & Row, 1986) p. 93.

Page

119   **Lasorda promises new suit:** "Lasorda Dresses Up Offense as Hershiser Does the Rest" by Ross Newhan, *Los Angeles Times* (n.d.)

121–122   **Bryant:** *Bear: The Hard Life and Good Times of Alabama's Coach Bryant* by Paul W. Bryant and John Underwood (Little, Brown, 1974) p. 117.

122   **Gooden salary:** *Los Angeles Times.*

124   **Bryant recalls cigarette lighter:** *Bear: The Hard Life and Good Times of Alabama's Coach Bryant* by Paul W. Bryant and John Underwood (Little, Brown, 1974) p. 120.

126   **Lasorda:** "Sunshine Boy," *Reader's Digest,* July 1982: 107 (from *Playboy*).

126–127   **Lasorda:** "Business Secrets of Tommy Lasorda" by Brian Dumaine, Lasorda interview, *Fortune,* July 3, 1989: 135.

CHAPTER 6: SENDING THE PLAYERS TO THE SHOWERS

131   **Lasorda:** *The Artful Dodger* by Tommy Lasorda and David Fisher (Arbor House, 1985) p. 140.

131–132   **Reeves fires Allen:** *The Coaches* by Bill Libby (Henry Regnery, 1972) pp. 5–7.

134   **Landry:** *The Man Inside . . . Landry* by Bob St. John, (Word Books, 1979) pp. 161–62.

135   **LaRussa:** *Baseball's Greatest Quotations,* compiled by Paul Dickson (Harper Perennial, 1992) p. 239.

   Sports Illustrated: Ibid., p. 75.

   Martin: Ibid., p. 270.

138   **Lombardi trades Ringo:** "The Toughest Man in Pro Football" by Leonard Schechter (reprinted from *Esquire,* 1967), in *Thirty Years of Best Sports Stories,* ed. by Irving T. Marsh and Edward Ehre, p. 240.

140   **Belmont hears on radio he was hired:** *The Coaches* by Bill Libby (Henry Regnery, 1972) p. 53.

Page

141 **Holzman lets player go:** *Speaker's Treasury of Sports Anecdotes Stories and Humor* by Gerald Tomlinson (Prentice Hall, 1990) p. 12.

141–142 **Weaver:** *Baseball's Greatest Quotations* compiled by Paul Dickson (HarperCollins, 1991) p. 466.

143 **Martin:** Ibid., p. 271.

Landry trades Richards: *The Man Inside . . . Landry* by Bob St. John, (Word Books, 1979) pp. 161–62.

146 **Ford fired by CBS:** *Slick* by Whitey Ford, with Phil Pepe (William Morrow, 1987) p. 223.

148 **Day fired by Smythe:** *Best, Worst and Most Unusual in Sports* by Stan and Shirley Fischler, (Crowell, 1977) p. 95.

149 **Lasorda trades Hough:** *The Artful Dodger*, by Tommy Lasorda and David Fisher (Arbor House, 1985) pp. 222–23.

150 **Gordinier on how to terminate:** Response to questionnaire.

151 **Holtz:** *Simpson's Contemporary Quotations: The Most Notable Quotes Since 1950* by James B. Simpson (Houghton Mifflin, 1988) p. 388.

Stengel fired from Yankees: *Best Sports Stories–1961*, ed. by Irving Marsh and Edward Ehre, pp. 69–71 (Arthur Daley, *New York Times*, 1960).

152 **Gillman devises plays for Vermiel:** "Screen Gem" by Paul Zimmerman, *Sports Illustrated*, September 2, 1992: 122.

Rickey: *1992 Baseball Engagement Book* by Michael Gershman (Houghton Mifflin, 1991).

153 **Cooke:** *The Coaches* by Bill Libby (Henry Regnery, 1972) p. 31.

CHAPTER 7: PRIME TIME

154 **Holtz:** *The Fighting Spirit: A Championship Season at Notre Dame* by Lou Holtz, with John Heisler (Pocket Books, 1989) p. 43.

Page

154–155 **Walsh:** "Stress in Coaching" by Bob Oates, *Los Angeles Times*, July 13, 1989: III, 1.

155 **Welch:** "The Mind of Jack Welch" by Stratford P. Sherman, *Fortune*, March 27, 1989: 46.

156 **Smith:** *Sportswit* by Lee Green (Fawcett, 1986) p. 109.

157 **Executives and unnecessary meetings:** "Time-Management Opportunity," *Boardroom Reports*, October 15, 1990: page 13 (Accountemps survey of 200 executives).

158 **Holtz time:** *The Fighting Spirit: A Championship Season at Notre Dame* by Lou Holtz, with John Heisler (Pocket Books, 1989) p. 278.

Lombardi time: "The Toughest Man in Pro Football" by Leonard Schecter (reprinted from *Esquire*, 1967), in *Thirty Years of Best Sports Stories*, ed. by Irving T. Marsh and Edward Ehre, p. 234.

GE's Medical Health Group and chairs: "Inside Track," *Executive Edge*, vol. 23, no. 5 (May 1992): 1.

160 **McKinsey's recommendation:** "The CEO's Secret of Managing Time", by Alan Deutschman, *Fortune*, June 1, 1992, page 140

Auerbach: *MBA: Management By Auerbach* by Red Auerbach, with Ken Dooley (Macmillan, 1991) p. 69.

161 **Katzman publishes diary:** "The Custom-Made Day Planner" by Teri Lammers, *Inc.*, February 1992: 62.

163 **Treybig keeps calendar outside door:** *Office Hours: A Guide to the Managerial Life* by Walter Kiechel III (HarperCollins, 1989) p. 5.

164 **Westhead:** *The Quotable Quote Book* by Merrit Malloy and Shauna Sorensen (Carol, 1990) p. 272.

Rodgers: *Baseball Lives* by Mike Bryan (Pantheon, 1989) p. 177.

165 **Parcells:** *No Medals For Trying: A Week in the Life of a Pro Football Team* by Jerry Izenberg (Macmillan, 1990) pp. 187–88.

Van with phones etc.: *Los Angeles Times*.

Page

166 **Warriors use private plane:** Interview with Dan Finanne.

Gallup study on cellular phones: Survey by Gallup Organization for Motorola Cellular Impact Survey, quoted in *Bottom Line*, August 30, 1991.

167–168 **Microsoft uses E-mail:** "Managing Creative People" by Anne R. Field, *Success*, October, 1988: 87.

168–169 **Braves' Nixon keeps notebook of opposing pitchers:** "Morning Briefings," *Los Angeles Times*, May 23, 1992: C2.

169 **Digital phones on airlines:** "Claircom Plans Digital Phones For Airlines" by Ken Yamada, *Wall Street Journal*.

169–170 **Fedex and Otis Elevator use hand-held computers:** "Hand-Held Computers Help Field Staff Cut Paper Work and Harvest More Data" by Gilbert Fuchsberg, *Wall Street Journal*, January 30, 1990: B1.

170 **Bryant:** *Bear: The Hard Life and Good Times of Alabama's Coach Bryant* by Paul W. Bryant and John Underwood (Little, Brown, 1974)

170–171 **Pickens launches wellness program:** John Durkin, quoted in *Incentive*, repeated in "Boardroom Reports," Dec. 15, 1990: 7.

CHAPTER 8: FILLING THE STANDS THROUGH SALES AND SERVICE

173–174 **Dalton:** *Baseball Lives: Men and Women of the Game Talk About Their Jobs, Their Lives and the National Pastime* by Mike Bryan (Pantheon, 1989)

174 **Riese:** Solicitation letter from American Express.

Egelmann: "Of Mice and Men" by Judson Gooding, *Across the Board*, March 1992: p. 40.

175 **Zaphiropouls defines business:** *Office Hours: A Guide to Managerial Life* by Walter Kiechel III (Little, Brown, 1988) p. 199.

Wegmann: *Star Teams, Key Players: Successful Career Strategies for Women in the 1990's* by Michele Jackman, with Susan Waggoner (Henry Holt, 1991) pp. 139–40.

Page

176   **Hornets' Shinn focuses on customer service:** *Practical Business Genius: 50 Smart Questions Successful Businesspeople Ask* by Craig R. Hickman (Wiley, 1991) pp. 120–22.

       McDonald's motto: *Service America!: Doing Business in the New Economy* by Karl Albrecht and Ron Zemke (Dow Jones-Irwin, 1985) p. 29.

       Stew Leonard's mission: *Delivering Knock Your Socks Off Service* by Kristen Anderson and Ron Zemke (AMACOM, 1991) p. 39.

       Midwest Express motto: "Midwest Express Rides Old Formula" by Brian S. Moskal, *Industry Week*, October 1, 1990: 59.

177   **Everyone in Hornet organization participates in community service:** *Practical Business Genius: 50 Smart Questions Successful Businesspeople Ask* by Craig R. Hickman (Wiley, 1991) pp. 120–22.

       Fedex's objective: "Optimas Award: Federal Express," *Personnel Journal*, January 1992: 52.

       Fidelity answers phone by third ring: *The Service Edge: 101 Companies That Profit from Customer Care* by Ron Zemke, with Dick Schaaf (NAL/Dutton, 1989) p. 212.

177–178   **AutoZone's special rule:** *The Executive Edge*, April 1992: 10.

178   **Domino's delivers in 30 minutes:** *Delivering Knock Your Socks Off Service* by Kristin Anderson and Ron Zemke (AMACOM, 1991) p. 15.

       Hampton's guarantee: "Customer Treatment As A Mirror of Employee Treatment" by Cliff Barbee and Valerie Bott, *SAM Advanced Management Journal*, Spring 1991: 29.

       Marriott: *What Works for Me: 16 CEOs Talk About Their Careers and Commitments* by Thomas R. Horton (AMACOM, 1986) p. 67.

179   **Disney World Street sweepers get 4 days training:** "Customer Treatment as a Mirror of Employee Treatment" by Cliff Barbee and Valerie Bott, *SAM Advanced Management Journal*, Spring 1991: 30.

       P&G Service reps: *The Service Edge: 101 Companies That Profit from Customer Care* by Ron Zemke, with Dick Schaaf (NAL/Dutton, 1989) p. 62.

Page

L.L. Bean service reps: Ibid.

Fedex emphasizes training: "Optimas Award: Federal Express," *Personnel Journal*, January 1992: 52.

180   **Walton:** "Sam Walton in His Own Words" by Sam Walton (excerpt from *Sam Walton: Made in America*), *Fortune*, June 29, 1992: 105.

Stew Leonard's senior citizen bus: "Stew Leonard's Fact Sheet" by Stew Leonard (provided by Stew Leonard).

Stew Leonard's suggestion box: *The Service Edge: 101 Companies That Profit from Customer Care* by Ron Zemke, with Dick Schaaf (NAL/Dalton, 1989) p. 318.

Beyer Volvo has night shift: Ibid., pp. 252–53.

180–181   **McIntyre-Kolpin creates courier service:** Personal interview.

181   **Zimbrick offers cab rides to customers:** "Exceptional Service," *Boardroom Reports*, March 15, 1992: 8 (quoted from *Dun & Bradstreet Reports*).

Porter: *Delivering Knock Your Socks Off Service* by Kristen Anderson and Ron Zemke (Amacom, 1991) p. 87.

182   **Stew Leonard responds to customer complaints:** "The Profitable Art of Service Recovery" by Christopher W. L. Hart, James L. Heskett, and W. Earl Sasser, Jr., *Harvard Business Review*, July–August 1990: 152.

British Airways installs video: Ibid.

182–183   **Club Med staff meet passengers at airport after bad flight:** Ibid., pp. 148–49.

184   **Carlzon:** *Delivering Knock Your Socks Off Service* by Kristen Anderson and Ron Zemke (AMACOM, 1991) p. 31.

Forbes: "Boston Beer Co. CEO Lays It on the Line" by Malcolm S. Forbes, *Forbes*, June 27, 1988: 32.

Page

185 **Chrysler announces "Customer One":** "For LH Models, Chrysler Maps New Way to Sell" by Bradley A. Stertz, *Wall Street Journal,* June 30, 1992: B1.

185–186 **Uniroyal develops "Adopt a Customer":** *Executive Management Forum* (insert to *AMA Management Review,* July 1992) p. 2.

187 **Lowe:** *Baseball Lives: Men and Women of the Game Talk about Their Jobs, Their Lives and the National Pastime* by Mike Bryan (Pantheon, 1989) p. 332.

Perot: *Best of "Business Quarterly,"* p. 89. (Year?)

Ditka: *Ditka: An Autobiography* by Mike Ditka, with Don Pierson (Bonus Books, 1986) p. 240.

188 **Herzog:** "Pressure Point" by Rob Rains, *Inside Sports.*

Knight: "Knight Takes His Hoosiers Beyond Mere Will to Win" by Gene Wojciechowski, *Los Angeles Times,* January 14, 1992.

Rothman: Personal interview.

188–189 **Herzog makes offer for Porter:** *White Rat: A Life in Baseball* by Whitey Herzog and Kevin Horrigan (Harper & Row, 1987) pp. 122–25.

189–190 **Woolf:** *Friendly Persuasion: My Life As A Negotiator* by Bob Woolf (G. P. Putnam's Sons, 1990) p. 52.

190 **Cohen:** *You Can Negotiate Anything* by Herb Cohen (Lyle Stuart, 1980) pp. 210–11.

190–191 **Woolf:** *Friendly Persuasion: My Life As A Negotiator* by Bob Woolf (G. P. Putnam Sons, 1990) p. 179.

191 **Nierenberg:** *The Art of Negotiating* by Gerard I. Nierenberg (Pocket Books, 1981) p. 89.

192 **Cohen:** *You Can Negotiate Anything* by Herb Cohen (Lyle Stuart, 1980) p. 217.

Cohen: Ibid., p. 216.

Page

192–193 **Veeck:** *Veeck—As in Wreck* by Bill Veeck, with Ed Linn (Bantam, 1962) p. 134.

193 **Ruth negotiates new contract with Yankees:** *Sports Quotes: The Insiders' View of the Sports World* by Bob Abel and Michael Valenti (Facts on File, 1983) p. 202.

193–194 **Woolf:** *Friendly Persuasion: My Life As A Negotiator*, Bob Woolf, G. P. Putnam's Sons, 1990, page 121–122

195 **Auerbach:** *MBA: Management by Auerbach* by Red Auerbach, with Ken Dooley (Macmillan, 1991) p. 59.

Cohen: *You Can Negotiate Anything* by Herb Cohen (Lyle Stuart, 1980).

196 **Nierenberg:** *The Art of Negotiating* by Gerard I. Nierenberg (Pocket Books, 1981) p. 242.

CHAPTER 9: GOOD GUYS FINISH FIRST

197 **Landry:** *The Man Inside . . . Landry* by Bob St. John (Word Books, 1979) p. 139.

197–198 **Dodgers choose Robinson:** *Nice Guys Finish Last* by Leo Durocher, with Ed Linn (Simon & Schuster, 1975) pp. 204–205.

198–199 **Schembechler:** *Bo* by Bo Schembechler and Mitch Albom (Warner, 1989) p. 229.

199 **Dykes receives immunity:** *Sports Illustrated.*

Stanley: *Women's Sports: A History* by Allen Guttmann (Columbia University Press, 1991) p. 213.

North Carolina universities fail to graduate basketball players: *Sports Illustrated.*

Duke committment to excellence in classroom: *Los Angeles Times; USA Today,* June 4, 1992: Sports, 1.

199–200 **Krzyzewski tells Laettner he must obtain degree:** *Los Angeles Times.*

Page

200 **Notre Dame's primary mission:** *The Fighting Spirit: A Championship Season at Notre Dame* by Lou Holtz, with John Heisler (Pocket Books, 1989) pp. 7–8.

Manville in Chapter 11: "Why 'Good' Managers Make Bad Ethical Choices" by Saul W. Gellerman, *Harvard Business Review*, January 1986.

200–201 **E.F. Hutton kites checks:** *Manage People, Not Personnel* by Harvard Business Review (Harvard Business School Publishing) pp. 21–22; "Corporate Accountability," *American Management Review*.

201 **Miller:** "A Question of Ethics" by Richard Weatherington, *Foresight Magazine*.

201–202 **Georgia Tech football players abuse two young women:** "Unsportsmanlike Conduct" by Austin Murphy, *Sports Illustrated*, July 1, 1991: 24.

202 **Holtz bars 3 top players for entire season:** *The Fighting Spirit: A Championship Season at Notre Dame* by Lou Holtz, with John Heisler (Pocket Books, 1989).

Kotter: "The Ultimate Ethics Test" by Andrew W. Singer, *Across the Board*, March 1992: 20.

203 **Munger:** Ibid.

Cadbury: "Ethical Managers Make Their Own Rules" by Sir Adrian Cadbury, *Harvard Business Review*, September–October 1987.

St. Paul Insurance Co.'s code: *Sloan Management Review*, Winter 1989: 85.

204 **Chemical Bank has extensive ethics program:** "Ethics Codes Spread Despite Skepticism" by Amanda Bennett, *The Wall Street Journal*, Friday, July 15, 1988.

Dimma develops policy against "flipping properties": "The Ultimate Ethics Test" by Andrew W. Singer, *Across the Board*, March 1992: 21–22.

Page

Study finds codes designed to protect company against employees: "An Ethics Roundtable: The Culprit Is Culture" by William C. Frederick, *Management Review*, August 1988: 49.

206 **Citicorp game, "The Work Ethic":** *Wall Street Journal*, April 18, 1989.

206–207 **Pop Warner uses red footballs:** *The Giant Book of Strange But True Sports Stories* by Howard Liss (Random House, 1976) p. 137.

207 **Durocher relays signals through sports writer:** *It Ain't Cheatin' If You Don't Get Caught* by Dan Gutman (Viking Penguin, 1990) p. 108.

Dressen puts on disguise: Ibid.

Veeck has fence moved: *Veeck—As in Wreck* by Bill Veeck, with Ed Linn (Bantam, 1962) p. 161.

Wills: *It Ain't Cheatin' If You Don't Get Caught* by Dan Gutman (Viking Penguin, 1990) p. 105.

208 **Cadbury:** "Ethical Managers Make Their Own Rules" by Sir Adrian Cadbury, *Harvard Business Review*, September–October 1987.

208–209 **Meyer uses snowplow to clear field:** *The Football Hall of Shame* by Bruce Nash and Allan Zullo (Pocket Books, 1986) p. 31.

210 **Lasorda refuses to appear in uniform:** "He Goes Where the In Crowd Goes," *Sports Illustrated*, January 30, 1984: 78.

211 **Only 3 percent of purchasing agents wouldn't accept favors:** "Vendor's Gifts Pose Problems for Purchasers" by Pamela Sebastian, *Wall Street Journal*, June 26, 1989.

Cadbury: "Ethical Managers Make Their Own Rules" by Sir Adrian Cadbury, *Harvard Business Review*, September–October 1987.

214 **Coryell:** *Don Coryell: Win with Honor* by Joe Stein and Diane Clark (Joyce Press, 1976) p. 17.

CHAPTER 10: TRADE-OFFS

Page

215 **Walton:** *Sam Walton: Made in America* by Sam Walton, with John Huey, excerpted in "Life of A Salesman," *Time,* June 15, 1992: 53.

Madden: *Los Angeles Times,* August 2, 1992.

216 **Lasorda:** *The Artful Dodger* by Tommy Lasorda and David Fisher (Arbor House, 1985) p. 253.

217 **Dickerson takes pay cut:** "Money Can't Buy Happiness" by Chris Baker, *Los Angeles Times,* July 21, 1992: C1, C4.

Durocher: *The Concise Columbia Dictionary of Quotations* by Robert Andrews (Columbia University Press, 1987).

Stoic: "Teamwork" by Mariah Burton Nelson, *Women's Sports & Fitness,* May/June 1992: 82.

217–218 **Special Olympics motto:** *The Quotable Quote Book* by Merrit Malloy and Shauna Sorensen, (Carol, 1990) p. 87.

218 **Krzyzewski:** "A Winner's Secret" by John Feinstein, *Reader's Digest,* January 1992: 47–50.

Nierenberg: *The Art of Negotiating* by Gerard I. Nierenberg (Pocket Books, 1981) p. 37.

218–219 **Anderson:** *Star Teams, Key Players: Successful Career Strategies for Women in the 1990's* by Michele Jackman, with Susan Waggoner (Henry Holt, 1991) p. 3.

219 **Herzog:** *White Rat: A Life in Baseball* by Whitey Herzog and Kevin Horrigan (Harper & Row, 1987) p. 9.

220–221 **Myers:** "The Search for the Organization of Tomorrow" by Thomas A. Stewart, *Fortune,* May 18, 1992: 98.

221 **Drucker:** *The New Realities* by Peter Drucker (Harper & Row, 1989).

Kohn: "Great Experiments in Team Chemistry" by Paul Chance, *Across the Board,* May 1989: 18–20.

Page

222   **DePalma:** "Turn Your Workers Into a Team" by Bradford McKee, *Nation's Business*, July 1992: 36.

222–223   **At Gencorp, all are called "associates," and received same benefits:** "Great Experiments in Team Chemistry", Paul Chance, *Across the Board*, May 1989: 25.

223   **Celtics' pay not based on individual stats:** *Corporate Players: Designs for Working and Winning Together* by Robert Keidel (Wiley, 1988).

        Riley: *Showtime: Running Away with the 1987 World Championship* by Pat Riley, Warner Books, 1988, page 143

223–224   **Meyer, leaves wife at game:** "The Son Also Rises" by Gene Wojcie-chowski, *Los Angeles Times*, January 19, 1992.

224   **Parseghian retires:** *The Fighting Irish: Notre Dame Football Through the Years*, William Gildea and Christopher Jennison, Pocket Books, 1989, pages 17–19

225–226   **Walsh:** Stanford Alumni publication, 1992, p. 17.

227   **Forbes:** *The Quotable Quote Book* by Merrit Malloy and Shauna Sorenson (Carol, 1990) p. 1.

227–228   **Prothro:** *The Coaches* by Bill Libby, (Henry Regnery, 1972) p. 13.

228   **Gibbs too involved with Redskins to go to dad's funeral:** "Gibbs Throws a Pass" by Tim Kawakami, *Los Angeles Times*, January 28, 1992: C4.

        Mornell: *Thank God It's Monday or How to Prevent Success From Ruining Your Marriage* by Pierre Mornell, M.D.

AFTERWORD

231–232   **Lasorda:** "Business Secrets of Tommy Lasorda" by Brian Dumaine (interview of Tommy Lasorda), *Fortune*, July 3, 1989: 131.

INDEX